What people are saying about *The Innovation SuperHighway:*

"Debra makes innovation a central topic with decentralized (but) networked organizations. This paradigm is an important finding, since most big companies tend to re-centralize their innovation-processes to have better control!!!"

Joachim Doering, Sr. Vice President, Information Communications network, Siemens A.G.

"Debra Amidon—a globally leading knowledge pioneer for decades—leverages how past experience is the key to visualizing the emerging longitude patterns of the Future through knowledge innovation. This book is a milestone in the knowledge field. She has put the spotlight on the two major dimensions—enterprising as well as innovations. The methodologies and international network outlined in this book represent a true global entrepreneurial spirit for nourishing intellectual capital."

Leif Edvinsson, CEO of UNIC and author of *Intellectual Capital* and *Corporate Longitude*

"If the 21st century is to be characterized by a profound shift towards a knowledge-based economic infrastructure then we cannot simply expect knowledge, innovation and learning to emerge serendipitously. Debra Amidon brings clarity of thought and a timely contribution to this important debate and demonstrates that we must develop strategies that connect hitherto compartmentalized components of our innovation pipelines.

Dr. Michael Kelleher, Director, the European Union KALiF Project

"This is truly a landmark book and highly recommended as essential reading for those needed to lead innovation practices between functions of an organization, companies within industries, across sectors of the economy and among nations of the world. Debra suggests—and I concur—that innovating our future through human creativity—beyond technology and beyond content—is the key for wealth-generation in the 21st century. In this decisive book, Debra has been exceptionally skilled in building consensus and working complex issues that require collaboration—with sensitivity and resoluteness"

Dr. George Kozmetsky, Founder of Teledyne and winner of the National Medal of Technology

"In this book, Debra Amidon provides a summary of the *new fundamentals* of Knowledge and Innovation— plus the 'how to's' for Leadership/Leverage of these forces into the future. This is a must-read for Board members and executives charged with the responsibility of choosing future directions and ensuring the sustainability of their organizations."

Doug Macnamara, CEO, Banff Executive Leadership Inc.

"Debra provides a sustainable path forward in what is a defining moment in the history of our society as we determine the kind of world our children's children will inherit. We should all take heed."

Dr. Thomas F. Malone, Distinguished Scholar Emeritus, North Carolina State University

"Debra's compelling vision of *The Innovation Superhighway*—beyond KM and information management— connects all multidisciplinary, planetary talents and uses collective intelligence to build the future. As many other words in the global context, the definition has evolved beyond invention into multi-facetted innovation: comportmental (new attitudes), organizational (new structures), educational (new ways of learning), economic (new values), and motivations. No one can stop our collective imagination."

Dr. Eunika Mercier-Laurent, CEO of EML Conseil and Professor of IAE Lyon University

"Debra Amidon combines vision and practice in this pioneering book. Her vision aims very high and her examples are very concrete. She herself has been practicing what she preaches and the book is full of live and powerful examples, many taken from her own experience. You will find out why we all need to move from knowledge management to innovation through collaboration and how it has already been done by an international network of experts led by the author."

Dr. Edna Pasher, author of *The Hidden Values of the Desert: the Intellectual Capital of Israel*, and co-editor of *From Knowledge to Value : Unfolding the Innovation Cube*

The Innovation Superhighway

Harnessing Intellectual Capital for Sustainable Collaborative Advantage

The Innovation Superhighway

Harnessing Intellectual Capital for Sustainable Collaborative Advantage

DEBRA M. AMIDON

Greg,
Welcome to Boston.
Imagine what we might
be able to innovate . . .
together !
Debra
8 June 2004

BUTTERWORTH
HEINEMANN

An imprint of Elsevier Science
www.bh.com

Amsterdam   Boston   London   New York   Oxford   Paris   San Diego
San Francisco   Singapore   Sydney   Tokyo

Library of Congress Cataloging-in-Publication Data

Includes bibliographical references and index.
ISBN: 0-7506-7592-6 (alk. paper)

British Library Cataloguing-in-Publication Data
A catalogue record for this book is available from the British Library.

About the Cover
The world is now our manageable landscape. Connections are made East to West and North to South with many nodes in between. But The Innovation Superhighway is not only a physical infrastructure, albeit a technical and electronic one. It is human—a function of insight, interaction, and imagination resident in the minds, hearts, and hands of people around the globe.

The publisher offers special discounts on bulk orders of this book.
For information, please contact:

Manager of Special Sales
Elsevier Science
225 Wildwood Avenue
Woburn, MA 01801-2041
Tel: 781-904-2500
Fax: 781-904-2620

For information on all Butterworth-Heinemann publications available, contact our World Wide Web home page at: http://www.bh.com

10 9 8 7 6 5 4 3 2 1

Printed in the United States of America

Dedication

*Dr. George Kozmetsky
and his wife, Ronya*

*In appreciation of your
inspiration to value
intellect,
innovation, and
international collaboration.*

*Through your demonstrated leadership,
guiding hands and open hearts,
you have both touched me
in ways too numerous to mention;
and I have grown,
both personally and professionally.*

*There is no substitute for genuine care,
supporting the road less traveled;
and it has made all the difference.*

Contents

Foreword   xvii

Preface   xxiii

Acknowledgments   xxvii

Part I   The Innovation Frontier   1

1   A Global Imperative for Sustainability—
The Knowledge Why   3

     1.1   Austin Roots   4
     1.2   From NII to GII   6
     1.3   Frame For Progress   8
     1.4   The Potential of Knowledge Societies   11
     1.5   Foundation for Sustainability   14
     1.6   Productivity Without Borders   16
     1.7   Summary   17
     Chapter Endnotes   18

2   The Knowledge Value Proposition—
The Knowledge What   19

     2.1   Resolving the Paradox   20

2.2   Creating the Proposition   22
2.3   From Transfer to Transformation   25
2.4   Innovation Redefined   29
2.5   Blending the Old and the New   32
2.6   Summary   34
Chapter Endnotes   34

3   From Planning to Innovation Strategy—
     The Knowledge How   35

3.1   The Downside of Planning   36
3.2   An Atlas for Innovation   37
3.3   Actualizing Innovation Strategy   40
3.4   Summary   44
Chapter Endnotes   45

Part II   Architecting a Future   47

4   Knowledge Performance Economics   49

4.1   Some Roots   51
4.2   Totally New Foundations   54
4.3   National Initiatives   56
4.4   Societal Level—New Indicators for Success   62
4.5   Architectural Considerations   64
4.6   Action Steps   65
4.7   Summary   65
Chapter Endnotes   66

5   Knowledge Structures   69

5.1   Some Roots   70
5.2   Back to the Productivity Paradox   72
5.3   Culture is Key   74
5.4   Platform for Collaborative Advantage   77

	5.5	Architectural Considerations	79
	5.6	Action Steps	80
	5.7	Summary	80
		Chapter Endnotes	81

6	Knowledge Workers		83
	6.1	Some Roots	84
	6.2	Emerging Practices	87
	6.3	Shaping of the Knowledge Profession	91
	6.4	Architectural Considerations	94
	6.5	Action Steps	94
	6.6	Summary	95
		Chapter Endnotes	96

7	Knowledge Processes		97
	7.1	Some Roots	98
	7.2	Envisioning the System as a Model	102
	7.3	Emerging Practices	104
	7.4	Operationalizing a Knowledge Strategy	105
	7.5	Innovation on the Radar Screen	106
	7.6	Architectural Considerations	109
	7.7	Action Steps	109
	7.8	Summary	110
		Chapter Endnotes	111

8	Knowledge-Processing Technology		113
	8.1	Some Roots	114
	8.2	Collaborative Technologies	116
	8.3	E-Business Implications	116
	8.4	Emerging Practices	118
	8.5	Evolution of the Gateway: Bridging the Digital Divide	120

8.6   Architectural Considerations   123
8.7   Action Steps   124
8.8   Summary   125
Chapter Endnotes   125

Part III   The Globe as a Network   127

9   ENTOVATION®: A Case Story   129

9.1   The Founding of the Network   130
9.2   The Engagement Process   132
9.3   Proof of Concept   133
9.4   Building the Social Capital   142
9.5   Lessons Learned: The Network in Retrospect   145
9.6   What Went Right?   146
9.7   What Went Wrong?   146
9.8   Summary   147
Chapter Endnotes

10   Global Momentum of Knowledge Strategy   149

10.1   The ENTOVATION 100   151
10.2   Global Responses: Similar yet Varied   154
10.3   Responses by Question   155
10.4   What They Said   161
10.5   Testimony: Value of the Global Network   165
10.6   Summary   171
Chapter Endnotes   171

11   Trends of Innovation Strategy   173

11.1   Meta-views of the E100   175
11.2   Ten dimensions of Innovation Strategy   179
11.3   Case study: Consortium for Advanced Manufacturing
International (CAM-I)   192

11.4 Key Findings 198
11.5 Summary: 199
Chapter Endnotes 200

Part IV Innovation Leadership in Practice 201

12 Modern Knowledge Leadership: the 7Cs 203

12.1 How Does Leadership Differ In A Knowledge
Economy? 205
12.2 Redefining the Management Agenda 206
12.3 Leadership Starts With You 218
12.4 Summary 220
Chapter Endnotes 221

13 Exemplar Ken Practitioners 223

13.1 Dr. Marcus Speh Birkenkrahe
(New Zealand/United Kingdom) 225
13.2 Yvonne Buma (The Netherlands) 227
13.3 Dr. Javier Carrillo (Mexico) 228
13.4 Joachim Doering (Germany) 230
13.5 Leif Edvinsson (Sweden) 232
13.6 Alejandro Fernandez (Venezuela) 233
13.7 Dr. Piero Formica (Italy) 235
13.8 Bob Franco (USA) 236
13.9 Cindy Gordon (Canada) 238
13.10 Admiral Bobby Ray Inman (USA) 239
13.11 Keith Jones (Canada) 241
13.12 Dr. George Kozmetsky (USA) 243
13.13 Chin Hoon Lau (Malaysia) 244
13.14 Doug Macnamara (Canada) 246
13.15 Dr. Tom Malone (USA) 248
13.16 Dr. Eunika Mercier-Laurent (France) 250

13.17   Dr. Edna Pasher (Israel)   251
13.18   Dr. Ante Pulic and Karmen Jelcic (Croatia)   253
13.19   Dr. Joerg Staeheli (Switzerland)   255
13.20   Xenia Stanford (Canada)   256
13.21   Hubert Saint Onge (Canada)   258
13.21   Summary   259
Chapter Endnotes   260

14   Evolving Innovation Infrastructures   261

14.1   Global Knowledge Partnership   262
14.2   Development Gateway   265
14.3   KALiF—The European Perspective   266
14.4   The Knowledge Wave—New Zealand   267
14.5   Singapore—"The innovation nation"   270
14.6   ShareNet: The Enterprise Model   271
14.7   CBIRD   274
14.8   NEPAD: Africa's Initiative   275
14.9   The United Nations   276
14.10   Summary   277
Chapter Endnotes

Part V   The Millennium Vision   281

15   The Knowledge-Millennium Generation   283

15.1   A Vision of the Future   285
15.2   Trends   288
15.3   Global Knowledge Partnership   289
15.4   World Congress of the Young
        Entrepreneur Association   292
15.5   Junior Alpbach   294
15.6   The Jade Network   294
15.7   New Zealand   296

15.8   Summary   298
Chapter Endnotes

16   Blueprint for Twenty-First Century Innovation   301
16.1   The Case for Innovation   302
16.2   A Solid Foundation   303
16.3   Creating an Innovation Culture   308
16.4   Multiple Economic Levels   309
16.5   Crafting an Enterprisewide Innovation Vision   312
16.6   Summary   314
Chapter Endnotes   315

17   Creating the World Trade of Ideas   317
17.1   A Vision-In-Progress   319
17.2   Five ENTOVATION Principles for Homeland
Security   321
17.3   A Global Holonomy   325
17.4   Prospectus   327
17.5   Summary   331
Chapter Endnotes

Appendix A: Knowledge Innovation®   333

Appendix B: Sample Definitions of Innovation   335

Appendix C: Calibrating the Innovation Strategy   338

Appendix D: The Momentum of Knowledge
Management   341
D.1   Collective findings are emerging   342
D.2   Conclusions   345

Appendix E: Knowledge Leaders and Laggards   347

    E.1   Ten Characteristics of Leaders   347
    E.2   Ten Characteristics of Laggards   348

References   351

About the Author   361

Index   365

Foreword

We are now embarking upon the Knowledge Economy; in fact, we have all played a role in its evolution. The opportunities are numerous and the managerial challenges multifold. The Future is just beyond the bend; and how are we equipped to take advantage of the opportunities? Do you see it…and have you envisioned your own role in it? Debra M. Amidon has outlined the 'future as an asset', which goes well beyond the traditional, Tayloristic forms of management.

In previous publications as a pioneer of innovation, Debra has defined the core principles and outlined a methodology for innovating enterprises. In this new publication—*The Innovation SuperHighway*, she defines the critical steps in envisioning our future. In essence, will we see the future as an asset or a liability? Amidon outlines a constructive path forward.

The newpapers of the present are full of stories of financial crises, failures and fraud. It is also sometimes referred to as the time of institutional failures, as phrased by the founder of VISA Mr. Dee W. Hock. We evidently have to step back like the impressionists and Claude Monet—what Amidon defined in her first book—and try to see and reshape the larger pattern. This is also what Amidon is offering in many ways in her work with Entovation—enterprise innovation—a network comprised of theorists and practitioners from around the world. She understands the global Gestalt and where it is going; with her words and collective wisdom, she illuminates our direction.

She is also accompanied by a group of thought leaders called the Entovation (E 100), among who Dr. Thomas F. Malone is saying: "We are at a historical choice point—a defining moment—in determining the kind of world our children will inherit. If we make these choices based only on the models of our industrial age past, we will almost certainly miss the true opportunities before us." We must learn to convert the future into an asset, not a liability, by addressing the opportunity cost of not innovating and continuously renewing.

Debra's assumptions are based upon a new Knowledge Value Proposition beyond cost, quality and time. There are many facets of the emerging future to be systematized and leveraged. Knowledge economics is one of the major patterns, contrasted by the present stories of the financial economics of failing institutions, where the economies seem to be shadowed by the lack of perspectives and insights behind the new intangible economics and intellectual capital. If we miss the perspectives, we might be the victims of impoverishing ourselves by forgetting the heritage. Our future always begins with an investment into what we now call the 'hidden value' of the firm. The core of the knowledge economics is knowledge innovation, or the capacity to shape future opportunities. It is think-oriented instead of thing-oriented. It is a momentum of natural evolution. It can also be referred to as a process of knowledge navigation, i.e. a quest for the enlarged and knowledge explorative learnings of the not knowing. Today organizations are labeled as complexity systems, chaordic systems and bio economics. Transaction values are replaced by interaction values.

Similarly, the new proposition is a function of the behavior of the organization—best exemplified by the emergent communities of knowledge within which new leadership lies. Now, we are dependent upon a trust-led leadership based upon values of openness, knowledge-sharing and respect for the competencies of one another. Interdependence takes on new meaning between functions, sectors, industries and even nations. Value is created in the interconnections and fostered through the quality of conversations virtually and face-to-face. No longer are we limited by the hierarchical, control policies of the past. Our future depends upon our capacity to share leadership, listen to the inquiries of others, be courageous in our ability to take responsible risk, and create cultures of knowledge-sharing. Dare we build institutions that seek collaborative—not competitive—advantage?

The Innovation SuperHighway is by definition global. The emergent technology removes all geographical boundaries. The full potential of these global networks for innovation largely remains untouched and unexplored. Debra maps it all out for us, a bit like explorers started to produce maps of the New World. The new innovation highway is comprised of a series of cross disciplinary forums where the quality of the conversation enabled by the technology and the forever expanding bandwidth is providing an unprecedented platform for innovation. Organizations that miss getting on the train will be irremediably left behind.

The Information SuperHighway was perceived as a vehicle of information, computers and technology. Within few years, it is obvious that the highway is actually one of social networks in addition to the technical infrastructures. Only through the motivations of people can the 'network' come alive; and only with the technology can the cultures of nations—industrialized and developing—realize their full potential. Amidon is right—the innovation process is what brings knowledge alive and puts it to work. Further, she has illustrated how the technology is only as useful as how it is used…and our sustainability as a world is only as effective as is our weakest nation. We now know that innovation is not a function of the technology and that knowledge is what drives the enterprise forward. Debra has placed innovation the central topic of enterprises. More important, she realizes the value of decentralized (and yet) networked organizations—something many big organizations are forgetting as they attempt to control the innovation process.

Once again, Amidon has moved the finish line—and appropriately so—to stretch our imaginations of how we might architect our future. She has been the guardian of the knowledge movement and with this publication steers our efforts toward profitability and prosperity. This can be viewed as a time element—the longitude dimensions of an organization. In other words, a lateral networked collaborative brain expands the frontiers for new knowing by knowledge insourcing through new alliances. We've more to gain with learning from, rather than defeating one another. Amidon's original concept of Ken— having the knowledge AND a range of vision to apply the knowledge—shape our current concepts of Intellectual Capital—something she was publishing in the mid 1980's.

But do not take it from Amidon alone. This book is rich with the insights and observations of professionals from around the world that also believe that a new world is emerging and we all have a role to play.

This might be called intelligent enterprising, as well as innovative societies. *The Innovation Superhighway* provides a tangible highway to serve as the multiplier of intangible value—the networked competence for shared prosperity. It offers to leverage the local human capital— primarily the component of the brain such as intellect, insight and imagination—multiplied by the global technology tools often called structural capital, into a growth spiral of innovative value and wealth creation. This will result in emerging intellectual capital, on the individual level, an enterprise level as well as a society level.

Innovation is what gives purpose to the exchange of knowledge. Innovation is the outcome of a knowledge-based interaction. Innovation is about shaping and architecting a desired future. *The Innovation Superhighway* tells us how this future will unfold and shows you how you can be part of it. As someone who lives and works in global networks, Debra is uniquely positioned to be our guide.

The Entovation superhighway is the bridging process of organizational capital on a global scale—a springboard opportunity to be grasped. The longitude value of an organization, enterprise or society is to be found in its capacity to reach out, connect and leverage the collective competence to take advantage of the future. How will the intelligence flow through the logistics of *The Innovation SuperHigh-*

way? According to Amidon, the opportunity is ours. Are we ready to accept the challenge?

One step toward 'innovating your future'…

August 2002

Leif Edvinsson,
former Senior Vice President for Intellectual Capital,
Skandia AFS and co-author of Intellectual Capital and
author of Corporate Longitude(Sweden).

Hubert Saint-Onge,
former Senior Vice President of Clarica and
co-author of Leveraging Communities of Practice (Canada).

Joachim Doering,
Senior Vice President, Information Communications Networks (ICN),
Siemens, AG (Germany).

Preface

I shall be retelling this with a sigh
Somewhere ages and ages hence:
Two roads diverged in a wood, and I—
I took the one less traveled by,
And that has made all the difference.

—Robert Frost

The knowledge movement has literally taken flight—and in only fifteen short years! The "ken"—gaining knowledge and having a range of vision to put the knowledge into action—has been awakened worldwide; now it is a matter of harnessing that collective intellectual talent to build a sustainable future that does not exist today. Hundreds of thousands of theorists and practitioners worldwide are traveling a new path—one destined to lead us to prosperous innovation.

In 1996, I documented the knowledge evolution in the book, *Innovation Strategy for the Knowledge Economy: The Ken Awakening*, with a conclusion that was—at the time—an immense stretch of a vision. I argued that such foresight should be bold enough that, when documented into a plan, it was not something that was outdated before actions were operationalized. A strategic vision must be simple, visceral, and magnetic enough to pull the competencies of the public forward.

Readers were invited to step into the next millennium, in which the "World Trade of Ideas" was described—"worldwide recognition that intellectual capital is the most valuable resource we have to manage enterprises, nations, and society as a whole." A challenge was asserted that the "flow of knowledge will enhance the standard of living in every country around the globe" and that a "global innovation infrastructure (GII) serves as the underpinning of the international network for the creation and application of new ideas."

Further, I described, "hundreds of theorists and practitioners in the new 'community of knowledge practice' who would convene…(where) the economic, behavioral, and technological issues are reconciled and opportunities abound for all who participate. Diversity of heritage is respected, and similarities in mission are discovered. A common language evolves that brings together the foundations of knowledge and the process of innovation that were never considered before." Speaking of the representatives, "They are distinguished in their fields, but convene together to collaborate with one another on how best to preserve and leverage the best innovation practices for the benefit of humankind."

Now in 2002, what has happened? Results have been so far beyond expectations that it seems impossible to project where all this might be headed; but we will give a try. The language has emerged. Respect for the value of an innovation culture is now obvious. Leaders in the knowledge community and innovation communities—heretofore separate professional directions—are beginning to converge. Innovation is no longer creativity…nor is it R&D. An appreciation of the 'innovation value-system' (vs. value-chain), customer success (not satisfaction) and establishing collaborative (not competitive) advantage is appreciated in all aspects of management—public and private. None of this was the case in 1996; today, it is common knowledge.

I refer those of you seeking the "how" of the knowledge economy to *Innovation Strategy for the Knowledge Economy*. There, you will find the rationale, the business proposition, and modern management practices embedded in an innovation methodology. It is designed for those who

have practiced the best of quality, incremental reengineering methodologies and are ready to transform their organizations with systematic
notions of knowledge creation and application.

Our intent with this publication, *The Innovation Superhighway*, is to
build on the frame and "move the finish line." In addition to strengthening the "advanced how," this book provides the "where next." Now
that a shared vision has emerged, and it has; how do we harness the
intellectual capital of the world for sustained prosperity? This book is
intended for those who have explored the principles of knowledge
exchange, knowledge sharing, and knowledge management and are
now ready for far more dynamic methods rooted in the basics of enterprise strategy, measurement of intangible value, and the symbiosis that
can come only from international leadership.

Part 1 defines the new *innovation frontier* illustrating the global
imperative in terms of the new knowledge value proposition resolving
the productivity paradox that has plagued enterprise performance for
decades. It positions innovation strategy—as opposed to strategic
planning—as core to the sustainability of an enterprise, sector, or
nation. Part 2 expands the *architectural foundation* linking measures,
structures, people, process, and technology in terms conducive for the
knowledge economy. Part 3 uses the evolution of our virtual competencies as an example of the *globe as a network*. Part 4 illustrates how these
concepts—purely theoretical only a decade ago—have become fundamental modern management modus operandi. These are examples of
innovation leadership in practice—the individuals and initiatives that are
shaping the future. The book closes with Part 5, *The Millennium Vision*,
which provides a blueprint for how individuals and organizations can
make a contribution to the future realization of building collaborative
advantage—a practice that could be a platform for world peace.

If you are ready to act on your accumulated learning, this book will
be your compass to use in riding the crest of the knowledge wave as
it moves toward unchartered territories. Let it be a beginning, an
unleashing of your own aspirations—what you know intuitively is
managerially obvious. We live in a kaleidoscopic economy, and the

complexity of its facets and the pace of change are destined to increase. The time is now to craft your own role, to journey on the "road not taken" and make a difference. Let me know your progress.

Always in your Network,

Debra
April 2002
Wilmington, Massachusetts
E-mail: debra@entovation.com
URL: http://www.entovation.com

Acknowledgments

"How you thank someone for taking you from crayons to perfume?" —words from *To Sir With Love*, a film that inspired individual and collective performance beyond established expectations.

The Entovation Network, which began as a Rolodex of 400 people from 20 nations, has grown into an international network of competencies spanning 90 countries. Of course, there are my mentors who have taken many of the steps with me—Dr. George Kozmetsky, Dr. Tom Malone, and Admiral Bobby Ray Inman. There are practitioners from the new school of knowledge practice, such as Leif Edvinsson, Hubert Saint-Onge, and Joachim Doering, who have been constant companions in the process. These are the people from whom I have learned on a daily basis, those who constantly fuel my own vision and the energy to contribute.

The Network itself has grown to tens of thousands, many of whom are registered colleagues; but many others have been participants in the many international forums in which I have been privileged to participate, throughout North and South America Eastern and Western Europe, Asia, Australia and South Africa. It includes the person who offers the invitation, another who serves as my host, and, in some cases, my translator, my driver, or even my minion. It includes the others with whom I have shared the podium—and helped to edit slides—who have deepened my learning, expanded my knowledge of a new culture, and strengthened my resolve.

One of the prime discoveries since writing the last book has been the importance of having materials translated into foreign languages. It is the only way that modern concepts can be disseminated in ways to influence the masses. But this is no small task, given the complexity, uniqueness, and progressive nature of the material. Each foreign edition has taken incredible dedication from both the primary translator(s) and, in many cases, capable graduate students put to task: Drs. Jin Zhouying and Chen Jin, responsible for the Chinese edition; Dr. Manfred Bornmann and Stefan Fazekas (both from Austria), responsible for the German edition; Gerardo Calderon Malagamba (Mexico), responsible for the Spanish edition; Dr. Eunika Mercier-Laurent, responsible for the French edition; and Peter Kuok Seng Hwee (Singapore), responsible for the second Chinese translation). There are several Entovation colleagues who have assumed responsibility for translations of various articles on the Entovation Web site into Norwegian, Turkish, Spanish, Dutch, Portuguese, Russian, Polish, Japanese, and Chinese.

The Entovation 100 represents a diagonal slice of the network as featured on the Global Knowledge Leadership Map—many of whom are referenced later in this book. Together with Dr. Silvard Kool, a Boston College professor and international concert pianist, we have made visible the contributions of experts around the world, all to extraordinary musical harmony and improvisation, essential criteria for successful modern management. There are several who serve as Entovation Fellows responsible for one of the ten dimensions of innovation strategy. In addition to those mentioned above, I have deep appreciation for the talents of Karl-Erik Sveiby (Australia), Sally-Ann Moore (Switzerland), Dr. Charles Savage and Elizabeth Sundrum (both from Germany), Jan Wyllie (UK), Larry Todd Wilson (USA), Larraine Segil (USA), Yvonne Buma (The Netherlands), Doug Macnamara (Canada), and Dr. David J. Skyrme (UK), who was also a co-author of our 1997 research report, *Creating the Knowledge-Based Business* and editor of our joint monthly electronic publication, "*I³ Update/ENTOVATION News.*"

In addition to those already named, several have played a pivotal role in the visibility of the Entovation materials and/or in personal support of my own endeavors that have been more of my own learning than they might imagine: Xenia Stanford (Canada), F. Javier Carrillo Gamboa (Mexico), Piero Formica (Italy), Olimpia Salas (Venezuela), Jose Gasalla (Spain), Stephen Denning (USA), Darius Mahdjoubi (USA), Jean Marc LeDuc (France), Baruch Lev (USA), Ante Pulic (Austria/Croatia), Esko Kilpi (Finland); Lynne Schneider (USA), Marcus Speh Birkenkrahe (New Zealand), Gülgün Kayakutlu (Turkey); Konstantin Golubev (Ukraine); Tomasz Rudolf (Poland), Leonardo Pineda (Colombia), Bob Wiele (Canada), Parry Norling (USA), Brian Davis (Canada), Jerry Ash (USA), John Hibbs (USA), Edna Pasher (Israel) and more, many more—too many to mention.

At the end of the day, though, it all boils down to a few individuals who maintain the strength of the vision through their own actions. I am deeply indebted to Laura Childs and Margaret Logan (both from Canada) who have helped develop and maintain the Entovation Web site—our own Entovation superhighway that has enabled the creation and dissemination of the wondrous works of the collective talent of the network. I should credit the able staff of Butterworth-Heinemann—especially Karen Maloney and Kathryn Grant—who believed in the follow-on work destined to make a qualitative difference in the status quo.

There are no words—no thoughts of adequate appreciation—for the tender loving care of my mother, Mildred. M. Amidon; my husband, Dr. Clinton C. Ackerman; and my daughter, Kendra Mae Amidon, who has been the closest, most constant confidant of all. I am indebted to their faith in my work and regular sacrifices they made to enable me to become a player in this emerging economy. Because of their relentless encouragement, we have a better chance for a foundation for future generations—beyond the competitive practices of today.

We have come together as a composite of diverse experience, but shared aspirations. Our innovation superhighway is destined to be both human and humane, not lost amidst the information and technological rhetoric. History will document how this transition will be led by many of those mentioned above. The transformation is inevitable now; it only matters what role each one of us will play in its realization. Thank you for all the gifts you have already provided along the way.

Innovating our future…together.

The Innovation Superhighway

Harnessing Intellectual Capital for Sustainable Collaborative Advantage

PART I

The Innovation Frontier

ONE

A Global Imperative
for Sustainability—
The Knowledge Why

I saw the earth without any borders
Without any fighting, without any fear;
So, captain, give the order,
We're going to the next frontier.

recollections of Apollo commander Eugene Cernan
as written in a song by Paul and Ralph Colwell

The world is experiencing unprecedented change in applications
of knowledge in every dimension of development, growth, revitali-
zation, and organization. The demands and opportunities of an
interdependent global economy have implications for private and
public decision making by enterprises and communities, whether local,
national, regional, or global. Most nations have launched major initiatives to harness their inherent capabilities within a transnational
context. All has been done in the name of international competitiveness. Economies have been transformed, communities revitalized,
emerging territories supported, and industrialized nations reposi-
tioned. We have much to learn from one another.

The foundation for a new economic world order has been laid—one
based on knowledge, innovation, and international collaboration. This

is a new landscape for which the managerial rules have significantly changed—but how, when and to what end?

1.1   AUSTIN ROOTS

In 1982, I had been working on the team assigned to bring the Microelectronics Computer and Technology Corporation (MCC) to Boston. After all, we had the most successful Route 128 high technology belt and the highest concentration of academic institutions of anywhere in the world. We were "the Massachusetts miracle" (Lampe, 1988). We expected that the San Francisco Bay area was our only formidable competitor with the then rapidly emerging Silicon Valley.

The principals of Control Data Corporation and Digital Equipment Corporation had been actively involved in charting a new course for their U.S. R&D and establishing a collaborative foundation for pre-competitive research. They had studied the principles of the then highly successful Japanese "Keiretsu"—horizontally and vertically integrated groupings of firms. They studied the plans for Tsukuba City, the first large-scale planned science city, which was designed to be a "knowledge-generation" site (Gibson & Rogers, 1994). And they studied the plans for the Technopolis strategy to link the castle towns of the nation with superhighway infrastructures (Tatsuno, 1986).

The economic development community was stunned when the announcement was made that this national treasure would be based in Austin, Texas. This was a pivotal decision orchestrated with a combined academia, government, and industrial bid that established new rules for the soon-to-be innovation landscape of the modern enterprise, although few realized its importance at the time. Collaboration—with all the difficulties if implementation—was to become the modern management modus operandi.

I remember my first trip to Austin in 1984 to review the initial research and technology transfer plans of this new research consortium. I was impressed by meeting with Admiral Bobby Ray Inman, the corporation's first CEO, who was the former Director of the National

Security Agency and Deputy Director of the Central Intelligence Agency. I marveled at the plans for a new MCC facility—a researcher's dream and an ideal location in which to create and exchange new knowledge in a spirit of collaboration that transcended the walls of significantly competitive firms. I must admit, however, that as I looked at the relatively barren landscape (sorry, but remember I was from Massachusetts), I wondered how the talent needed to succeed would be recruited to Texas.

I returned only 18 short months later, and it seemed that a city had been built overnight! Already there were highways and skyways to rival a mature industrial complex, and that was only the beginning. It did not take long for us to realize, in fact, that the "infrastructure" that had been so eloquently crafted by local leaders, such as Dr. George Kozmetsky, founder and director of the IC² Institute, was not one of bricks and mortar. It was, instead, a vibrant "social capital" infrastructure founded on the intelligence and interactions of people sharing a common purpose and vision.

They called it "collaborative individualism"—these managerial architects of MCC. It was similar to "entrepreneurial teamwork"— the core value of Digital Equipment Corporation, the third official company to join. It was based on a "technopolis wheel," emphasizing the public/private collaboration across the academic, business, and governmental sectors (Smilor, Gibson, and Kozmetsky, 1988). A new form of technology transfer was being innovated, one that relied on the flow of knowledge (not technology per se) to and from MCC. Success would be based on the quality and intensity of those interactions.

There was considerable energy in the deliberations and excitement, if you will, that a new era was coming—and indeed, it was. The severe antitrust laws of the country were rewritten, arch-competitors were collaborating, and people were discussing possibilities—across functions, across businesses, and even across nations.[1] The process of innovation was being redefined forever, and we were all participating in that evolution.

1.2   FROM NII TO GII

About the same time, representatives in the scientific community were already witnessing the benefits of electronic communication. What originally began as ARPA-net in 1972 as the network for the Defense Advanced Research Projects Agency (DARPA), used by a few university military laboratories, was expanded as a general science network and became NSF-net in 1986. Once success had been proven, the growth was explosive; and it eventually evolved into the platform for what was called the National Information Infrastructure (NII) and later described in editorial shorthand as "the information superhighway."

The NII perspective, as originally intended, was based on the assumptions that now seem an understatement: the pace of network communications would accelerate over the next decade; the boundaries of the traditional research scientific community were fading; and networks would link science and society in ways yet unimaginable.[2]

The platform, as stated in the original *National Information Infrastructure* (1994), was to provide "The facilities and services that enable the efficient creation and diffusion of useful information (in order) to

- Enhance the competitiveness of our manufacturing base.
- Increase the speed and efficiency of electronic commerce, or business-to-business communication, to promote economic growth.
- Improve health care delivery and control costs.
- Promote the development and accessibility of quality educational and lifelong learning for all Americans.
- Make us more effective at environmental monitoring and assessing our impacts on the earth.
- Sustain the role of libraries as agents of democratic and equal access to information.
- Provide government services to the public faster, more responsively, and more efficiently.

In short, the NII was an agenda for national competitiveness. But even when it was broadened and renamed the Global Information Infrastructure (GII) during a subsequent G7 discussion, it was never intended to be the "information" infrastructure at all. The "facilities and services" were actually the network, and the "network" was both technical and human. "Useful information" could be considered "knowledge" that resides in the minds of people, whatever their cultural or professional origins. And "creation and diffusion" is actually the innovation process, however defined, such as theory to practice, idea to market, cradle to grave, or creation to application.

Therefore, the NII/GII was in reality the design of an *innovation* (not information) infrastructure—thus, the *innovation* superhighway. Now with the geometric growth in the acceptance of the Internet and the globalization of its application, the innovation intent can be realized: to move ideas from the point of origin to the point of opportunity (e.g., global business) or the point of need (e.g., to eradicate world poverty).

Today, if you do a search on the World Wide Web for "the information superhighway," you will get everything from "Smart cars running on smart highways" (Weisenfelder, 1996) to a recent winner of the American Society for Information Science and Technology's 2001 Best Book Award: *From Gutenberg to the Global Information Infrastructure: Access to Information in a Networked World* (2000) by Professor Christine L. Borgman, Presidential Chair in Information Studies at the University of California, Los Angeles. She explores, with well-researched material, the implications of electronic commerce, electronic publishing, distance-independent education, distributed entertainment, and cooperative work that depends on the ability to discover and locate information, whether about products, services, people, places, facts, or ideas of interest.

Borgman suggests, "None of these applications are new. What is new is the process by which they are conducted....Much is known about the information-related behavior of individuals and institutions, yet relatively little of that knowledge is being applied to the design of digital libraries, national and global information infrastructures, or information policy." I would add that when the GII is viewed as an *innovation* infrastructure (i.e., looking carefully at the "how" and "to what end"), we might be able to use the network—admittedly human and technical—to more prosperous advantage.

Progressive managers and other enterprise leaders are already seeing the benefits and the application of these learning and networking technologies to the knowledge economy. Such an *innovation* superhighway can bring together leading thinkers and practitioners from around the world, from different industry sectors and types of organizations, from governments and public policy agencies, and from professional organizations. Only with this level of cross-fertilization will it be possible to build a truly global infrastructure from which all sectors, functions, and regions of the world can benefit.

1.3   FRAME FOR PROGRESS

The dawn of the new millennium has been met with great enthusiasm and an equivalent commitment to change—or, as we prefer to call it—innovation (i.e., the capacity to preserve the best of the old and realign the rest to take advantage of future opportunity). Individuals and organizations from every function, sector, and corner of the globe are envisioning a new economic world order, one based on intellectual, not financial, capital. Of course, knowledge has always been an essential element in the advancement of civilization, but today's emerging economy proposes that knowledge be managed explicitly.

Certainly there are numerous facets to understand with this complex evolution; but there are three primary underlying themes fundamental to the new infrastructure needed to create prosperity in this new economy:

- *Knowledge* is the new, expandable source of economic wealth. There is an emerging recognition that the inherent intellectual assets, effectively exploited through innovation, are the most valuable resource of any country.

- *Innovation* encompasses the full spectrum, from creative idea generation through full profitable commercialization. Successful innovation depends on converting knowledge stocks and flows into marketable goods and services.
- *Collaboration* replaces the competitive (win/lose) paradigm, which is prevalent in many businesses today, with win/win benefits based on pooling competencies: knowledge, know-how, and skills.

Today, we know that the knowledge agenda is worldwide, pervades every function and every industry, and has implications for industrialized and developing nations alike. Indeed, it has evolved well beyond the borders of a nation; it has become an agenda of international collaboration. Although originally thought to refer to white-collar, high technology workers, there is no such thing as a non-knowledge worker. And, originally to have been the focus of the services sector, there is no such thing as a non–knowledge-intensive industry. The knowledge of all individuals is important. Knowledge is what makes companies unique, even within the same industry. We have more to gain by building on the competencies of one another as individuals and nations.

By now the shift in orientation from "data" to "information" to "knowledge"—or reasonable facsimiles—seems commonplace. However, we still hear about national initiatives for the Information Society and the needs for ICT (i.e., information, computers and technology). There are still many who lack a fundamental understanding of the difference. Our simple explanation is that data is a base representation of fact, information is data with context, and knowledge is information with meaning and fully actionable.

The innovation of which we speak—and must manage—is not a function of the flow of technology or even the flow of materials into viable products and services. Rather, it is the learning process—the pace and effectiveness with which knowledge is exchanged—and how

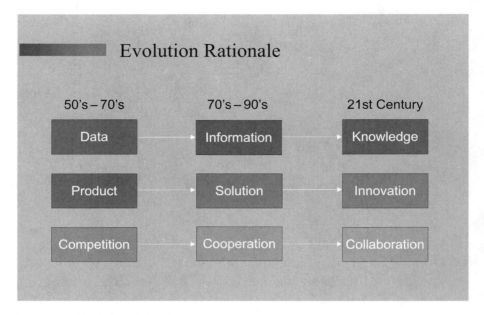

FIGURE 1.1   *Evolution of thought.*

swiftly ideas (old and new) are applied. Customers have become so sophisticated and the realities of hypercompetition so prevalent that companies can no longer focus on products from a technology-push perspective. In fact, most customers are not even satisfied with a solution-based product offering. Instead, their knowledge needs to be considered part and parcel of an organization's ability to innovate.

We now know that win/lose scenarios are suboptimal at best. Even cooperative ventures (i.e., sharing the pie) may create win/win interaction but do not capitalize of the real value of human interactions and the potential knowledge-sharing therein. On the other hand, collaboration can provide a synergistic win/win in which opponents and partners develop a shared understanding of what's possible and make decisions on what might be created (and actualized) in consort with one another, rather than as separate entities.

We are just beginning to discover how to value knowledge in our organizations and the fact that knowledge has no value until it is put to use. Leaders in technological innovation and knowledge management are beginning to converge in their concepts and in their practices. University research initiatives are beginning to proliferate. Nations are launching initiatives for twenty-first century positioning, and societal organizations (e.g., The World Bank, the United Nations, the European Union, and the OECD) have placed knowledge and learning at center stage for future sustainable economic development. It is only the beginning.

1.4   The Potential of Knowledge Societies

There has been a compounding effect from the rapid advances and acceptance of virtual reality and the phenomenon of virtual networks. Advances in one area appear to affect the other and vice versa. In other words, communications technology—visible within the past decade as research experiments and "skunk works"—is now embodied in a plethora of products and services ranging from the most complex simulations to child video games. This symbiosis makes possible the virtual organizational structures, defined by Steven L. Goldman, Roger N. Nagel and Kenneth Preiss (1995) as "an opportunistic alliance of core competencies distributed among a number of distinct operating entities within a single large company or group of companies." Such innovation enables organizations to operate with more fluid, flexible management practices and on a global scale.

In 1987, we held the first nation's Roundtable for *Managing the Knowledge Assets into the 21ˢᵗ Century* (Amidon and Dimancescu, 1987) during which we concluded:

> *If we can agree that the knowledge base of the United States is our most precious resource, then we can begin to manage it more effectively. This requires a re-thinking of how the intellectual capital of each sector— education, government and industry – should be developed and applied to the dual goals of the advancement of science and technology as well as the international competitiveness of our nation."*

And so, the journey began with an exploration of the process of innovation: knowledge creation, knowledge translation, and knowledge commercialization. Given the exploding receptivity of Internet capability, the concepts diffused quickly through all sectors of the economy and manifested in Europe, where there were already roots[3] laid by Karl-Eric Sveiby (1987) and in Japan by Hiroyuki Itami (1987) and Ikujiru Nonaka (1991).

These progressive concepts that initially focused on the enterprise level (e.g., Know-How Company, Knowledge Creating Company, et al) were elevated swiftly with adoption to the realm of economic development by various countries, such as France and Poland. Having been exposed to a U.S. Study Mission on technological commercialization, Prime Minister Pawlak of Poland brought his entire cabinet to New York City—hosted by Dr. Michael Crow, Vice Provost of Columbia

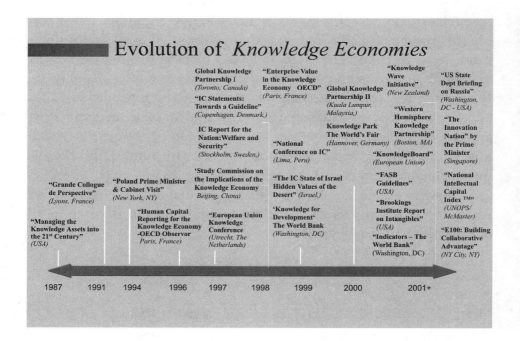

Figure 1.2   *Evolution of knowledge economies*[4]

University—to understand the implications of the use of the technology for the sustainability of his country.

Soon, we saw evidence of the attention of industrialized nations through the initiatives by the Organization of Economic Co-operation and Development (OECD) with lead articles in the OECD Observer by Jean-Claude Paye (1996) on policies for a knowledge-based economy and Riel Miller (1996) on Human Capital Accounting. The World Bank followed suit with major initiatives including the publication of the World Development Report with the title *Knowledge for Development* (1999) that set to convert the institution into the World Knowledge Bank for developing nations. They followed up with major Global Partnership Conferences—the GKI in Toronto, Canada and GKII in Kuala Lumpur, Malaysia, which drew 1,200 participants from 90 nations. By the time I visited Beijing in 1998, there were already several study commissions on the implications of the knowledge society for China.

By now, the notion of intellectual capital (IC) Reporting, originating at Skandia AFS, began to focus on the "power of innovation" (1995) and was adapted to the level of the nation's economy in Sweden. At the same time, several countries—namely Denmark, The Netherlands, and Israel—were experimenting with the schema adapted for their countries. The European Union hosted a meeting in Utrecht bringing together Ministries of Education, Ministries of Commerce, and leading knowledge professionals to explore the "European Knowledge Union." Even such nations as Peru were holding National Conferences on IC as early as 1999, and the World's Fair in Hannover, Germany, created a sizable "Knowledge Park."

Most recently, the Brookings Institute has released its study on intangibles (Lev, 2000), the FASB has issued guidelines, The World Bank has issued new economic indicators, and the United Nations —together with McMaster University—has defined a national intellectual capital index (Bontis, 2002). The U.S. State Department has held briefings on converting nations such as Russia to a knowledge economy; there are proposals for the western hemisphere knowledge partnership (WHKP); and the Prime Minister of Singapore has declared his intention for his country to be "The Innovation Nation."

We need more demonstration projects to create prototypes for new ways of thinking about how research scientists and bench engineers—across disciplinary, industry, and national boundaries—can collaborate on problems of mutual interest. We need more examples of the progress of developing nations and how aboriginal communities are establishing new mechanisms to preserve and leverage their own cultural heritage. We need more success stories of how the accelerated creation, movement, and application of new ideas into products and services can ensure the profitable growth of an enterprise—a large scale organization as well as a small start-up entrepreneurial firm—and ultimately benefit society. We need more incentives for individuals to value their knowledge and the knowledge of others and work toward collaboration for the common good.

Such international multi-year projects should not focus on the flow of information per se, but on the interdependent creation and utilization of three types of knowledge: core knowledge (data, information, and expertise); new knowledge (ideas and inventions); and applied knowledge (products, services and know-how). Evaluation of such systems will provide insight into the interdependence of the economic, behavioral; and technological factors referenced earlier. It will provide some understanding of the managerial principles inherent in virtual networked learning—the challenge of The Innovation Superhighway.

1.5   FOUNDATION FOR SUSTAINABILITY

It was Dr. Tom Malone, formerly at MIT and now a Distinguished Scholar at North Carolina State University, who introduced many of us to the real opportunity at hand with his comments on Global Learn Day:[5]

> *The path to a prosperous, sustainable, and equitable society is long, winding, and difficult, but a start can now be made with a knowledge-based and human-centered strategy. This strategy*

empowers individuals to renew rather than degrade the physical and biological environment, and to enrich rather than impoverish the social and cultural environment. Entry into this knowledge society will require new patterns of collaboration among the scholarly disciplines. New modes of partnership must also be established among all levels of government, academia, business and industry, and local community organizations.

Using the foundation for sustainability outlined for the Western Hemisphere Knowledge Partnership (WHKP)—see Chapter 14— that was premiered in Boston in July, 2001, participants formulated a vision (and relevant strategies) for nations and regions of the world:

1. *Education*—life-long learning is a sine qua non for a knowledge-based economy. Distance education is a promising tool with which to pursue life-long learning.

2. *Health and resilience of natural ecosystems*—requires the development of indicators for the pressures on, extent of, and output by agricultural, coastal, forest, freshwater, and grassland ecosystems. As civilization expands, hazards from natural disasters increase. Extensive use of *collaboratories* is envisioned in this and subsequent agenda items

3. *Eco-efficiency in the production and consumption of goods and services*—environmentally benign to alleviate the impact of further economic growth on world ecosystems.

4. *Energy to power economic growth, and conservation and exploration of environmentally friendly sources of energy*—the accumulation of greenhouse gases in the atmosphere is emerging as a regional as well as a global problem.

5. *National income accounts*—extension to include environmental impacts and make realistic the consequences of contemporary patterns of production and consumption.

6. *Intellectual property rights*—the knowledge-based economy is transforming legal and measurement standards.

7. *Delivery of health care*—now entering an era of profound change in which integration with the sciences and sharing of new knowledge and its applications to health care are increasingly important.

8. *Community networks*—to foster interactive participation by individuals at all levels (local, regional, and global), from indigenous communities to major urban centers.

It is not these factors individually, but how these economic elements combine to establish an environment conducive to attracting foreign investment, stimulating entrepreneurial management, and taking advantage of the opportunities technological advancement provides.

1.6   PRODUCTIVITY WITHOUT BORDERS

Singapore's Prime Minister Goh Chok Tong (recently reelected to office) in a keynote address provided the vision of an innovative society:

> To many people, the word "innovate" conjures up images of science labs, high-tech computers, and people with a string of degrees working in a faraway place called Silicon Valley. But that is incorrect. Innovation is nothing more than coming up with good ideas and implementing them to realize their value. It is about value creation.... Throughout the history of mankind and civilizations, countries and corporations, which were able to anticipate, respond and adapt to changes quickly, have triumphed over others. Those that failed to act and react quickly fell by the wayside."

He suggested that to realize a vision of an innovative society, Singapore needs a concerted, deliberate effort to transform the mindsets and processes that choke and kill innovation. A national focus on innovation is required; and the Prime Minister has put resources behind the words to actualize the vision. The Singapore Productivity and Standards Board (PSB), Economic Development Board (EDB), and other agencies are working close together to cultivate the innovation culture among students, the workforce, businessmen, the civil service, and leaders in society.

Ultimately, it is people who will make the difference in transforming Singapore into an innovative society, admits the Prime Minister. The government provides the infrastructure and creates the environment for more people to take business risks; but it is each individual who must act. With a call for action, he inspired his nation: "Each of you can and must innovate. Together, we can transform Singapore and ride the crest of change in the world."

What better foundation for The Innovation Superhighway than such a vision of borders minimized? Indeed, the intent of this conference was a search for world synergy—not inappropriate given the events of 9/11/2001. Indeed, by the leadership shown at this recent IPC conference, Singapore—with the help of the APO—could set the standards for creating the innovation region of the world!

In 1945, Vannevar Bush submitted a seminal Report to the National Science Foundation in Washington D.C., called *Science—The Endless Frontier*. Now, we have an opportunity—not just with a single chief of state but with the academic, governmental, and industrial leaders of the world to see innovation in a new light. No longer need we focus only on information, computers, and technology. In fact, we need no longer focus only on financial capital, for it is the intangible value hidden in the interactions among people, nations, and societies that creates the true value; and innovation is how that value is realized.

1.7 SUMMARY

In fifteen short years, an agenda that was in the minds and hearts of a few has become the dominant theme of promoting the new millennium. Knowledge—often defined in terms of intellectual capital—is the source of new economic wealth. Innovation is the process by which that wealth is converted into action—products, services, or initiatives. Although activities can be based at the level of the group, function, enterprise, or nation, ultimately real value is in what flows between the borders, creating collaborative advantage.

The variables for sustainability—economics, education, environment, and more—are interdependent. Similarly, we represent nations that are treasured for their diversity, but true value is discovered in the collective—what we have to offer one another. All innovation begins with the individual within whom lie intuition, intellect, and imagination. Innovation is a call to action, for it is only when knowledge is acted on is there a benefit to society. The dramatic effects of the acceleration of technology—its receptivity and promise—are providing an infrastructure within which our knowledge can be created, shared, and applied—in real time.

The global information infrastructure—the information superhighway—captured the imagination of professionals in every corner of the globe. Now, we can step back and see that the network—both technical and human—was never intended to be about information per se. It was the design in practice of The Innovation Superhighway that has spread in versatility and with global reach unimagined only a decade ago. We've all become participants in the exploration of the new innovation frontier.

CHAPTER ENDNOTES

[1] There was an international intelligence function designed to scout information beyond national boundaries.

[2] Assumptions in a workshop, "Management of a National Telecommunications Highway" that was presented to NASK, the Polish equivalent of the NII, by Willem Scholten and Debra Amidon, October 1994.

[3] Visit the detailed ENTOVATION Timeline based on *Innovation Strategy for the Knowledge Economy: The Ken Awakening* for the evolution of the knowledge movement: http://www.entovation.com/timeline/timeline.htm.

[4] This listing is intended only as a representative sample of national and societal initiatives.

[5] For a detailed description of the 24-hour dialog described in seven vignettes of global interactions, visit http://www.entovation.com/whatsnew/learn-day-entovation.htm.

TWO

The Knowledge Value Proposition— The Knowledge What

The firm's most valuable assets
may become professional know-how,
flexible response,
capabilities for innovation,
information and management systems,
and knowledge about customers and markets.

National Research Council Report

Today's companies measure success based on cost, quality, and time. However, as the marketplace becomes hyper-competitive, the performance metrics become more complex and intangible, the organization becomes more networked, people become more empowered and energized, processes become boundless, and the enterprise will increasingly rely upon technology.

In addition, as enterprises become more reliant on technology and its attendant complexity, they will become more dependent on the knowledge and behavior of employees as well as other stakeholders—both inside and external to the firm. Simultaneously, performance metrics will become more hidden and intangible—related to what leading management philosophers have defined as intellectual capital. Therefore, the traditional value proposition of cost, quality, and time—although still very important—is just not enough.

We live in an era of "kaleidoscopic change."[1] It is not the speed of change of one variable, or the speed of change of multiple variables challenging today's management executives. It is the compounding effects[2] of the speed of change of multiple variables creating a business landscape in which old traditional policies and practices are not sufficient. Just as with a kaleidoscope, one may not know how the weight, shape, or texture of pieces combines to form a new image. We do know that there is no turning back. Executives are challenged to manage enterprises in a world where the economic rules have changed and the new ones have yet to be invented.

2.1   RESOLVING THE PARADOX

The research goes back to the mid-1980s when engineering and marketing experts worldwide were trying to understand why companies were not getting bottom-line results when they were modernizing with information technology.

The phenomenon was described originally as the *technology paradox* and then relabeled the *productivity paradox*. Productivity is a concept that relates the level of output to the level of input and is understood to be more of a multivariable problem than a linear cause-effect relationship.

We know that innovation is no longer a value chain of activities (i.e., R&D to engineering to manufacturing to sales and service). This outdated mode of production has been displaced along with Tayloristic management. New concepts of the strategic business networks and extended enterprises demand far more dynamic, ecological management. Given the systems nature of innovation and the interdependent effects of variables, results are difficult to quantify and seemingly impossible to measure and predict. With two major studies sponsored by the National Research Council in Washington, D.C., we learned that the complex problems were a function of behavior—specifically, the sociology, psychology, and anthropology of a firm.

One NRC report (1994) notes that on the enterprise level there are great difficulties in predicting strategic effects, measuring certain types of output, assessing benefits that might be diffused or delayed, and separating the contributions of information technology (IT) from those of other factors. Today, these assets are also not—as a rule —reflected in the organization's financial statements or in the nation's accounting system. It suggests that

> IT (information technology) has value only if surrounded by appropriate policy, strategy, methods for measuring results, project controls, talented and committed people, sound organizational relationships, and well-designed information systems....Indeed the management of intellectual capital may be a major factor in who survives and who does not in the coming years.

Much progress has been made in our quest for harnessing intellectual capital. During the past decade, we have learned that there is a difference between tacit and explicit knowledge; and there are ways to make our insights visible and even convert them to structural and/or financial capital. We also know that those companies able to explicitly manage their innovation infrastructure—within which ideas are created and commercialized—are considered market leaders.

According to a CMA Report (Amidon et al., 1998), we also know that the challenge for management of knowledge and intangible or invisible assets may also include, but is by no means limited to:

- Facilitation of access to knowledge
- Rapid obsolescence of knowledge
- Corporate memory loss
- Distribution of knowledge power
- Coping with information overload amidst (meaningful) knowledge scarcity
- Arrogance (there is still much to know)

- Reduction of the knowledge gap between the haves and have-nots
- Adaptation to accelerating change, change paralysis, and resistance to change
- Protection of knowledge assets and intellectual property
- Knowledge absorption and assimilation
- Inclusion of local knowledge in decision making
- Volatility inherent in rapid diffusion
- Enhancing interfaces for knowledge visualization
- Openness to alternative ways of knowing
- Protection of privacy and personal knowledge rights
- Need for appropriate standards, policies and metrics

Technology has been used to increase cross-competition among industries and among individual activities within enterprises in different industries. However, at the same time it has stimulated entirely new forms of collaborative economic activity, such as worldwide research networks, global sourcing arrangements, large-scale development and sharing of databases, new training and education capabilities, faster-response innovation systems, and alliances and networks of companies.

Therefore, if we perceive that the innovation highway is as people-intensive as it is technology-intensive, we need to understand the linkages that contribute to performance of an individual, the productivity of an enterprise, or the prosperity of a nation.

2.2   CREATING THE PROPOSITION

Modern value propositions, then, must balance these three complex, interdependent factors: performance, behavior, and technology. A focus on one will have an automatic effect on the other two elements. Only a balance among the three in an innovation process enables an enterprise to be centered and capable of managing to achieve sustained prosperity. The knowledge movement has taken flight in every function, every industry, and every corner of the globe—developing and industrialized nations alike.

What follows are some of the items to consider under each management factor. The actual elements will differ between organizations, industries, and countries. However, the universal concept is that a management system requires the balance of all three, and the interrelationship among the factors may be more important than the categories themselves.

- *Performance economics (intellectual capital)*—Metrics for investments and profitability; asset identification (financial, technological and intellectual); qualitative/quantitative success measures; budget level; resource mix; rewards/incentives; tax structure; and creative financing mechanisms.

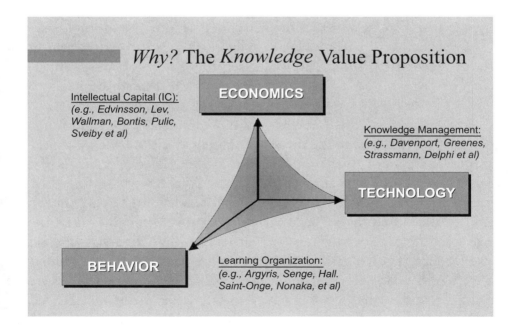

FIGURE 2.1 *The knowledge value proposition.*

- *Behavior (social capital)*—Learning networks of expertise; system dynamics; reporting relationships; staffing patterns; cultural and cross-cultural aspects; liaison relationships; collaborative strategies; sense of purpose; work imperatives; individual/organizational balance; development plans; learning philosophy; role responsibilities; work design; simultaneous parallel activities; cross-fertilization of ideas; cross-functional teaming; global sourcing; benchmarking best practices; periodic review and evaluation; and communication strategies.

- *Technology (technological capital)*—Electronic communication infrastructure; intelligence system; service delivery techniques; technology advancements; transformation; shared technology resources; collaborative groupware; workflow documentation; intranets; corporate portals; decision support; computer memory; and network management tools.

It is easy to recognize that the behavioral aspects (for example psychology, sociology, anthropology, and political science) are the crux of the productivity paradox. This is precisely the driver that has led executives to begin to assess the implications of the human capital as a tangible, measurable asset. How can it be measured and leveraged?

The themes of the knowledge value proposition—interestingly enough—correspond to the three sub-themes of the knowledge movement The intent to calculate and monitor the intellectual capital is best exemplified by Leif Edvinsson of Skandia AFS (Sweden), Karl-Eric Sveiby (Australia), Ante Pulic (Austria), Baruch Lev (United States), and Charles Goldfinger (Belgium). Social capital embodies the concepts of the learning organization, articulated by Chris Argyris and Peter Senge (United States), Charles Savage (Germany), and Hubert St. Onge (Canada). Technological capital, or IT as knowledge processing, is articulated by Tom Davenport, Peter Keen, and David Coleman (United States); Joachim Doering (Germany); and Kent Greenes (UK).

During the past decade, we have seen the convergence of language and practices wherein proponents of one facet embrace the facets of the other. Practitioners in particular are realizing the need to have a holistic, enterprisewide strategy that brings together the aspects of all three; and leadership executives understand that the architecture required is far more complex.

The most important—and least understood—aspect might be how to account for the behavioral aspects of the organization. According to surveys, managing culture is by far the most difficult and critical challenge facing organizations today. How does one encourage a culture of knowledge sharing in an organization steeped in competitive values and suffering the aftermath of reengineering and downsizing? This is precisely the dimension the traditional business planning models do not take into account, but executives must grapple with the question in order to migrate toward a more robust knowledge-innovation strategy approach to the business.

2.3 FROM TRANSFER TO TRANSFORMATION

With the passage of the National Cooperative Research Act of 1984, there was a new emphasis on the process of technology transfer. Corporations established dedicated offices and staff, Congress passed legislation to enable more rapid movement of scientific information into the private sector, state governments initiated local economic development initiatives, and a National Center for Technology Transfer was established.[3]

Just as there were unprecedented changes in the R&D environment, the technology transfer profession experienced a parallel reorientation to a focus on knowledge, the entire process of innovation and systems thinking. What once was considered a discrete activity between functions (or nations) became an integral activity in interconnecting the research organization with business units within the firm, alliances and joint ventures external to the firm, and the leading-edge customer base itself.

In our 1989 management research laboratories that also included the faculty from business schools (e.g., MIT, London School of Economics, et al.), we began to focus on the innovation process as the process to be managed rather than left to serendipity. We performed detailed value chain process analysis across all functions, business units, and other stakeholders such as suppliers, distributors, customers, and the customer's customer. In search of a management architecture that was simple, elegant, and memorable, we realized that all other processes and practices could be put under the universal rubric of innovation. In fact, as we analyzed other aspects of transformation, innovation was the one process that would provide a common language and allow a universal architecture to make connections across all economic levels.

We determined five primary interdependent management domains (see Figure 2.2), which when in balance provide for optimal effectiveness and efficiency: Performance, structure, people, process, and technology—these elements shape the chapter[4] on architecture in *Innovation Strategy for the Knowledge Economy* (Amidon 1997). The elements are also further explored in Part 2 of this book.

Similarly, in an article in Research-Technology Management (Amidon, 1993), we documented five evolutionary stages we might identify to depict some of these differences from managing from a "transfer" perspective into what is likely to become the foundation of modern knowledge innovation systems in a dynamic knowledge, but technology-intensive economy.

The following list illustrates the evolution from one stage of a relationship between two parties (i.e., member of a team, function, enterprise, or nation). Because these may appear to represent sweeping generalizations and may be incomplete, they must be taken in the illustrative spirit with which they were defined.

1. *Stage I: Technology transfer*—moving from one place to another; the "passer/receiver" language applied to labs, within consortia or country to country.

2. Stage II: Technology exchange—technology transfers through people; the "contact sport" analogy; dual communications links; dialog among parties; ideas from either side.

3. Stage III: Knowledge exchange—shift to viewing that which is transferred from "widgets" to ideas and insights as a function of human interaction; realization of something beyond "information"; timely access provides the competitive advantage.

4. Stage IV: Technology/knowledge management—recognition that the "process" cannot be left to serendipity; organizations must pay "sweat dues" in addition to the enrollment fee; emergence of a new discipline: the management of technology; building staff and mechanisms to manage the process.

5. Stage V: Knowledge innovation systems—realization of the dynamic nature of the total process of innovation; emergence of the "virtual" research enterprise without functional, industry, sector, or geographic borders; takes systemic view of "knowledge flow"; shifts focus from monitoring discrete deliverables to creation of a learning system designed to enable profitable growth.

A matrix below illustrates the characteristics within each stage and provides insight into how we have evolved during the past fifteen years into prevalent concepts of knowledge management (KM). Most who are practicing the modern knowledge concepts have begun to realize that the real value lies in understanding and influencing the innovation system of an enterprise.

Note the fourth stage—knowledge management (KM), which is currently the state of progressive practice. Perhaps the best articulation of the benefits (and drawbacks) of KM comes from Tom Stewart, an editor of *Fortune*, who was the first to put "brainpower" and "intellectual capital" into the business press. In his newest book (2002), he states, "The response to the need for knowledge management has been astounding." And referencing his *Intellectual Capital* (1997), he foresaw that "If the subject of intellectual capital ever spawns a business fad, it will be under the guise of 'knowledge management,' because there's money to be made selling software, systems, and consulting services with the touted goal of allowing every person in an organization to be able to lay his hands on the collected know-how, experience, and wisdom of all his colleagues."

In fact, Stewart documents, "By IDC's estimate, knowledge management software and services will be a $6 billion industry in 2002," and then uses some case examples to illustrate his points. He describes knowledge management software designed to manage a network of thousands of technical experts and analysts; but the real value comes when it is integrated into the business processes—and, we would suggest, the business strategies—of the firm (see Chapter 3).

5-Stage Analysis

	Performance	Structure	People	Process	Technology
I. Technology Transfer	• Quantitative • Tabulations	• Functionally-Driven	• Technology-Push • Skill Dependent	• Linear Sequential • Transactional	• Data-Based
II. Technology Exchange	• Qualitative • Quid pro quo	• Functionally Interconnected	• Market-Pull • Relationship Dependent	• Dual Communications • Mutual Exchange	• Information-Based
III. Knowledge Exchange	• Qualitative • Quid pro quo	• Decentralized • Local Autonomy	• Push-Pull Balance • Learning Process	• Cross-Functional Communication • Change-Oriented	• Knowledge-Based
IV. Knowledge Management	• Productivity • Partner Satisfaction	• Centralized • Command and Control	• Role Definition • Accountability	• Integrated Interaction • Transformational	• Collective Knowledge-Based
V. Knowledge Innovation	• Investment Strategy • Partner Success	• Distributed Networks • Multiple, Dynamic Modes	• Self-Managing System • Empowerment	• 'Real-Time' Global Learning • Symbiotic	• Intelligent Knowledge Processors

FIGURE 2.2   *Five-stage knowledge innovation analysis.*[5]

For the purpose of determining the technical underpinning of today's innovation superhighway, we see management systems that are investments based on mutual success; now we know they are based on the identification and measurement of intangible value. The organization structures are distributed networks with multiple, dynamic nodes of interaction and the workers are empowered—in fact, called to innovation action. The processes enable "real-time" global learning in a symbiosis that can build upon the knowledge, learning, and capabilities of others. And the technology, in addition to the proliferation of intranets and the increasing use of the Internet, is moving toward intelligence knowledge processing and collaborative learning technologies.

2.4   INNOVATION REDEFINED

Dr. Peter Drucker, in the *Harvard Business Review* (1995), wrote that innovation is the one competence needed for the future along with the ability to measure the performance thereof. We have, however, realized that very few people have a fundamental understanding of the difference between invention and innovation. What we are discussing is not technological innovation, but knowledge innovation—complete with the learning systems necessary for exemplary practice.

We have researched over forty definitions of innovation, ten of which appear in Appendix B. Basically, these definitions boil down to two perspectives:

- Invention is a process in and of itself, separate from the process of innovation.
- Invention is the first—and integral—stage in the process of innovation.

We adhere to the second view since we believe that the process, in order to be effectively managed, must operate as a complete value system. We have simplified the innovation process into the 3Cs: knowledge creation, knowledge conversion, and knowledge commercialization. Why have we selected innovation as the focus of policy, process, and practice? Innovation is "knowledge in action." We believe that an enterprise should be a learning organization—but to what end? The end is in the full realization of the idea, not the invention itself.

Professor James Brian Quinn, Dartmouth College, suggests that we should expect the randomness, chaos, and disorderliness that are inherent in the innovation process:

> *Innovative organizations tend to be "ad hoc," fluid, cross-disciplinary, and cooperative. There are many different types of adhocracies from which to choose for a specific innovative purpose. Tasks tend to define relationships more than formal authority or control systems do. Processes tend to be chaotic rather than orderly as in the professions, more cooperative than political, and more subject to challenge, vision and interaction with users.*

If you were asked who you consider to be great innovators, you would likely reply that they are usually men and women who had the ability to convert their ideas or inventions into practice, such as viable businesses or other prosperous enterprises. Consider the characteristics of an innovator, even as opposed to an inventor.

Execution is absolutely critical. But execution is not the end of a value chain process. Execution is required throughout each of the three stages (3Cs) in the process—creaton, conversion, and commercialization. First, managers must envision the entire process (i.e., from cradle to grave, from seed to need, etc.). Then, strategies can be developed to ensure proper execution and optimal results. Indeed, an enterprise has not fully innovated until customers demand more of the technology or service innovation!

I also believe effective execution will set one enterprise apart from the rest; but it is because they are innovating and establishing new standards, not because they are following best practices—internal or external—per se. In terms of what venture capitalists are funding today, there are some lessons to be learned. Not only should they be concerned about funding a specific technology—which is generally the case—and the execution of the idea through an effective management team. These are important to be sure, but equally important is the capability of that team and organization to continue to innovate. Shareholders invest in the future of an organization. As an investor, I would be more concerned with how effectively the organization will continuously innovate (i.e., create new ideas and put them into the marketplace effectively and efficiently in advance of the competition). A good idea or technology is only the beginning.

The meaning of the foregoing is made clear in the following case examples:

- Xerox PARC is a good example of a company that is excellent at "inventing" but not innovating (i.e., putting the invention into commercial gain).
- Dell actually did completely innovate the delivery process. And yes, their execution of their business model makes them the enterprise to emulate.
- Hoffman LaRoche improved time to market for new drugs by a factor of years. Gathering and packaging information for delivery for efficient FDA approval is all part of the innovation process.

The organization needs to perform more at an enterprisewide level than in a few isolated pockets. Our point is that if there is no explicit innovation process and no one—with whatever C*O title—is responsible for optimizing that process, business results are left to serendipity. There must be methods—both human interaction and technical—to systematically share that new knowledge in a way that will get frontline individuals to use it, support it, and find it when they need it, instead of searching through inscrutable archives.

Moreover, we believe that those on the front lines—often the sales and service professionals—have access to more valuable information than the rest of the organization. Oftentimes that customer interaction process is not appreciated and not monitored. Customer Relationship

Management (CRM), as a movement, has improved the process, just as the quality initiative placed attention on the process. But even the most progressive CRM programs appear to focus more on "knowledge of the customer," than on "customer knowledge"—two very different things! In my article "Customer: Innovation: A Function of Knowledge" (1997), I suggested ways to innovate with the customer as a pathway to success.

The front lines—as often represented by the sales or service personnel —add to the knowledge base of a company through a continuous process of "kaizen," without going through a lot of intermediaries and without forcing people to spend a lot of time looking for or monitoring the new insights. If managers do not take advantage of this interface opportunity, the innovation is wasted or—at the least—is operating at suboptimal performance.

Innovation is the primary management problem of most companies, large and small, start-up or mature. Keeping the ideas flowing into prosperous implementation is the name of the management game. Many inventions (they are not innovations) will die or languish, precisely because the distribution system does not exist, is broken, or is underperforming. This distribution system is part of the third stage in the process of innovation (i.e., commercialization, application, diffusion, etc.).

The agenda, then, is one of transformation—integrating with corporate business strategy in systematic ways that balance the economic, behavioral, and technological factors of the enterprise. Creating such dynamic innovation systems requires experimental modes of modern management. No longer will traditional value chain methodologies suffice. In fact, the new value-system paradigm is one that transcends conventional organizational boundaries and uses the technology to support the formulation and implementation of real-time strategies to meet the business opportunities of the global marketplace.

2.5   BLENDING THE OLD AND THE NEW

The topic of the knowledge value proposition was first detailed in a monograph published by the Society of Canadian Management

Accountants—*Collaborative Innovation and the Knowledge Economy* (1998). In addition to providing insight on the variables, a differentiation can be outlined between Traditional/Industrial and Knowledge/ Innovation Management, as outlined in Table 2.1.

There is a mistake made by many, however. In our eagerness to move toward the newer modes of management, we may forget that many of the traditional methods and practices are not only still useful; they are essential for success. The solution is not either/or; but both. There are certain operations in the enterprise that demand competitive and cause-effect practices; and in other instances, the lack of flexible, adaptive, and interdependent initiatives will result in duplication of effort and suboptimization of resources, the most precious of which is the human talent.

TABLE 2.1   *Contrast in Management Styles*

	Traditional/Industrial (Financial Capital)	Knowledge/Innovation (Human Capital)
Performance	Financial	Comprehensive
Measures	Static	Dynamic
	$$$ as assets	Relationships as assets
Structure/Culture	Competitive	Collaborative
	Market share	Sets of alliances
	Distrust of borders	Value-adding
	Cost/expense	Revenue/investment
People/Leadership	Profitability	Sustained growth
Process	Independence	Interdependence
	Cause-effect	Value system
Technology	Information processing	Knowledge processing
	Data/information	Tacit/explicit knowledge
	Things/warehouse	Flow/process

2.6   SUMMARY

The technology/productivity paradox has plagued enterprises for decades and with little or no resolution. With the increased complexity of globalization and organizational dynamics, new performance measures are essential. The traditional variables of cost, quality, and time are no longer a market differentiator; they are a rite of passage. These new measures, more likely indicators of progress than metrics for success, can be found in understanding the intangible value of a firm—a combination of the intellectual capital, social capital, and technological capital.

Further, these variables operate not as independent but as interdependent factors. Indeed, the infusion of computer and communications technology can have an impact on the performance of a enterprise —or a nation for that matter—if, and only if, strategies are crafted to balance the economic, behavioral and technological factors in consort.

The changes occurring throughout the economy are fundamental. There are dramatic shifts in demography, advancements in technology, increasing global interdependence, and economic shifts in power; these are all external factors that must be considered in creating sustainable strategies for success.

CHAPTER ENDNOTES

[1] Chapter 2: *Innovation Strategy for the Knowledge Economy*, pp 15–26.

[2] Each economic factor taken separately is significant; but the compounding effects described by Lester Thurow (1997) demand a new management philosophy.

[3] This was the same period of time when the Alvey program in the UK and the ESPRIT program in Europe provided the collaborative foundation for what we know today as the European Union—best and most recently exemplified in the KnowledgeBoard electronic activity—"Made in Europe."

[4] Chapter 6: "An Innovation Management Architecture," pp. 77–89.

[5] Knowledge Innovation® is a registered trademark of Entovation International, Ltd.

THREE

From Planning to Innovation Strategy—The Knowledge How

Those who are skilled in executing a Strategy
Bend the strategy of others without conflict;
Uproot the Fortification of others without Attacking;
Absorb the organizations of others without prolonged operations.
It is essential to engage completely with the Entire System.
Thus the Strategy is never-ending and the gains are complete."

R.L. Wing Translation of Sun Tzu

Over the years, I have given considerable thought to the essence of modern management—the vision, the language, the culture, the practices—and ultimately the strategy for optimal results. Ours has been a quest for the universal architecture, one that would connect relevant disciplines (e.g., economics, sociology, psychology, anthropology, and information science, to mention a few); and at the same time, we researched trends on all levels of the economy (i.e., micro-, meso- and macroeconomic). All this has been done in an era of unprecedented and kaleidoscopic change.

Consider the competitive landscape, becoming more so each day on every front. With the anticipation of accelerated communications and the shelf life of existing knowledge, we might envision this intensity to increase, not decrease. You need not agree, but consider for a moment that we will soon reach the law of diminishing returns with competitive strategies. The rules of the game have changed; but the management practices have not yet evolved.

That being the case, any architecture we might embrace must maintain necessary controls and consistency while, at the same time, being flexible enough to take advantage of novelty and the (yet unseen) opportunities. The answers might lie in collaborative policies, processes, and practices. Positioning for the knowledge economy requires explicit management of the process of innovation for enterprise success, national vitality, and societal advancement.

3.1 THE DOWNSIDE OF PLANNING

In 1989, an external consultant had concluded that our company had no vision. This was the result of numerous executive interviews from various functions, business units both inside and external to the firm. This had not been my experience—quite the contrary. The company could be faulted for having too much vision; but these various aspects were fragmented, not coalesced and not articulated in a cohesive, compelling form. Thus, I was put to task to analyze all the planning documents of the company and define what, in fact, might be that magnetic vision to catapult the company forward.

You can guess the results after I had reviewed thousands of pages of the output of a well-architected strategic planning process for the company. I knew little about where the company was really headed, other than some possible new technologies, expansion of markets, and how resources—primarily financial—would be allocated over the next five years. Not that this was bad; it wasn't. It just was not enough.

Henry Mintzberg in his *The Rise and fall of Strategic Planning* (1994) describes it best. In a chapter dedicated to the pitfalls of planning (e.g., planning and freedom, commitment versus calculation, inflexibility of plans, the politics of planning, obsession with control), he discussed how planning could actually impede creativity. "Planning by its very nature defines and preserves categories. Creativity, by its very nature, creates categories or rearranges established ones…And that is why the entrepreneurial types fought the system at TI and GE, why innovation was never institutionalized. "

3.2 AN ATLAS FOR INNOVATION

A strategy requires a deliberate plan of action and the leadership capability to see the plan through to execution.. An innovation strategy is similar to a road map that assists an enterprise to articulate where it is to go and organizes the resources needed to get there. However, there may be no perfect map; and the measuring devices may not be as accurate. A competitor may change the whole landscape even before we reach there. Key to developing an innovation strategy is looking at knowledge as a resource. Knowledge and innovation are the key players in the path of progress. An innovation strategy is also distinct from business planning. For example, business planning is an *analytic* routine based on the tacit assumption of the continuation of current situation (status quo). Innovation strategy, on the other hand, is a *synthetic* practice based on creativity and uncertainty.

The first step in an effective innovation strategy is to make the process explicit. It is that simple and that complex at the same time. If the process is not managed systematically, it is left to serendipity. Most organizations expect innovation from R&D, the function where new ideas are funded. With a global and interdependent perspective of the enterprise, ideas can and must come from every function and external stakeholders as well.

In an article[1] co-authored with Darius Mahdjoubi, a Ph.D. student at the University of Texas at Austin, published in the 2000 *Handbook for Business Strategy* (Amidon and Mahdjoubi, 1999), we explored the dramatic shift needed to navigate organizations into the future. We used the analogy of an atlas (i.e., a system for depicting and measuring world views) and the metaphor of road maps to illustrate the migration from business planning to a knowledge-innovation strategy.

A geographic atlas provides a systematic presentation of the World—or a part of it—on a flat surface, although the earth is a globe.

It provides a methodology needed for planning and implementing travel. It is generally considered a comprehensive representation of the world as we might know it today. Usually, it consists of three distinct, albeit interrelated, parts: mapping for organizing commonalties; scaling to provide measurement and relational information; and a compass for direction.

Shortly after the astronauts of Apollo 17 reached the moon, the world awakened to a new perspective of bringing a vision into reality. It required more collaboration and faith than anyone previously dared to dream. Results were wondrous and beyond expectations. Similarly, executives today are caught in a quandary. They can continue to utilize the tried-and-true methodologies (unsuited for today's economic environment), or they can experiment with the unknown and venture forth with management initiatives that project innovation, creativity, and responsible risk. New assumptions[2] must be formed, as follows:

FIGURE 3.1   *Migration to innovation strategy.*

1. Knowledge is the primary driver of innovation, not technology.

2. The value of human potential can and should be linked to economic results.

3. It is a systems dynamic—not a cause-effect value chain—that is operating.

4. A prosperous future is based increasingly on interdependence, interaction, and collaboration.

5. It is the flow of knowledge that must be visualized, monitored, and incentivized.

Integration of knowledge as an interdependent variable into conventional business methodologies creates a dynamic no less dramatic than the shift from a flat-earth view of the world to a global view. Initially, the world was seen as two-dimensional, similar to the way many business managers perceive their business environment today. Design a market matrix, create a balance sheet, and manage the process in a simple methodical linear mode. Build the better mousetrap, and the market will beat a path to your door.

Similarly, business planning is the current representation of the process and plans necessary to position a particular enterprise with competitive advantage in a particular industry or region of the world. It provides a methodology to define business plans usually based on a product/market portfolio.

In contrast, a three-dimensional global view capitalizes on the dynamics of the multiple compounding effects of what we might describe as a kaleidoscopic economy. It is not the speed of change of a variable, or the speed of change of multiple variables. It is the compounding effect of the speed of change of multiple variables creating a business environment that is difficult to understand, much less manage. The challenge is not to make existing businesses bigger; it is to create new businesses. It is not to evolve existing technologies as much as it is to envision products and services that meet the unarticulated needs of customers or an unserved market and do so ahead of the competition. Today, the market operates with a system dynamic we do not yet understand.

3.3   Actualizing Innovation Strategy

From several years of management systems research and application of core concepts in a variety of academic, industrial, and governmental settings, the following ten dimensions of management strategy have emerged as an excellent way to calibrate an organizations capacity to innovate (see Figure 3.2). There are similar dimensions defined in *Innovation Strategy for the Knowledge Economy*, the book that now includes a Business Literacy 2000 Study Guide and Knowledge Innovation® software application.

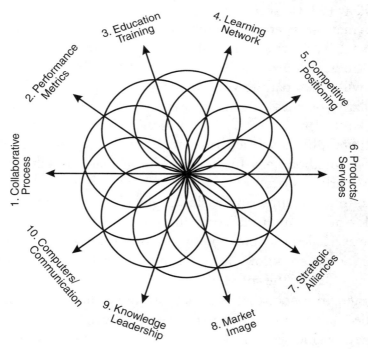

Figure 3.2   *Ten dimensions of innovation strategy.*[3]

Each of these domains is often managed in isolation, usually with its own language, priorities, and practices. For example, there is often little respect found between the finance, human resource, and information technology organizations. These functions and business units often compete for limited resources through the budgeting process without a coherent sense of purpose and vision. The results lead to fragmentation, unnecessary duplication, conflict, and underutilized competencies.

What is needed is a dialog among the principals of the organizations—across functions, business units, and managerial levels. An administrative tool is needed to stimulate the strategy formulation process with a focus on the managerial aspects of the firm, not just the financial or technological elements. Remember that all three must be in balance for optimal leverage.

Similarly, business units will compete for resources and not collaborate based on their own relative strengths and weaknesses to optimize the results of the organization. Those that do not succeed are vulnerable to being amputated. Unfortunately, business planning to date, with its primary foci on finances, products, and markets has intensified the competition to the point that business units within the same company often compete for the same customers.

One way to begin to calibrate the innovation process is to view the system as a whole by answering the ten questions outlined on the Litmus Test (see Appendix C). These ten steps enable a company to see where it is on the scale of innovation management capability and provide a foundation for strategy formulation. As with any corporate-wide initiatives, companies must establish key players, agree upon a framework for dialog, create an implementation plan (ideally after all stakeholders have been interviewed), manage the process, evaluate results, and be open to new ideas and unexpected business opportunities.

1. Foremost, the innovation process should be made explicit by identifying a corporate officer and a cross-functional team

responsible for the process. Innovation can be stated as a core value of the firm, thereby ensuring that all participants in the process recognize its importance.

2. Once the process is defined (i.e., cradle to grave, seed to need), including the roles and responsibilities of all stakeholders, the attempt should be made to define the metrics of progress—both tangible and intangible—that define optimal performance of the system. Recognize that metrics that are difficult to define may be the best measure of success. Develop the business case based on the knowledge value proposition (i.e., the relationship between economics, behavior, and technology) that promote the creation, exchange, and application of new (or reused) ideas. Develop key indicators and early warning signals that might be tracked in a periodic review. Be attentive to what incentives can be built into the system to foster behavior necessary in an innovative environment.

3. Take stock of the education and training capability of the firm and whence ideas originate. Consider the implications of a real-time learning environment that may not be classroom based. Provide an infrastructure for the incubation of new business ideas that might develop into products and services and even new businesses that might contribute to the bottom line.

4. Consider your local, national, regional, and worldwide presence. How might these locations be converted into a distributed learning network that treats stakeholders, including customers, as sources of knowledge, rather than as those to whom services are delivered? The network, however it is defined, operates far more as a system of conversations than a value chain transfer or delivery mechanism.

5. Pay attention to the competitive environment, but be sure that your radar searches wide enough to capture potential competitors who may not even be a factor in your industry today. Ensure that any intelligence activity is designed as a feed-

forward that automatically distributes insights to those with a need to know. Where appropriate, rely upon available computer and communications resources to facilitate the process.

6. Review the metrics of your own product and service development—for example, the number of new products or services yielded in a given business period as a percentage of sales. Perform an in-depth analysis of the knowledge economy (i.e., projected trends) and determine the implications for your business. Consider some new adaptations that capitalize upon knowledge-based products and a new knowledge-delivery channel.

7. Take stock of the variety of your strategic alliances—research, joint venture, cooperative marketing, etc. Determine how they are being managed in ways that are consistent and aligned with your values and corporate strategy. Document successes and failures. Consider the portfolio of research alliances developed by your competitors—their inherent strategy and the potential impact on your performance.

8. Review your media/advertising strategy to assess how it portrays your intellectual and innovation capability. Furthermore, review your current level of customer intimacy from a sales, relationship, and partnering perspective. Could a focus on customer knowledge—rather than knowledge of the customer —reframe prospects for customer innovation?

9. Rethink your leadership strategy—both internal and external. The knowledge economy is an economy of opportunity, not of problem solving. It is an era of collaborative, not competitive, strategy. It requires visible sharing of your own knowledge and on a worldwide stage. Determine your sphere of influence and how to best leverage the talents of your own workforce.

10. Assess your technical infrastructure for internal and external communication capability (e.g., computers, software, multimedia, intranets, the Internet, videoconferencing, collaborative

applications, e-markets) and their management effectiveness. Consider the overall behavior necessary in the innovative environment and determine whether the given systems afford opportunities to manage the corporate memory, foster e-commerce, enhance electronic dialog, deliver on-site training, and learn from participation for continuous process improvement.

In short, leaders will position innovation strategy and management as a core competency. Make the process—and the management and measurement thereof—explicit. Illustrate how it can be seen as the migration from business planning with more dynamic, robust models for ensuring future success instead of documenting past performance. Ensure that individuals—ideally representing the 3Gs (generations) —are motivated and rewarded for enhancing innovation[4]. Take into consideration the relationships inherent in the "extended enterprise" or the strategic business network—suppliers, distributors, alliance partners, customers, customer's customers, and even competitors. Avoid punishing failure as you are building a common innovation language and culture of constructive innovation. And by all means, celebrate progress, even the little victories.

Just as with the Egyptians, the Persians, the Minoans, the Greeks, the Chinese, the Abyssinians, and the Europeans of times past, the future belongs to those who have the willingness to venture into the unknown. They used their intuition, imagination, sense of adventure, and the tools they innovated to explore the environment beyond its limits.

3.4 SUMMARY

Even though moving beyond traditional business planning practices will not be easy; the rewards will be great. Today we measure what we can measure, rather than measuring what is important. Now we underestimate the true potential of information technology, knowledge processing, and worldwide communications. Today we have little sense of how to measure the true value of social capital, which is far more a function of interaction, interdependence, and collaboration. To do so and to understand the relationship among the three requires multidimensional visioning and courageous leadership.

The Innovation Superhighway could scope the new classification schema, the scaling and measurements systems, and the compass to chart new directions. Because something hasn't been done before is no reason not to innovate. We must learn to create the business plans for emerging markets. Thus, we will unleash the bountiful opportunities afforded during the next millennium. We will do so systematically and with renewed purpose.

Although much has been written about knowledge management and the knowledge economy, the reality is that we know very little about the real implications of this inevitable transformation. One thing is certain: the journey into the next frontier will bring forth new value for knowledge and the innovation processes in ways today unimagined.

CHAPTER ENDNOTES

[1] For a summary of the article, see http://www.entovation.com/whatsnew/atlas1.htm

[2] Assumptions defined as a collective discussion in a meeting for the Society of Management Accountants of Canada (1998).

[3] These ten dimensions are detailed as an assessment in Chapters 7 and 8 of *Innovation Strategy for the Knowledge Economy*.

[4] 3G planning (i.e., three generations) was pioneered by Skandia AFS and their Vaxholm Futures Center.

PART II

*Architecting
a Future*

FOUR
Knowledge Performance Economics

Economic theory has a problem with knowledge;
it seems to defy the basic economic principle of scarcity...
The more you use it and pass it on,
The more it proliferates—
Infinitely expansible.
What is scarce in the new economy
Is the ability to understand and use knowledge.

Survey of the World Economy[1]

I can still remember the day Ken Olsen (CEO of Digital at the time) insisted that we develop some management metrics as part of our company's transformation. "But sir," said we, "such measurements do not exist". "Yes," he responded, "and this is precisely why it must be addressed". We set about to research the potential metrics—no small task. Of course, today, twelve years later, we understand that it is a matter of measuring intangible value; and, moreover, that there are multiple ways to do so!

Although there are earlier examples of the use of the term "intellectual premium" in the 1950s, my understanding is that John Kenneth Galbraith, an American economist born in Ontario, may be credited as one of the first, if not the first, to write about "intellectual capital" as a financial concept, as he did in 1969[2], saying, "Intellectual Capital can be seen as a process of value creation in addition to an asset, an action more than just knowledge or pure intellect." Nobel Laureate Gary Becker, influenced by Milton Friedman and spending time with the National Bureau of Economics, produced books on human behavior (1978) and human capital (Becker 1993).

Michael Polanyi, originally from Budapest, was writing about personal knowledge (1974) and the tacit dimension (1983); he is credited with providing insight on the interrelationship of economics, philosophy, and learning. The Michael Polanyi Society,[3] formed to preserve and promote his heritage, provides this quote:

> *Tacit assent intellectual passions, the sharing of an idiom and of a cultural heritage, affiliation to a like-minded community: such are the impulses that shape our vision our on the nature of things upon which we rely for our mastery of things. No intelligence, however critical or original, can operate outside such a fiduciary framework.*

Dr. Peter F. Drucker may be the first international management expert to crystallize the opportunity into the knowledge economy. Although his book on the topic, *Post-Capitalists Society*, was not published until 1993, he began making references to the "knowledge worker" many years earlier.

There is perhaps no functional area of management that has been more affected by the new agenda than finance. An entire new language has evolved, characterized by heavy debates—pro and con—about the validity of the new view. A community of leadership has emerged in aggressive pursuit of the new performance metrics of the "new" economy. Professional societies on various continents have published monographs on the topic and, in some instances, on managing principles. World-renowned research think tanks have pursued multi-year studies on the topic; and some of the quasi-governing organizations have released new guidelines for accounting for the intangible value of a firm. Societal organizations (e.g., the OECD and The World Bank) have been catalysts in the international dialog. National leaders have launched nationwide initiatives to determine the new indicators for success, and suggestions for navigational systems abound.

4.1 SOME ROOTS

Clearly, we are in a transition period in which the old rules do not apply and the new ones have yet to be invented.

When I was writing about intellectual capital in 1986, one person to shed light on the subject was Karl-Erik Sveiby (Sweden) who produced the *Know-How Company*,[4] still one of the best resources in the field. He has since written another book (Sveiby, 1997) differentiating between knowledge as "the capacity to act" and competence as embracing "factual knowledge, skill, experience, value judgments, and social networks"—a perspective that is especially useful in the business context. Tom Stewart, editor of *Fortune* magazine, is credited with bringing the agenda into the popular business press in 1991 and 1993. His book[5] (Stewart, 1997) includes a chapter on the new economics of information, where he suggests, "In the knowledge economy, the scarce resource (amidst information overload) is ignorance."

At the same time, Hiroyuki Itami, then a student of Ikujiru Nonaka (Japan), was writing about invisible assets (Itami, 1987). Several years later, there appeared *The Balanced Scorecard* (Nolan & Norton, 1992), which expanded the perspective beyond financial metrics. In addition, Leif Edvinsson was producing his renowned supplements to the Annual Reports[6] between 1994 and 1998 as one way to navigate into the future. (see the profile in Chapter 13). He has published a book on the topic (Edvinsson and Malone, 1997) in which he described in detail his Skandia Navigator (Figure 4.1)—the "house"—which has become the foundation of hundreds of company and national reports on intellectual capital.

As described in 1996,[7] this shift in orientation to intangible assets will revolutionize the way enterprises are measured. Whether dealing on the level of the enterprise, the nation, or society as a whole, there is an entire new way to value economic wealth. For many of today's executives, whatever cannot be measured is not of value. And yet, as we now understand the "productivity paradox," we realize that these factors—a new knowledge value proposition (see Chapter 2)—must be defined, monitored, and evaluated as an essential foundation of the knowledge economy.

In fact, intangible assets are now recognized as being integral to the functioning of any organization. With the new global knowledge economy and the removal of trade barriers, cross-cultural knowledge—simply because of economies of scale and scope—becomes a competence any major firm must leverage. Even the smallest performance entity—the factor of one—may be the individual entrepreneur; and economies of learning become the universal measurement.

There are several other significant researchers and practitioners in addition to Sveiby (now in Australia) and Edvinsson (Sweden) who drive the knowledge agenda from the perspective of performance. Dr. Ante Pulic (Austria) has defined the Value Creation Efficiency Analysis (VAIC^{TM}), a software management tool designed to assist managers in monitoring and measuring the utilization of company's resources—intellectual (human), physical, and financial capital. Brian and Stuart Henshall (New Zealand) have produced material on a Knowledge Capital Engine for Wealth Creation (1988); and Brian Davis (Canada) is researching performance as it relates to e-Knowledge Markets[8] with a diagram of the Enterprise Ideas Economy (See Chapter 8).

Baruch Lev (USA) has convened annual conferences on the topic at the Stern School of Management at New York University and has provided leadership with the studies of the Brookings Institute that resulted in a seminal report—"Understanding Intangible Sources of Value: Managing, Measuring and Reporting" (2000)[9] and a prominent article in *CFO Magazine* that featured a "Knowledge Capital Scorecard" charting the progress of several companies within various industries.

In the 2000 edition reported top companies in 20 industries were ranked according to their levels of knowledge capital, from a high of $211 billion at mighty Microsoft Corp., down to $332 million at our smallest knowledge-rated company, Adolph Coors Co. At our median company, $21 billion of knowledge capital amounted to three times book value.

Lev has also been instrumental in decisions of the Financial Accounting Standards Board (FASB) to pursue rigorous research efforts to determine the implications of which new accounting metrics and standards might be suitable for the knowledge economy. Other related initiatives are occurring within the SEC regarding GAAP, as reported in the *BusinessWeek* article "New Yardsticks for Investors" (November 5, 2001).[10]

Nick Bontis (Canada)[11] established the first Institute for Intellectual Capital Research, based at McMaster University in Hamilton, Ontario. For several years, he has chaired the World Congress on Intellectual Capital, the most recent of which resulted in a publication (Bontis, 2002) in which he provides a frame for advancing the field. Dr. Bontis is also the CKO of KNEXA,[12] one of the new "knowledge trading companies." His revolutionary method as illustrated by the causal map diagram in Figure 4.2, outlines how variables such as Human Capital, Structured Capital, and Customer Capital might influence the bottom line performance of an enterprise or national economy.

Dr. David Skyrme (UK) and I produced a report (Skyrme and Amidon, 1997)[13] with several case study examples of exemplary practice with a chapter dedicated to measurement and justification. Our conclusions are as follows:

- Measurement is the area in this new knowledge field that shows largest gap between management expectations and actual achievement of results.
- It may be the least understood and the most critical for future success.

- Traditional accounting mechanisms developed over hundreds of years do not provide much light on measuring intangibles. They are very effective in counting the past, showing where a company has been. They are not very effective in pointing the direction for future results and impact—precisely what is required by investing executives.
- Justifying investment in knowledge management programs is problematic and requires a leap of faith.
- Whatever the ambiguity in numbers, there are now some demonstrable links to the new value proposition resulting in increased performance—however defined.

4.2   TOTALLY NEW FOUNDATIONS

Michael Rothschild with his book *Bionomics* in 1990 set the stage for a new way to look at the economics of a firm—and a nation, for that matter —as an ecosystem. By tracing the history and the intellectual influence of Adam Smith's *Wealth of Nations*, Malthus's theories of the dire effects of population increase, and Darwin's theories of evolution and natural selection, he suggests that capitalism has been impossible to comprehend because we have been viewing it from the wrong angle. We'd accepted blindly the notion of "economy as a machine."

But, documenting the trends of the middle of the twentieth century, only after DNA was discovered and its code cracked did biology attain its status of a science worth emulating. By the 1970s, it was possible to completely rethink economics, using the new discoveries of biology as a guide: The paradigm of the "economy as a cyclical machine" at last could be discarded. In its place one could imagine the "economy as an evolving ecosystem."[14]

Now, bionomics—the study of the relationship between organisms and their environment—provides the best starting point for a new way of thinking about the human economy. The essence of this "global coevolution" is an economic platform for The Innovation Superhighway—the new knowledge economics.

In a seminal *Sloan Management Review* article (1987), Chris Bartlett and Sumantra Ghoshal outline the three simultaneous flows that must be analyzed in the innovation process: (1) the flow of parts, components, and finished goods; (2) the flow of funds, skills, and other scarce resources; and (3) the flow of intelligence, ideas, and knowledge. Until now, most managers have viewed innovation as the movement of technology, not as an infrastructure for rapid learning. The article's description of the process transcended geographic borders, thus providing a foundation for what is now known as the (globally) extended enterprise or The Innovation Superhighway.

Dorothy Leonard-Barton of Harvard University described the process of building and sustaining the sources of innovation as the wellsprings of knowledge. In a significant passage, she says

> *The most useful wellsprings are constant, reliable and their waters pure. As flows of water from such wellsprings feed the biological systems around them, so in the same way flows of appropriate knowledge into and within companies enable them to develop competitively advantageous capabilities. However, without sources of renewal, wellsprings can run dry; moreover, the channels feeding out of them require tending, clearing, adapting. Within corporations, managers at all levels of the organization are the keepers of the wellsprings of knowledge.*

Using this imagery, she is able to document with case examples some of the fundamental innovation concepts, such as fostering and inhibiting factors, continuous interaction, shared problem solving, and learning from the market. Karl-Erik Sveiby would concur: "Very little of knowledge has to do with money, so why measure in monetary terms?"[15]

We need to be thinking of radically new ways in which the world is structured—how it evolves and the interdependence of its parts. Moreover, not all the measures will be financial, as the experts are espousing. Of course, there are those who believe that the "new" thinking is not that radical at all; it's just a natural evolution of the field. In a

2000 Global Valuation and Accounting Report[16] released by Morgan Stanley Dean Witter, "new" domains for indicators are defined: Flexibility, Agility, Scale, Scope, Talent, Education, Servicing Customers, and Technological Edge. However, if we contrast these with the variables defined by Sveiby, Pulic, Lev, and others, we will find considerable congruence.

In his new book, *Corporate Longitude,* Leif Edvinsson (2002) suggests we need to have a sense of where we are going in order to navigate the knowledge economy. Further, he affirms the need to change direction at a moment's notice. And in a subsequent article, "The Knowledge Capital of Nations,"[17] he applied the concepts to the national level.

> *Plotting a course solely based on traditional financial reference points leaves them blind to the opportunities on the lateral horizon. Lost on a turbulent sea of change and without lateral navigational tools to guide them, they cannot navigate the unchartered challenges the management of intangibles is presenting, in particular to the public sector.*

4.3   NATIONAL INITIATIVES

Some nations have been more progressive than others in establishing formal, systematic measurement criteria to document and report their progress according to key factors that undergird the prosperity of the nation. Sweden was first. Announcing that 1996 would be the "Year of Innovation," the government leadership together with Stockholm University modified the Skandia Navigator at the national level to quantify Sweden's critical success factors. The resulting report, *Welfare and Security,* details a barometer of indicators that have been charted over a period of time:

- *Financial focus*—including per capita GDP, national debt, and the mean value of the U.S. dollar.

- *Market focus*—including tourism statistics, standards of honesty, balance of service, balance of trade, and balance of trade for intellectual property.
- *Human focus*—including quality of life, average age expectancy, infant survival rate, smoking, education, level of education for immigrants, crime rate, and age statistics.
- *Process focus*—including service-producing organizations, public consumption as a percentage of GDP, business leadership, information technology (e.g., personal computers connected by LANs), survivors of traffic accidents, and employment.
- *Renewal and development focus*—including R&D expenses as a percentage of GDP, the number of genuine business start-ups, trademarks, and factors important to high school youth.

Sweden was only the beginning for architects such as Leif Edvinsson and Caroline Stenfelt, the principals involved in the study. Believing that intellectual capital (IC) is the driving force for the future wealth creation and provides the roots for the "future fruits of nations as well as organizations," they hosted the Vaxholm Summit, the First International Meeting on Visualizing and Measuring the IC of Nations in August 1998. The result has been a flurry of activity in different nations and an informative report—*An Invitation to the Future*. The original meeting was intended to have an open, imaginative and collaborative exploration of the IC of nations in order to share past experience, identify issues, and develop new perspectives. The process of measuring the IC of nations includes four steps:

1. Defining and agreeing on the meanings of measurement
2. Identifying key driving success factors
3. Refining navigation indicators
4. Collecting, processing, and visualizing measurement data

In addition to the Swedish report, there are several others available for review. Under the leadership of Dr. Edna Pasher (see the profile in Chapter 13), an IC report was produced on the State of Israel—*A Look to the Future: The Hidden Values of the Desert*, released in 1999. This IC picture of Israel presents the hidden values and the key driving success factors during its 50 years of existence in such areas as education, patents, scientists engaged in research and development, international openness, and computer and communication infrastructure. The report concludes:

> *(global competition) trends are creating opportunities and new businesses based upon the Knowledge Revolution...dependent upon knowledge from the technological and scientific fields, upon information concerning world markets, and upon the optimal acquisition and exploitation of knowledge!*

This courageous report was intended to present a holistic and organized picture of the knowledge and intellectual assets that Israel enjoys as contrasted with other nations. It was also to be seen as a basis for assessing the knowledge, expertise, and capabilities of the country as a navigator for government in various policy-making forums in order to upgrade the tools needed to exploit knowledge and accelerate the process of long-term economic and social growth. In addition to indicators outlined in the Swedish report, they added:

- *Financial capital*—including dollar exchange rates, external debt, unemployment, sector productivity rates, and exports by industry and inflation.
- *Market capital*—including international events, openness to different cultures, language skills.
- *Process capital*—including extent of Internet use, software use, teaching effectiveness, freedom of expression, agriculture added-value, entrepreneurship and risk-taking, venture capital funds, and immigration and absorption.

- *Human capital*—including advanced degrees, equal opportunities, women in the professional workforce, book publishing, museum visits, physicians in the medical system, alcohol consumption, and crime.
- *Renewal and development capital*—including civilian R&D, scientific publications. and biotechnology companies.

It was concluded that in a number of fields, Israel is at parity with other developed nations; and in some instances (e.g., the scientific activity and quality of its workforce), Israel even surpasses the leading developed nations.

In July 1997, The Danish government published a study, "A Structural Monitoring System for Denmark" that is believed to be the first of its kind. The publishing group, the House of Mandag Morgen, has a think tank that analyzes main trends of economic and societal importance and has developed a concept to unite the competence development of the country with a national vision.

The Danish leadership believes that a global knowledge economy poses quite different conditions from those of an industrialized society. Intellectual capital statements—similar to those originally produced by Skandia—are used as both an internal management tool and an external communication tool to attract new staff, new clients, and perhaps new investment capital. In a unique effort to establish the national IC guidelines, the Danish Agency for Trade and Industry has been publishing a series of IC Statements that systematically collect experience from nineteen companies for a couple of years. A complete package of the summary report, *IC Statements: Toward a Guideline*, as well as the individual company reports are available upon request[18].

The Ministry of Economic Affairs in The Netherlands, in a shift from "technology policy" to "innovation policy," published a 1998 report, *The Immeasurable Wealth of Knowledge*. Subsequent reports included *Intangible Assets: Balancing Accounts with Knowledge.*"[19] The study, administered by the Central Planning Bureau, showed that in 1992 over 35 percent of national investments were of an intangible

nature—an indication of the evolution of the knowledge-based economy. In 1995, KPMG was asked to assess the feasibility of creating a
"knowledge balance sheet." KPMG advocated establishing appendices
to the corporate annual reports and the creation of a database for
benchmarking purposes. The Cabinet, the standing Committee Par-
liamentary Committee for Economic Affairs, the Royal Netherlands
Institute of Chartered Accountants, and the Netherlands Order of
Management Consultant Accountants—to mention a few—have been
involved in subsequent studies.

In March 2000, an executive summary, *Benchmarking the Netherlands 2000: On the Threshold of the new Millennium*, was released.
Somewhat modeled after the Israeli report, the study is used by the
leadership to illuminate the major challenges that must be addressed by
the Dutch economy. Indicators (and related analysis) are organized
according to macroeconomic and fiscal climate, human capital, climate
for innovation, physical infrastructure, product markets, and the capital market. The express aim of the study was not only to show how The
Netherlands was performing, but also to learn from the best practices
in other benchmark countries.

The report does suggest one caveat. Nations do not compete, as do
companies. Rather, governments influence the basic conditions for
those companies (e.g., quality of living environment, climate for innovation, physical environment). A healthy competitive position, then, is
ultimately expressed in the level of growth and prosperity. The second
challenge is to shape the economic policy in such a way that the country
can benefit from the trends, such as demographic changes, globalization, increasing demand for individual freedom of choice, information
technology, growing mobility, and greater environmental awareness.
In turn, this provides for:

1.   A knowledge and participation economy.
2.   An economy that calls for macroeconomic stability and a com-
     petitive fiscal climate.

3. An economy that calls for macroeconomic flexibility and innovation.

4. An economy that must reconcile growing demand for mobilty
and space with the concern for a clean environment.

The report surveys all these factors and places the analysis in the
context of actionable policy initiatives to move the country forward.

Now it is evident that the benefits to be reaped with a focus on a
knowledge –not even an information—society extend far beyond the
context of company profitability. Indeed, those nations that seek to
establish viable and sustainable economic prosperity will inevitably
turn toward managing (and measuring) what we now consider the
intangible wealth of the nation. As more nations focus upon the
human capital and the innovation process (i.e., how knowledge is created, converted into products and services, and applied), we have an
opportunity to increase the standard of living worldwide.

There has been considerable activity, sometimes from unexpected
places. The Peruvian Ministry of Economic Affairs convened a conference on Intellectual Capital in 1998. The Latvian Cabinet of Ministers
has accepted "a National Concept of Innovation" (Stabulnieks, 2001).
The Prime Minister if Singapore has declared the intention to become
"The Innovation Nation" (see Chapter 14).

The Conference Board of Canada has produced several reports, the
most recent being its third annual report, "Investing in Innovation."[20]
The province of Alberta, Canada has produced a GPI Blueprint
(Anielski, 2002), "The Genuine Progress Indicator (GPI) Sustainability Well-being Accounting System." John Prior has produced a
comprehensive glossary of terms, "Knowledge Management and the
Wealth of Intangibles." The Commonwealth of Massachusetts has
issued the Index of the Massachusetts Innovation Economy 2000,[21]
outlining nine industry clusters and indicators for results, the innovation process, and allocation of resources. And all this appears to be only
the beginning

4.4   SOCIETAL LEVEL—NEW INDICATORS FOR SUCCESS

In the *World Economic Survey* (1996), Charles Goldfinger, an economic consultant, argues that

> *The shift from material goods to intangibles is the defining feature of the new economy. Not only have the services such as finance, communications and the media multiplied in size, but even tangible goods have more and more knowledge embedded in them: smart tires that tell you when the pressure is too low, vending machines that call distributors when they need restocking. Intangible inputs now account for 70% of the value of a car. And according to one estimate, the value of America's stock of intangible investment (R&D, education and training) overtook the value of physical capital stock during the 1980's.*

In the same report,[22] a 1996 OECD Observer is cited for its estimates that more than half of total GDP in the rich economies is now knowledge based, including such industries as telecommunications, computers, software, pharmaceuticals, education, and television. By one reckoning, it suggests that "knowledge workers—from brain surgeons to journalists—account for eight out of ten new jobs."

The OECD has produced a series of reports that have provided both leadership and direction on the topics of human capital, learning and society, national systems of innovation, and, most recently, the knowledge-based economy. A bimonthly OECD Observer features the most recent thinking and research results.

The April–May 1995 issue addressed the topic of measuring human capital. Riel Miller and Gregory Wurzburg describe how the contribution of human capital goes largely unreflected on the balance sheets because no one knows how to define and evaluate it. They describe how national accounts and economic analysis treat labor as a homogeneous input. However, the differentiated skills and expertise of workers are even more important as countries move away from goods toward services and other knowledge- and information-intensive outputs.

Because of these shifts and the increasingly competitive climate in which economic activity takes place, the economic survival of enterprises and the employability and earning power of individuals depend more on learning as the basis for agile adaptation. But the tools available to measure and attach economic value to human capital, and the investment in upgrading it, have not kept up with these changes (Miller and Wurzburg, 1995, p. 16).

In June 1999, an OECD congress on the topic took place in The Netherlands. That body has also been driving a project for national innovation systems (NIS). The findings indicate that: innovative firms grow through transitions; firms have differing degrees of freedom and innovation cycles; capital investments are important for knowledge flows; and nontechnological innovation is key in its own right and generates returns on technological innovation.

The World Bank has developed its set of indicators for developing nations—"2001 Knowledge Assets"[23]—using a knowledge assessment methodology (KAM) consisting of a set of sixty-nine structural and qualitative variables that benchmark how an economy compares with its neighbors, competitors, or countries it wishes to emulate. It helps to identify the problems and opportunities that a country faces, and where it may need to focus policy attention or future investments. The comparison is undertaken for a group of 100 countries, which includes most of the developed OECD economies and about 60 developing economies.

In addition, the World Bank Institute (WBI) has designed a new program, Knowledge for Development (K4D), which helps client countries achieve these objectives, thereby supporting the World Bank's knowledge and learning agenda. The program consists of four main components: Course/Policy Forum; Policy Services; TechNet, and Knowledge Economy Tools.

Although many of these principles may have been around for decades, few organizations have implemented them in a major way. Fewer have discovered a systematic way to measure the results. Measurement in the management development field is uncomfortable and time consuming. Now, with the significant research being done with the Brookings Institute and a variety of accounting/finance academic research centers and professional societies, we are beginning to comprehend the power behind the intangible value of the enterprise.

At the dawn of the new millennium, knowledge and information are becoming key factors of development. Increasing scientific understanding and rapid advances in information and communication technologies are leading to unprecedented changes in how knowledge is produced and disseminated. Developing countries now have the opportunity to exploit the knowledge revolution to help reduce poverty and promote sustainable development.

4.5   ARCHITECTURAL CONSIDERATIONS

1. Are there universal research metrics for investment and profitability?

2. Can the assets (e.g., financial, technological and intellectual) be well determined?

3. Can the critical success factors be defined in quantitative and qualitative terms?

4. Is the budget level and resource mix appropriate to the research mission?

5. Are there adequate rewards/incentives (e.g., travel support, release time, awards) to motivate involvement of key contributors.

6. Do internal tax structures provide shared risk in the cost accounting?

7. Are there more creative financing mechanisms (e.g., joint venturing, profit centers, limited partnerships) to be employed?

4.6   ACTION STEPS[24]

The good news is that considerable progress has been made. There is a major research project affiliated with the Brookings Institute providing guidance. Accounting Boards and professional organizations world-wide have placed the intangibles agenda as a priority. Best practice guidelines[25]—even in this emerging field—are surfacing: Some of these are given in the following list.

1. Draw up your own categories of intellectual capital and knowledge assets.

2. Estimate ("guesstimate") for each their overall value and their future revenue-generating potential.

3. Develop some form of balanced scorecard reporting.

4. Explore, as an experiment, some of the newer methodologies, such as the economic value-added models.

5. Create a matrix linking the assets you have identified with business impact.

6. Initiate pilot measurement and investment appraisal systems.

7. Develop the value proposition.

8. Don't despair if you cannot "prove" bottom-line business benefit. Take the leap of faith, as others are doing.

4.7   SUMMARY

Many now agree that we would rather be "roughly right than precisely wrong," as Leif Edvinsson espouses. Most executives today are measuring what they can measure because it can be measured. But this is like looking for the lost keys by the light—because there is light—rather than near the car where they were dropped! Those who do not get a better handle on measuring intangible value or intellectual capital are likely to be left behind those that do. This is one of the reasons that the accounting profession and research groups such as The Brookings

Institute are dedicating considerable resources to find some answers —and if not answers, at least some direction to navigate.

Measurements monitor the performance of the system such that inputs are measured against the outputs of valuable products and services given the time-value of the investment. This dynamic measure holds for a network of organizations, for a network of businesses, for a country, or for a global interrelated set of countries evolving in the new economy. This focus has put us on a new path toward understanding the real value of intangible wealth—how it is created and how it contributes to profitability and prosperity.

Millennium leadership will not avoid the issues of measurement. They will embrace innovative mechanisms, tools, and methodologies to navigate into the future. We will not avoid the issue of results on investment in building leadership capability. We will discover the human and humane methods to document progress. Our generations to come deserve nothing less.

CHAPTER ENDNOTES

[1] *The Economist*, September 26, 1996, p. 23.

[2] *Ambassador's Journal: A Personal Account of the Kennedy Years* (1969).

[3] For the Michael Polanyi Society, visit http://griffon.mwsc.edu/~polanyi/

[4] Copy downloadable from Web site http://www.sveiby.com

[5] *Intellectual Capital*, pp. 169–180.

[6] Scandia Annual Reports; see http://www.entovation.com/innovation/skandia.htm

[7] *Innovation Strategy for the Knowledge Economy*, Ch. 6.

[8] e-Knowledge Markets; see http://www.kikm.org/portal/markets.htm

[9] See http://www.brookings.org/dybdocroot/es/research/projects/intangibles/ic.htm

[10] For the article, visit
   http://www.businessweek.com/magazine/content/01_45/b3756103.htm

[11] For further information, visit http://www.bontis.com/

[12] KNEXA, see http://www.knexa.com/

[13] *Creating the Knowledge-Based Business.* pp 125–174.

[14] *Bionomics*, p. 334–335.

[15] *Collaborative Innovation and the Knowledge Economy*, p.15.

[16] "Valuing and Measuring a Technological Edge," pp 3–7.

[17] *Knowledge Management*, April 2002, p 27–30.

[18] For further information, visit http://www.efs.dk/icaccounts/

[19] For further information, visit http://www.minez.nl

[20] For further information, visit http://www.conferenceboard.ca/

[21] For further information, visit http://www.mtpc.org/

[22] p. 23.

[23] For further information, visit http://www1.worldbank.org/gdln/kam.htm

[24] Adapted from *Creating the Knowledge-Based Business* (Skyrne/Amidon, 1997)

[25] "Measuring the Value of Knowledge," p. 179.

FIVE

Knowledge Structures

*Knowledge-based service systems and technologies
have radically reordered the power relationships,
competitive environments,
and leveragable opportunities in most industries—
whether in services or manufacturing....
Organization follows strategy....
Structure follows technology.*

James Brian Quinn[1]

If performance measures provide the economic understanding of management, then the structure of the organization defines the sociology or anthropology (i.e., culture) of the enterprise.

Some progressive managers have realized that there is strength in interdependence (i.e., the value of the whole in addition to the operations of individual parts). In fact, the whole has expanded to include suppliers, alliances, partners, customers and even competitors. As organizations develop a deeper commitment to cross-functional teaming, real-time learning, communities of practice, symbiotic partnering relationships with customers and other stakeholders, the value of human networking will be obvious.[2]

The reality is that many companies that have gone through the reengineering effort (often a Trojan horse for downsizing) have lost considerable intellectual wealth, because they restructured for the

69

wrong reasons and had no knowledge management system to guide their judgments. For some companies, it may be a matter of unlearning the recent practices that have now stagnated innovation and relearning or rediscovering their heritage and sense of purpose. Is that radical? I'm not sure it need be; but it is not just continuous process improvement either. For each organization, it would be different, for knowledge is what makes each organization unique.

5.1   SOME ROOTS

We have seen quite an evolution of a variety of structures—experimentation increasing in recent years since the original "M-Form" instituted by Alfred P. Sloan at General Motors. Please don't hold me to the dates—nor should this be considered a comprehensive list, but in Figure 5.1 there are a few examples to illustrate the pace of experimentation.

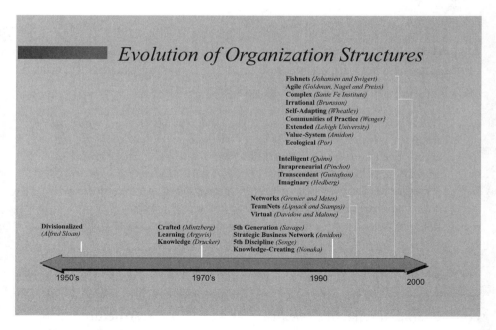

FIGURE 5.1   *Evolution of organization structures.*

These examples of alternative ways of describing the social structure of a firm may seem like different labels for the same phenomenon—more complex, highly interdependent, human variables; and in some instances, this may be true. However, there have been some fundamental concepts that underlie these various schools of thought. There are many, but we will select five for the purpose of illustration.

- *Role of learning.* Several authors in the late 1980s (DeGeus, 1989; Stata, 1989; and Senge, 1990) were experimenting with concepts for the learning organization, learning as a competitive weapon, envisioning the role an individual might plan in an organization and an organization as part of an expanding enterprise. This was the predecessor of the concepts researched with Society of Learning[3] and the European-funded KALiF Project (see Chapter 14).
- *Role of knowledge creation.* With the article on "The Knowledge Creating Company" (Nonaka and Takeuchi, 1991), the world paid attention to many of the concepts Professor Nonaka had been writing about years before in Japanese. These writings, which delineate in detail the socialization processes, provided a language to describe tacit and explicit knowledge so that we have a sense of the intangible value we were trying to measure in Chapter 4. The concept has evolved into the "Ba"[4]—something that is closer to my definition of the environment for innovation that includes knowledge creation and extends to knowledge conversion and commercialization.
- *Role of networks.* The experts in defining a working knowledge of creating and sustaining virtual teams in organizations are the principals from The Networking Institute[5] (Lipnack and Stamps, 1994). These concepts have also been researched and tied to dynamic mapping technologies by Valdes Krebs,[6] who is able to quantitatively illuminate network analysis of interactions, the quality of work interactions, and "communities of

knowledge." These have even evolved into competency networks, as described by Kuan-Tsae Huang.[7]

- *Role of communities.* Although John Seely Brown (Brown, 1995)
  may have been one of the first to put the notion of communities of practice "into practice," Etienne Wenger invented the
  concept and finally published his book in 2002. These concepts
  have led to more advanced views of the value of "social capital"
  (Portes, 2000) for both enterprise communities and nations.[8]
  Some progressive companies (e.g., AT&T) have begun to
  view themselves as smart businesses with systematic knowledge
  community advancements from market-driven foundations to
  community-driven sharing and ultimately into self-sustaining
  collaboration.[9]
- *Role of ecology.* George Por, now at INSEAD, developed the
  concept of knowledge ecology (Por, 2000), including university
  courses on the topic. In his most recent writings, he describes
  how knowledge communities evolve with their body of knowledge and with the tools and protocols for upgrading that
  knowledge. At the heart of the knowledge ecology is the art
  and science of gleaning meaning and value from the interplay
  of knowledge bases and productive conversations—another
  concept pioneered by Fernando Flores (Chile) and Dan Kim
  (MIT).

In short, we see the foundation of a multileveled networked organization system structured for collaborative advantage. Boundaries have
faded between functions, internal and external to the firm, across functions and nations. Connections have become more and more intimate
and the interdependence more obvious.

5.2 Back to the Productivity Paradox

As described in Chapter 2, the lack of performance in organizations, in
spite of the rapid infusion of technology, is due to the behavioral fac-

tors—the psychology, sociology, and anthropology of the enterprise. This applies to the nonprofit as well as the profit center. In the compendium report of the National Research Council,[10] there are multiple managerial levels and reciprocal linkages. It is a study of the conditions under which performance occurs and its structural characteristics.

> *Changing a single aspect of an organization almost never results in a substantial change in organizational performance. Organizations are too complex, their performance too multi-determined, and their inertia great for single innovation at the individual level to have an impact on organizational performance.*

We now know, however, that with the significant advances in organizational behavior methodologies referenced above we are discovering ways to make such changes. In fact, we are looking at the individual to make the difference in the organization—assuming he or she has an innovation mindset.

The report suggests that processes at and across individual, group, and organizational levels intertact and affect one another. The performance of an organization is a function of at least seven interrelated criteria: effectiveness, efficiency, quality, productivity, innovation, the quality of work life, and profitability.

There is "simultaneity" in operation. Functions remain single and important variables in the firm; but value is created at the intersections, the overlaps, and the connections between variables. For instance, where R&D meets marketing, we can develop new ways to meet customer demands with new products and services (i.e., innovation).

For a graphic example of the value in the overlaps, Karl Wiig[11] has developed an illustration of sole and shared responsibility as it relates to enterprisewide management, human resources (HR), and competency-based HR management, research and development, and information management and technology. At the heart lies the operation of the intranet with personal homepages and the knowledge-related personal review system.

Similarly, the educational, governmental, industrial, and nonprofit sectors are separate entities; but when they come together with shared purpose, leverage of resources—financial, human, and technical—can be found. Each nation within the European Union retains a heritage, culture, and identity of its own. But the important thing is the areas in which they can come together on common ground and mutual interest (e.g., the European currency, regional research funding initiatives, and international trade positioning)

5.3   CULTURE IS KEY

These connections—managing at the interface—are integral to value creation. How they are managed, however, may be more a function of intangibles than was reflected in Chapter 4—especially when related to the meso- and macroeconomic levels of the economy.

Consider this excerpt from an article in *The Economist*:[12]

> *Research has increasingly concentrated on clusters—places (such as Hollywood or Silicon Valley) or communities (such as the overseas Chinese) where there is "something in the air" that encourages risk-taking. This suggests that culture, irritatingly vague though it may sound, is more important to Silicon Valley's success than economic or technological factors.*

The article continues to outline a description of the integral variables that are essential to any innovation culture: tolerance of failure, tolerance of treachery, risk-seeking, reinvestment in the community, enthusiasm for change, obsession with the product (service), collaboration, and variety. Anybody can play.

These represent critical and rather nontraditional variables in catalyzing the innovation mindset required both individually and organizationally. Note how they contrast with the variables described in the foregoing quotation from the NRC Report.

The article concludes that culture and structure reinforce one another.

Do not regard it as some sort of economic machine, where various raw materials being poured into one end and firms like Cisco and Apple roll out at the other, but rather it is a form of ecosystem that breeds companies: without the right soil and climate, nothing will grow,

This is similar to the research findings reported in our study (Skyrme and Amidon, 1997).[13] That book's chapter on the knowledge-enhancing organization reviewed a variety of case study examples illustrating ways to improve knowledge creating and sharing.

- Creating a culture where knowledge is valued and shared is one of the most difficult challenge to be faced in practice.
- Appropriate cultures are those that engender change, learning, innovation, openness, and trust. They recognize and reward people for their knowledge contribution (i.e., sharing knowledge can be part of the performance and review reward system).
- Conditions for effective knowledge creation and sharing now require more flexible "networked" organizational structures, multiple types of teams, and a climate of intensive and purposeful networking.
- Factors can help establish the conditions that encourage knowledge sharing, such as moving people through job rotation, appropriate events, effective teaming, and a comprehensive networking technology infrastructure.
- Communities of practice are loosely formed teams with a shared purpose that emerge through informal networking, but they are now being incentivized and "managed" in various enterprises.
- Physical settings do play a role in creating the conditions for informal knowledge exchange.
- Once connections are made, attention should be given to purposeful conversations.

These are the implications for the enterprise level; but many of the same principles apply to developing an innovative national economy and stimulating innovation on a worldwide basis.

Take a country perspective. Elana Granell in her book *Managing Culture for Success*,[14] explores the uniqueness of Venezuela. She describes how certain (economic) assumptions about cultural superiority and parochial ethnocentrisms have been used to justify the imposition of one culture over another. Indeed, this has been the case to date with industrialized countries vis à vis. developing nations. Even the societal structures (e.g., the OECD and the World Bank) lend themselves to that differentiation.

This is what Granell argues:

> *That does not mean that you cannot learn from experience (from the success or failure or others), but the concept of a globalized business world should not imply conquest or imposition of one culture over another. It should give us the opportunity to know ourselves better and obtain maximum benefit from cultural exchanges.*

But the knowledge economy, enabled by The Innovation Superhighway, levels the playing field—knowledge being the asset to be managed, innovation the process, and the supporting technical infrastructure enabling the smallest voice to be heard around the world. Thus, we now see more evidence of cross-boundary initiatives where the heritage and uniqueness of cultural heritage is valued and respected for the contribution that might be made.

East is meeting West; and North is meeting South with international learning that has become a daily part of our lives. CNN, the international broadcast of the Olympics, television programs such as "Survivor," and even the events of 9/11/2001 have triggered in all of us an awareness of the need to respect the values of one another and work toward developing a shared purpose for global sustainability overall.

5.4 PLATFORM FOR COLLABORATIVE ADVANTAGE

Innovation, redefined in terms of the flow of knowledge, requires an environment of collaboration, not competition. However, many of the industrialized economies of the world have developed cultures that reward individualism, independence, and autonomy. The rage of the 1980s and early 1990s was international competitiveness. Organizations constantly compared, contrasted, and subsequently built initiatives to compete, by hoarding and protecting information at both enterprise and cultural borders.

Emerging economic conditions require a collaborative view of the organization. With concepts such as cross-boundary processes and the extended enterprise, which include stakeholders external to the enterprise, it may be necessary to consider collaborative relationships with those who may be competitors today. In *Cooperate to Compete: Building Agile Business Relationships*, the authors describe fuzzy boundaries and measures for success (e.g., concurrent operations, integrated product and process development, interactive customer relationships, virtual partnering, and electronic commerce, among others).[15]

> *Collaboration across functions and divisions within a company as well as with other companies is the operational strategy of first choice. Trying first to operate in a self-contained way and turning to others only as a last resort is a luxury that companies cannot afford when dealing with dynamic customer opportunities.*

In the simplest terms, competition is a win/lose scenario: one party wins the pie and the other loses it. On a cooperative playing field, both agree to divide the pie and thereby secure half of it. The synergistic approach is to discover ways to work together to create more than one pie and to reap the benefits of mutual goals. Both parties enjoy the benefits of a whole pie because they have been able to learn from, and collectively innovate with, one another.

Most major consulting firms are now releasing major research reports on the topics of innovation and collaborative knowledge networks, one of which comes from Deloitte Research.[16] With case study examples, they illustrate various facets of the knowledge innovation opportunity: "Creating Competitive Advantage" (Royal Dutch/Shell), "Building a Community of Developers" (Oracle), "Community-Driven Innovation" (National Semiconductor), "Harmonizing Systems" (Chevron), "The Power behind Stories" (Xerox PARC), "Unlocking Tacit Knowledge" (Nippon Roche), and "Creating Knowledge-Sharing Cultures" (AMS and The World Bank).

Collective findings reveal why collaborative knowledge networks are gaining momentum, as shown in the following list:

1.   Shareholder pressure
2.   Knowledge as a critical asset
3.   Blurring of corporate boundaries
4.   Customer imperatives
5.   Transformations of traditional organization structures

How then do individuals, corporations, and nations realize that in the end they are truly dependent upon the success of one another? They recognize that far more is accomplished together—economically, behaviorally and technologically—than alone. This is the essence of the knowledge transformation occurring globally.

Organizations worldwide have begun to embrace the knowledge agenda. Invariably, they describe the process of innovation in one form or another. However, this is not the technological innovation with which most people have been familiar. Success in this environment requires a fundamental understanding of progressive concepts: intellectual capital, intangible assets, real-time learning, knowledge management, and global conferencing, among others. Societal organizations such as the OECD, the Securities and Exchange Commission (SEC), the United Nations, and The World Bank have launched major efforts in this arena, and initiatives must be brought together in a common agenda.

Nations have begun to adopt strategies to capitalize upon the benefits of symbiotic relationships (i.e., building upon the capacities of one another). The Conference Board of Canada produced its Second Annual Innovation Report—"Collaborating for Innovation"— which states: "We strongly believe that collaboration and the ability to build linkages among all players in the economy are critical to building a high-performing and innovative nation."[17]

Just as was described in the Atlas of Knowledge Innovation (Chapter 3), to maintain leadership requires that you position yourself against where your competitors are going, not where they have been. The good news is that many nations are awakening to the opportunity. The bad (good) news is that their competitive (collaborative) nations are not standing still!

5.5 ARCHITECTURAL CONSIDERATIONS

1. Does the current learning network of expertise operate as an interrelated set of fully functioning contributors of knowledge?

2. Do the system dynamics provide for flexibility, adaptability, and the ability to capitalize upon technological breakthroughs in timely ways?

3. Do reporting relationships foster shallow hierarchies, virtual teaming, and authority based on knowledge?

4. Do staffing patterns take advantage of worldwide scientific expertise (e.g., visiting scientists, research fellows, technology scouts)?

5. Have the cultural and cross-cultural aspects of the research enterprise been defined sufficiently to leverage the diversity of talent?

6. Are liaison relationships assigned to monitor project progress and ensure optimal leverage of research results?

7. Does the structure promote collaborative strategy as a means to competitive positioning?

5.6   ACTION STEPS[18]

1. Develop clarity of understanding—terms, values, conditions, and intent.

2. Start somewhere and learn from successes and mistakes.

3. Apply a multidisciplinary research approach, often in the form of action research.

4. Treat customers and other stakeholders as sources of knowledge.

5. Integrate the workspace into a work-systems model.

6. Practice leadership and minimize resistance to change.

7. Apply lessons in-house and actively participate externally.

8. Trigger imagination—which in the end—is more important than knowledge.

5.7   SUMMARY

Developing a knowledge-sharing culture is the most difficult aspect of knowledge strategy; it may also be the most important. There are many new models from which to choose; and we are learning from the experimentation underway in all types of enterprises and nations, thanks to the technology affording "real-time" learning.

This dynamic economic climate demands a networked, fluid organizational structure that balances accountability with responsible risk taking. It is not the parts themselves that add value, but the synergistic nature of the whole, the value of which is greater than the sum of the parts. This is the nature of fusion and the result of symbiotic learning networks, both human and technical. Demonstrated value resides in the interfaces between the boxes, sometimes described as the white space, which must be the object of our performance management systems.

Treasure the discovery of diversity, not because it is politically correct but because it is a foundation for learning. Gaining insights and putting new ideas into motion faster than the competition is critical to economic survival. The Innovation Superhighway—operating as both a technical and human network—can afford connection opportunities heretofore unimagined.

We are beginning to see rapid and increasing evidence of the acceptance of these concepts, which only a half a decade ago were considered renegade. Today, they are not only possible; but they may indicate the only true path to a sustainable world and a platform for world peace.

CHAPTER ENDNOTES

[1] Quinn, "Revolutionizing Organization Strategies" (1992), p. 101.

[2] *Innovation Strategy for the Knowledge Economy*, Ch. 6

[3] For further information, visit http://solonline.org/

[4] *California Management Review* (1998).

[5] For further information, visit http://www.virtualteams.com/

[6] *Managing Core Competencies of the Corporation* (1996), pp. 393–409.

[7] Huang (1999). p. 358.

[8] "Social capital: Its Origins and Applications in Modern Sociology," p. 59.

[9] Botkin (1999), p. 87.

[10] *Organizational Linkages*, pp. 6, 8, 291–293.

[11] Wiig article in *Knowledge Horizons* (2000), p. 15.

[12] "Vital Intangibles," pp. 7–12.

[13] *Creating the Knowledge-Based Business* (1997), Ch. 6.

[14] Granell (1997), p. 7.

[15] Preiss, Goldman, and Nagel (1996), p. 255.

[16] Deloitte Research (2002).

[17] The Conference Board of Canada (2001), p. iii.

[18] Adapted from Creating the Knowledge-Based Business (Skyrne/Amidon, 1997)

SIX
Knowledge Workers

A society of "knowledge employees"
who are neither exploited nor exploiters;
who individually are not capitalists
but who collectively own the means of production;
who are subordinates but often bosses themselves.
These people are both independent and dependent.
They have mobility.
But they also need access to an organization—
As "consultants" if not as "employees"—
To have any effectiveness at all.

Peter F. Drucker[1]

The knowledge economy has placed our attention on the human being—where it belongs! It is not information nor is it digital technology, it is individuals—how they create knowledge, share it with one another and put it into use to add value. Now we know that people are important, as is how they are organized in structures to optimize learning as individuals and as organizations. But the real architectural issue may not be a matter of expertise, skills, or know-how; it may be a matter of psychology, how they are motivated to innovate[2].

When people originally referred to knowledge workers, they were describing the skills necessary for high technology industries. Others described the Knowledge Industry as the Services sector. People have realized that all industries—and, indeed, all professions—are knowledge-intensive. If they aren't now, they soon will be. A true knowledge-intensive organization is comprised of self-motivating, empowered workers who know that their knowledge is important to the performance of their organizations. They understand that their knowledge and expertise can be applied along multiple dimensions. In fact, their motivation to contribute to the enterprise may be based upon how the knowledge and skill base is utilized, recognized and rewarded."[3]

For years, we have been tracing the demographics, such as the age of the workforce and increase in telecommuting. We've charted the mobility indices, including that changing colors and complexions of the worldwide workforce and their relative economic positioning. We've assessed changing values, such as loss of allegiance to the company and the work ethic of one culture compared with that of the next. And we know from Chapter 5 the "new" cultural realities of the enterprise and national economies.

"People are important" read the sign behind the marketing director when I was interviewing for a position in 1979. Individuals have always been important; but now, having labeled the knowledge economy, we have a sense of "what" might be important about the people and how to incentive the behavior that fosters the development of both the individual and the organization.

6.1   SOME ROOTS

Since Peter Drucker first put a label on the "knowledge worker," we've developed a new focus on what might constitute the talents and competencies of individuals in the "new" economy. The focus on knowledge and learning is not new per se; what is new is our attention to the value of the knowledge and modern management philosophies, policies, and practices that enhance the development and contribution of that knowledge.

In *The Rise of the Knowledge Worker*,[4] James W. Cortada, author of over a dozen books on the history of computing and the management of information processing, tracks this modern evolution as follows:

1. Since the beginning of humankind, people have recognized the value of consciously collecting and using information.

2. Humans have always tried to augment human memory with writing to aid their preservation of information and knowledge for subsequent use.

3. Humankind has constantly developed physical objects in which to store and manipulate information.

4. Every major institution in society has collected, preserved, and exploited information.

5. Information begets information (leading to deep insights, to knowledge).

Drucker now describes the "knowledge worker" as the new majority, and this was long before it was common knowledge that manufacturing firms were as knowledge-intensive as the service sector. This was before the knowledge movement has diffused worldwide, especially into those communities previously excluded from the worldwide economic action.

Of course, the Internet has changed a great deal; and most of the advances have been more than simply technological in as much as they inspired individuals to participate. The real revolution, however, was in the psychology (i.e., motivation) of individuals, linking what they learn to what they do. Again there have been some fundamental concepts operating as influencing themes that have contributed to this evolution. They are as follows:

- *The role of entrepreneurialism.* Some of our current knowledge leaders were writing books on this topic early in the 1980s and were instituting programs and courses in many business schools around the world. Several began to link it to innovation in the early 1990s (Kozmetsky, 1989; Drucker, 1993). Several CEOs have been featured for their entrepreneurial prowess (e.g., Ken Olsen, the ultimate entrepreneur). Most recently, we find books on the "virtual" entrepreneur. There are books on civic entrepreneurship, economics, and black entrepreneurs along with an emerging discipline of "social entrepreneuring."[5]

- *The role of the intrapreneur*. Gifford and Elizabeth Pinchot[6] can be credited with defining the term that enables those *within* the corporation to make sense of the complexity of their organizations and determine ways to make a contribution. "The hallmark of an effective entrepreneurial network is the flexibility and ingenuity demanded for survival in an open market structure—the freedom to innovate, to get rapid feedback from customers, to learn and change."

- *The role of competence*. Computer-based education (CBE) has evolved into competency-based learning. In many instances, the capacity to learn, as individuals and organizations, is more important than skill development. Bill Miller,[7] former Vice President of Steelcase North America, has integrated these learning concepts into the theories and practice of innovation management.

- *The role of tacit and explicit knowledge*. Ikujiru Nonaka was the one to make this distinction visible, and Hubert Saint-Onge, Vice President of Clarica (see the profile in Chapter 13) was the one to put it into practice. These notions have evolved into the concept of the hidden, intangible value of organizations, which must be identified and managed—as difficult as that may seem. These are the right questions to ask.

- *The role of partnering*. Although the concept of customer relationship management (CRM) focuses on the value of the customer interface, it is those who understand the next horizon—collaborating and innovating with stakeholders (Amidon, 1997;[8] Dawson, 2000)— who are likely to maintain the competitive edge in the future. As Tom Petzinger suggests, "Nobody's as smart as everybody."[9]

For what Barry C. Carter might call the "infinite economy," he makes the integral connection between the individual and society:

> *Social order comes through norms, principles, and a shared vision of the interdependent whole of which we are a part. Each individual is connected and has the same relationship with every other individual globally, either directly or indirectly. It is a system whereby all boats rise together. An individual's wealth increases directly as the wealth of other individuals and the whole group increases; thus win/win and collaboration are the primary norm."*[10]

He suggests that with the advances in information technology, people have been empowered to connect, collaborate, and create wealth and self-order without bureaucracy or even representative government.

6.2   Emerging practices

In our research report (Amidon and Skyrme, 1997), we have an entire chapter dedicated to roles and skills for the knowledge age[11]. Reviewing several case study examples (e.g., TelTech, the U.S. Army, and Anglian Waters, among others), we discovered that the summary findings from the case studies include the following conclusions:

- As organizations become more knowledge based, new knowledge roles are emerging and the roles of existing knowledge workers are changing.
- Some of the new roles encountered were knowledge editors, knowledge navigators, knowledge analysts, and knowledge brokers. All play a part in linking some knowledge process to day-to-day activities.
- All roles require more knowledge creation (creativity) and knowledge sharing. This shift requires more hybrid knowledge

and skills, including organizational and business knowledge as well as general management skills (e.g., networking, communication, and relationship-building skills.

- No strong correlation was found between competency planning and knowledge management initiatives. There seems to be a consensus that competence is as much about behaviors as it is knowledge and skills.
- There is a growing focus on learning. In turn, this reflects a shift from a training focus to student-centered learning linked to on-the-job activities. Several methods are used to create such a learning environment, including open learning centers, links with universities, and the use of "safe to fail" simulation tools and board games.
- There is a strong correlation between knowledge-based organizations and learning organizations, with strong interest shown in Senge's *Five Disciplines.* However, the linkage between learning and knowledge activities is not explicitly developed in many organizations, such as through "lessons learned" centers.

Therefore, a strong management system is composed of talented, dedicated, self-managing knowledge workers who can balance entrepreneurial contributions with the business imperative of the team. Individuals—each as a "unit of one"—are encouraged to seek new ways to add knowledge value to the system to advance the state of the business. Role and goal agreements are carefully negotiated to optimize the decision-making capability of the whole.

Perhaps Peter Senge, author of *The Fifth Discipline*, produced one of the most influential books on the topic because he dealt with the personal mastery necessary. In the Table 6.1 David Sktrne and I have contrasted the five disciplines defined by Senge with some of the modern managerial concepts pervading the knowledge profession.

Thus, there is significant correspondence between some of Senge's learning disciplines and the knowledge processes described by Nonaka and Takeuchi.[12] Although our research revealed a growing awareness

TABLE 6.1   *Relationship of the Five Disciplines to Knowledge*
Source: *Creating the Knowledge-Based Business*

Discipline (from Senge et. al.)	Contribution to Knowledge Management
Systems thinking—structures, relatedness, systemic (holistic perspectives; the specific methods of systems dynamics)	This discipline is about widening and deepening knowledge, "seeking out interrelationships never discussed (or noticed) before". Thus, systems dynamics helps people gain insights into what is often counterintuitive behavior of a system (such as a supply chain). It's like Garvin's know-why knowledge.
Personal mastery—developing greater understanding of personal goals and today's reality, values and reality, interdependence with others.	This is self-knowledge. It is about making sense of your own position, by being more explicit. It is about articulating your knowledge in ways that are helpful to others.
Mental models—the models in your mind that shape actions and decisions. Two key tools are reflection and inquiry. Argyris's "ladder of inference" and action science are described, as is "the left-hand column". This is the most difficult discipline but the one with the greatest leverage, according to Senge.	Here the book makes an explicit link to knowledge. Mental models are "the tacit knowledge in personal cognitive maps," The "left-hand column" is "what I'm thinking" (vs. the right-hand column or " what is said"). The processes of enquiry and reflection aid the surfacing of tacit knowledge make tacit knowledge explicit. This correlates with Nonaka and Takeuchi's "knowledge spiral"
Shared vision—This is the bringing together in shared processes a collective vision of co-creating the future: "bringing together multiple visions in an organic interdependent whole," Dialog is an important tool.	The book describes a shared vision as a tacit shared sense of purpose. This is very much about knowledge building through knowledge sharing. It is moving personal knowledge into team knowledge and ultimately organizational knowledge. It requires a common language so that diverse perspectives can contribute to the overall whole and sense of purpose.

TABLE 6.1 (continued)

Discipline (from Senge et. al.)	Contribution to Knowledge Management
Team learning—Developing a collective understanding and capability alignment so that the team acts as a whole. Unity results because members "know each others hearts and minds." Dialog and skillful discussion are its two key methods.	This represents two aspects—the process of moving from tacit to explicit and vice versa, and the diffusion of individual knowledge to collective knowledge. It relates mostly to Nonaka's processes of socialization, though to some extent of externalization.

of the links between learning and knowledge, we suspect that most knowledge management programs have yet to make these links explicit at the operational or technique level.

On the other hand, there has been a considerable increase in the number of managerial positions as chief knowledge officer, chief learning officer, chief leadership officer, and chief innovation officer, among others. In an Action Series publication[13] produced by the American Society of Training and Development (ASTD), Dr. Dede Bonner provided an array of eighteen case study examples of this leadership in practice, including the one featuring the Entovation Network (see Chapter 9). She synthesizes the lessons learned across the diverse group of leaders and focuses on the action verbs found in the language of the new leadership: align, benchmark, design, develop, identify, implement, integrate, leverage, partner, plan, and strategize.

We cannot underestimate the role of the "new" leadership competencies required for twenty-first century leverage. In our research study, another entire chapter was dedicated to the topic; and in this text alone there are three references—Chapters 12, 13, and 15. As Tom Peters suggests, "You think the past five years were nuts? You ain't seen nothin' yet! It's only going to get weirder, tougher, and more turbulent. Which means that leadership will be more important than ever—and more confusing."

As the Cluetrain Manifesto[14] suggests, "A powerful global conversation has begun."

6.3   SHAPING OF THE KNOWLEDGE PROFESSION

Just as we are seeing different professions converging on the "Emerging Community of Knowledge Practice,"[15] we are seeing the emergence of specialist knowledge professionals. New titles and job responsibilities appearing in a variety of functions—knowledge engineer, knowledge editor, knowledge analyst, knowledge navigator, knowledge gatekeeper, knowledge brokers, knowledge handyman, knowledge asset manager, and knowledge steward or shepherd. And these do not include the facilitation and coaching roles or the functional job titles, which are assuming the leadership role in many companies. The schema shown in Table 6.2 provides a scope of the emerging professional responsibilities:

TABLE 6.2   *Knowledge Profession Classification Schema*

Classification Schema:

1.   *Knowledge and Innovation Professionals*

Individuals have strong backgrounds in shaping and formulating knowledge-based programs. Many have developed best practices for global Fortune 1000 companies. Most are highly skilled in a variety of disciplines, including business process improvement, innovation, dialogue, performance measurement and modeling, case history, facilitation, strategic integration, and developing best practices. Chief knowledge officers are part of this group as are consultants.

2.   *Knowledge Management Professionals*

Knowledge management professionals have expertise in implementation. They ensure that a company gains from management of knowledge. They are involved in all phases of innovation (knowledge creation, knowledge acquisition, knowledge sharing, knowledge conversion, knowledge commercialization. Career background may be in any function (e.g., Finance, human resources, quality, IT, R&D, manufacturing, sales, service).

TABLE 6.2 (continued)

Classification Schema:

3. *Knowledge Catalogers, Researchers and Media Specialists*

These are contributors who have skills as Web site, Internet, and intranet developers; librarians; catalog specialists; content developers; communicators; software designers and developers; middle managers; and others who create knowledge networks and links.

4. *Knowledge and Competitive Intelligence Professionals*

Emphasis focuses on competitive intelligence. Heavy research, the ability to create and develop solid positions, online research savvy mixed with the ability to cogently and concisely present ideas in a clear and concise format are well-developed skills. Writing and presentation skills are strong.

5. *Knowledge and Strategic Integration Professionals*

Composed of top strategists, thinkers, planners, marketers, and individuals with senior management experience. These individuals make planning and strategy the engine for business improvement and growth.

6. *Knowledge Academicians, Theorists, and Visionaries*

This group focuses primarily on discussion within an academic setting and developing and testing models and applications. Visionaries are thought leaders who are frequently well in front of the practice. These individuals make outstanding speakers and can stimulate your organization's thinking.

7. *Knowledge Facilitators, Trainers, and Corporate Educators*

These individuals focus on learning and education in a corporate setting. Many have created outstanding models and programs for linking external and internal audiences, designing and developing curriculums, implementing distance learning, and creating custom-tailored courses for executives and senior managers.

8. *Knowledge and Expert Systems Professionals*

One facet of knowledge and knowledge management is expert systems, a field concentrated on how to institutionalize corporate knowledge. Individuals in this area include systems specialists, technologists, chief information officers, technology transfer specialists, expert systems engineers, Project managers and others who primarily focus on information technology.

The knowledge profession itself has organized into a variety of professional societies, accreditation program offerings, and standards of operation. Ultimately, more responsibility shifts to the individual as he or she determines the role to play in a given organization.

Andrew Mayo[16] defines capability as "all that a person brings that enables them to achieve both their goals and those of the organization. It is such an important input to the process of adding value that it requires serious analysis and measurement." The question, of course, is how might it be assessed? What do we measure that might relate directly to the knowledge value proposition outlined in Chapter 2?

Mayo further tackles those characteristics that promote innovation[17]—one of the competencies we believe necessary for The Innovation Superhighway to be successful. These characteristics include:

- Acceptance of and readiness for change in every person throughout the organization along with dedication to the continuous improvement of processes
- Willingness to experiment and explore new ways of working, new suppliers, and new technologies
- Eagerness to learn from others
- Creating new markets and customers
- Building new relationships and alliances
- Establishing new approaches to markets, channels, and pricing
- Encouraging new and varied approaches to organization, management, and performance measurement

Further, professionals are gaining a respect for understanding the future. Claus Otto Scharmer, at Massachusetts Institute of Technology, calls it "Presencing—Learning from the Future as It Emerges."[18] John Simpson and others focus on scenarios for "Future Work in the Knowledge Economy"[19] understanding the KM Task Force and its relationships for the European KM Forum. And Tom Asacker brings it home with his "sandbox wisdom":

True leaders never try to acquire success and fame at the expense of others. They're other focused and lead through influence. And they don't choose their destiny. Their destiny chooses them. You are a group of people living together at a unique time. How you communicate this wisdom, and care for each other, means everything.[20]

6.4   ARCHITECTURAL CONSIDERATIONS

1. Do individuals have a clear sense of the purpose of the entire search enterprise?

2. Have people aligned their own work imperatives with their contributions to the innovation system?

3. Are people expected to balance their own individual research contributions with the performance of the system as a whole?

4. Do people possess the appropriate level of skills and knowledge required to perform their roles and, if not, what development plans have been put into place?

5. Does the environment promote a learning philosophy such that people are rewarded for continuous growth?

6. Are role responsibilities clearly defined?

7. Does the work design allow for both creativity and quality within a robust innovation system?

6.5   ACTION STEPS[21]

1. Recognize the emergence of new knowledge roles and support their development through competency planning and career development.

2. Understand how your best performers work—successful competencies and behaviors.

3. Develop more hybrid ("T-shaped") skills with vertical depth and horizontal scope.

4. Understand what motivates knowledge workers and how to manage them.

5. Create a strategy for learning (as opposed to training), one that is individual-focused rather than instructor-focused and one that includes "lessons learned."

6. Consider coaching and mentoring as key skills for your managers.

7. Ensure that you have an external "sensing" system— one that taps into the knowledge and development of your stakeholders, including customers.

8. Allocate sufficient time for learning and inspire insights to action. True learning may be more a function of conversations than of courses.

6.6 SUMMARY

Successful knowledge-based companies depend on how successful individual knowledge workers create and apply new ideas productively and efficiently (i.e., how they innovate). This requires new roles, new skills, and new ways of developing organization capabilities that continuously improve, such as through organizational learning.

New roles are emerging as we "speak;" and the profession is rapidly becoming a "discipline"—some would suggest prematurely so. The reality is that in fifteen short years, a dedicated community of knowledge practice is making a difference in every function, industry, and geographic region. The collective learning—yet to be fully realized—is enormous. The intellectual talent of the world is being unleashed—one person at a time.

Bottom-line results rely on the unit of one, and that "unit" is the human being. Knowledge-based companies place a premium on learning—how it is developed for the individual and how it relates to the organization and resulting performance—however that might be measured.

Every person represents a potential learning node on The Innovation Superhighway. If we all became more adept at connecting socially and technologically, our insights can feed forward to those who have a need to know. The bountiful resource continues to expand, but, more important, it finds its way to where it can best be applied in the name of progress.

CHAPTER ENDNOTES

[1] *The New Realities* (1989). p. 85.

[2] Note that in the previous chapters, performance was a matter of economics and structure a matter of sociology and anthropology.

[3] *Innovation Strategy for the Knowledge Economy*, Ch. 6.

[4] Cortada (1998), pp. 5–8.

[5] For further information, visit http://www.ashoka.org/home/

[6] Pinchot (1994), pp. xvii–xviii.

[7] Miller and Morris (1999).

[8] "Customer Innovation: A Function of Knowledge" (1997).

[9] Petzinger (1999), p. 146.

[10] Carter (1999), pp. 185–186.

[11] *Creating the Knowledge-Based Business*, Ch. 7, pp. 333–369.

[12] Nonaka and Takeuchi (1991).

[13] Bonner (2000), p. 16.

[14] Levin et al. (2000).

[15] *Innovation for the Knowledge Economy*, Ch. 4.

[16] Mayo (2001), p. 88.

[17] Mayo (2000), p. 190.

[18] Scharmer (May 25–26, 2000).

[19] Simpson et al. (2001).

[20] Asacker (2001), p. 139.

[21] Adapted from *Creating the Knowledge-Based Business*, Skyrne/Amidon, 1997.

SEVEN
Knowledge Processes

I will not go
where the path may lead;
I will go
where there is no path;
and I will leave a trail

adadapted from Ralph Waldo Emerson

It's about innovation; it has always been about innovation!

"Theory to practice," "Seed to need," "Cradle to grave;" however the phases may be labeled or segmented, each description refers to the process of innovation. Each implies the value chain (Porter, 1985) and stage gate (Cooper and Edgett, 1999) processes that have been defined by researchers and put into practice with great success. Drucker (1995) reinforces our need to have one competence—innovation—and the ability to measure the performance thereof. It is that simple and that complex.

> *Perhaps the greatest contribution of the quality community to business management has been the focus on process. The nature of the process-to-date has been linear/service delivery models. The systems dynamic constructs of the future are complex and multi-directional. Not only does the ability to listen (and hear) become important, the ability to learn and share those learnings becomes paramount in an organization that*

leverages intellectual capital. In the postwar era of cooperation, it is more essential that nations realize the potential value of regional collaboration.[1]

The knowledge economy, however, is an economy of kaleidoscopic change. Time-consuming, linear processes are no longer sufficient to capitalize on the opportunities afforded a global economy. It is not the speed of change of a variable or the speed of change of multiple variables. It is the compounding effect of the speed of change of multiple variables creating a business landscape that demands additional systems approaches.

The process of innovation, however, is not creativity. The process of innovation is not R&D. The process of innovation is the creation, evolution, and commercialization of new ideas into products and services to benefit a constituency.

7.1   SOME ROOTS

Michael Porter made a major contribution to the field of innovation management by outlining the managerial concepts inherent in the value chain. Although he defined innovation in terms of technological change, the model he developed is utilized today as managers attempt systematically to divide the firm into discrete processes and activities. The value chain initiative was designed as a basic tool for diagnosing competitive advantage and discovering ways to create and sustain it. Porter did cite the need for creating and managing linkages among organizational units as an important issue in the implementation of strategy. However, his illustrations remained linear in design and unidirectional, even as he expanded his view of the value system for a diversified firm that included value chains for suppliers, channels, and buyers.

With the advent of learning systems and networked organizations and the adoption of the systems dynamics principles advocated by Jay W. Forrester,[2] organizations are now able to adopt a more dynamic perspective on innovation strategy. The process is an innovation value system of interdependent activities influencing and being influenced by one another. Because of the foundation established by Porter, organizations are in a better position to understand the complexity of the modern day enterprise.

This refocus, although necessary, is still difficult. It requires a view of the organization as a whole prior to understanding the interrelationship of its parts. This is the holistic management that bridges Eastern and Western thought. Although the effects of change are considered unpredictable, there are management conditions that can be established to optimize results. It is this combination of natural evolution (i.e., chaos theory and adaptive systems) together with more rational, analytic schools of thought that will constitute viable management policies and practices for the future.

In previous publications[3], we defined innovation as a value system, not a value chain of activities—complete with diagrams may help in visualizing the difference between a chain and a system. By examining the chain of activities, one can see that all functions are evolving toward a focus on innovation. Figure 7.1 illustrates how the world of systems dynamics values the interdependencies within the functions as well as the reciprocal communication nature of the innovation process. In other words, ideas may, and must, flow anywhere in the value system. Expertise and activities in one function affect several other functions simultaneously. The knowledge gleaned from a customer at the point of delivery has as much value for research into new product development as it has for sales and marketing. This notion can be adopted in the nonprofit sector as well as in organizations converting to a success, rather than satisfaction, model of interaction.

Value chain thinking is simplistic and inadequate. Although originally useful in defining linear relationships and discrete activities, it does not provide a durable framework for modern innovation strategy. It hardly provides for the real-time decision making demanded by a constantly changing marketplace, nor does it allow for optimal resource integration from a global perspective. The interdependent knowledge economy demands a more fluid management system to

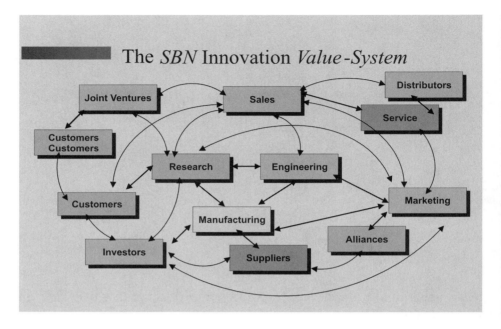

FIGURE 7.1   *The innovation value system.*

enable highly leveraged business decisions. As incomplete as the inno-vation value system is, it represents some of the possibilities afforded by a different view of management structure and linkages.

The newly defined innovation process (i.e., according to knowledge, not technology) is critical to the successful functioning of any organi-zation. Organizations can view the future of the business based on an innovation strategy and process. All stakeholders can contribute to the increased intellectual wealth of the enterprise.

It is only one step further to visualize the technology infrastructure that might underlie such a systems dynamic and the opportunities for e-learning, B2B business, e-commerce, and more seem obvious. But still, the figure is just a diagram—a concept if you will. Only when you envision the people in the process and explore the interrelationships between the parts and the value of storytelling (Denning 2001) as one way to manage the strategic conversations referenced elsewhere in this book does the figure become meaningful.

Of course, the focus on learning described in Chapter 5 is fundamental to the successful functioning of modern innovation systems. In *Strategic Learning and the Knowledge Economy*, we learn that "The source of innovation lies at the interface between an organization and its environment. And the process of innovating involves actively constructing a conceptual framework, imposing it on the environment and reflecting on the interaction."[4]

We also know that the treatment of networks in Chapter 5—on both enterprise and global scales—illustrates how they are fundamental to the innovation as it is now defined according to the flow of knowledge. In *Knowledge Networking*, David Skyrme illustrates[5] the elements in developing winning collaborative strategies—building the connections between knowledge, technology, and virtualization and integrating electronic networks, human networks, and collaborative strategies, "knowledge networking"[6] being at the heart.

And some new underlying themes are emerging:

- There has been a realization that context is important—perhaps critical—in sense-making activities surrounding strategic conversations.
- With all the downsizing and subsequent loss of knowledge in the process, there has been considerable attention given to intervention strategies, the most comprehensive and sensible being continuity management (Hamilton, Boenish, and Harden, 2002).
- Storytelling is the one way to get complex messages across quickly, especially those involving success events upon which to build (Shell, 2001).
- "All innovation has an improvisational aspect," says Rosabeth Moss Kanter (2001). Decades of research show that innovation combines the discipline of skilled players with serendipity and chance and that even strategy formulation can be discovery

based. "Innovators create value by working on things that are not fully known."[7]

- Many biological metaphors are emerging, such as "Corporate Anorexia," (Hamel and Prahalad); "Alzheimer" (Neilson, 1997) and "Schizophrenia" (Goldfinger, 1997).
- Links are being made with the cultural and performing arts and the environment—for example at The Banff Centre in Calgary, Canada.

7.2   Envisioning the System as a Model

Cross-organizational processes are described in a variety of terms, including the following models:

- The business intelligence model (create → gather → share → leverage)
- The Arthur Anderson/APQC model (identify → collect → adapt → organize → use)
- An Ernst & Young model (generate → codify → transfer)
- A second Ernst & Young model (acquire → categorize/store or package/format → develop → distribute/disseminate)
- The Karl Wiig model (acquire → arrange/organize → use)
- The Entovation model (create → convert → commercialize)

These models all represent attempts to define the various elements in the process. The problem is this: even if they are drawn in a circle with feedback loops, they are usually implemented as linear processes.

It isn't easy to think about the whole—not really. But this is precisely what the modern manager needs. Only when one can fully envision the scope of activity and the potential influencing factors can one determine the optimal relationship between the parts (never mind when and which resources—financial, human or technical—might be put to task).

Another approach is to envision the various elements as a system dynamic in which subprocesses operate simultaneously. Learning from Chapter 5, we now know that if one element is changed, there is likely a concurrent effect on other elements.

In Figure 7.2, we identify the core elements as credibility, access, competency, and delivery. In one way or another, all of these elements have been previously mentioned as integral to a successful "system." As a first-tier effect, we want our customers to be successful,[8] to increase learning for both the customer and/or other internal and external stakeholders, and to drive new standards in the industry.[9] The second-tier effect will automatically increase the reputation that provides increased access and builds credibility. It also increases the intellectual capital of the firm in ways that can be structuralized and result (eventually) in enhanced bottom-line performance.

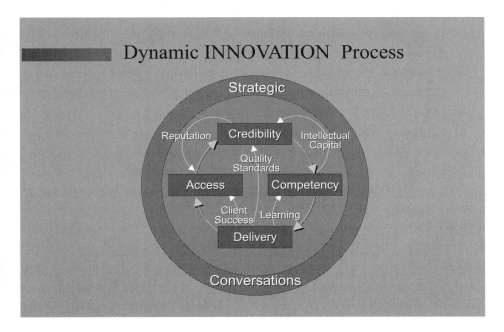

FIGURE 7.2   *The dynamic innovation process.*

7.3   EMERGING PRACTICES

In our research report (Skyrme and Amidon, 1997)[10], there is a chapter dedicated to "Value-Adding Process" in which we explore several case studies, such as Hoffman LaRoche, Booz Allan & Hamilton, Price Waterhouse, GIGNA, and the UK Department of Trade. We discovered that organizations should develop knowledge processes at three levels. The top level is a strategic coordinating one. The next level is for the specific tools and methods to underpin each subprocess. The third is for the skills and techniques to perform the knowledge work.

A key function of knowledge processes is to give better support to "knowledge workers" (see Chapter 6) in their day-to-day activities. However, an in-depth understanding of knowledge work is still at an early stage. Researchers are finding that social science methods, such as ethnography and situation theory, can help improve our understanding of these basic work processes.

Analysis of our research data shows that six main factors underpin success in the day-to-day practice of knowledge management:

1. *Strategic awareness*—building the links between knowledge processes and business processes and linking knowledge to the business value proposition.

2. *Making the implicit explicit*—identifying sources of knowledge, recording them and codifying them for later re-use, learning more about how knowledge creation and conversion processes can be made effective, and articulating them for transfer of learning.

3. *Systematisation of information and knowledge processes*—seeking to improve the efficiency and effectiveness of all processes for generating and sharing information and knowledge; facilitating knowledge flows is an important focus.

4. *Understanding the processes at multiple levels*—three clear levels are the strategy (enabling) level; the practice (leverage) level, where the processes are carried out; and the practitioner (skills)

level. Integrating all three levels simultaneously is one of the keys to unlocking knowledge potential in an organization.

5. *Striking a suitable balance between opposite pulls*—systematisation vs. creative chaos; rigorous detail vs. big picture; analytical precision vs. serendipitous opportunities.

6. *Finding the little things that make a big difference*—at Standard Life, for example, a simple change in the type of questions asked during information audit significantly improved progress; at Thomas Miller, a change of name from "the library" to "the information center" changed perceptions overnight; a U.S. West manager stated "the pivotal insight was finding a language that engages operational managers."

The benefits of knowledge management will come through when the perspectives of information management, human learning and innovation processes, and supporting technologies are fully integrated. Now that we have a better understanding of the knowledge value proposition (see Chapter 2), we must also add that the performance measurement of intellectual capital can and should also be added to the enterprise system architecture.

These cross-organizational processes should ensure streamlined practices that provide efficient and effective planning, review, and monitoring of investment strategies. Activities should cross the boundaries of functions, businesses, industries, and geographies. Knowledge capability and accountability is valued more than hierarchical authority. The system enables real-time innovation and global resource optimization.

7.4   OPERATIONALIZING A KNOWLEDGE STRATEGY

Clarica may be the most revealing demonstration of how these examples can be put into practice to lead an organization forward. Hubert Saint-Onge (see profile in Chapter 13), formerly from Clarica (now

Sun Life) and originally the chief human resources manager, moved on to his position as vice president of strategic capabilities. Early on, he began to use the language of knowledge strategy, rather than knowledge management (KM). He understood fundamentally the "value" of values, valuation, and valuing—the 3Vs, the appreciation of the intricate role of customer knowledge (not knowledge of the customers), and how to unleash tacit knowledge in the organization enterprisewide.

The strategy document that is used internally is one mechanism to develop a common language and a shared sense of purpose. The same document shared externally informs investors that the company is, indeed, managing its intangible wealth systematically, efficiently, and (probably) effectively. It also illustrates the new knowledge leadership—share what you know as one way of learning more.

The document outlines the business rationale, the vision, a blueprint to achieve the vision and implementation strategies. All is backed up by a company intranet that stimulates and monitors conversation to stakeholder advantage. Saint-Onge has offered his six precursors to success:[11]

1. Cross-functional collaboration
2. Support of senior management
3. The evolution of a receptive culture
4. Justifying the use of scarce resources
5. Measuring the use and performance of knowledge assets
6. Setting the appropriate scope of activities.

7.5 INNOVATION ON THE RADAR SCREEN

By now, several of the major consulting houses have generated reports on innovation, realizing that this is the agenda forward. And, for the most part, they are describing this "new" perspective on the innovation process with more emphasis on the flow of knowledge, the learning systems, the national economic implications, and more.

PriceWaterhouse Coopers[12] surveyed the CEOs of 327 product and service companies to discover that innovation pays off handsomely for the 75 percent of fast-growth companies making it an organizationwide priority. Most innovation programs have not yet reached their full potential. Steve Hamm concludes:

> *I would suggest that many aspects of innovation are cultural. Innovation need not originate entirely from within an organization. Interactions with outsiders through an alliance would be an eye-openers as to the possibilities, but businesses must also have a substantial level of readiness to accept change within their organization. They must strive to be open, curious, objective and flexible.*

The Gartner Research Group has launched some major new initiatives that feature innovation from both internal and external perspectives. They query innovation as the core competence and the manageability thereof. They've been analyzing how enterprises harness innovation and the environmental forces and indicators. They've explored best practices and developed a scorecard against which an enterprise might assess its innovation capabilities. In its own electronic Gartner Advisory,[13] the firm has made available some preliminary findings that appear to be the tip of its research iceberg.

The Gartner projection is, "Leading enterprises will have a dual focus: Embrace the innovations of others and drive the marketplace with their own innovations."[14] Environmental (external) innovation is an ongoing phenomenon within industries, market segments, or the general business environment. Enterprise (internal) innovation suggest that individual enterprises must continually innovate internally to remain competitive, build new market share, retain market share, reduce costs, and increase effectiveness. It applies to processes, technologies, organizational structure, and management or leadership styles.

Morgan Stanley's Report has already been mentioned as has the Deloitte Research Study on Collaborative Networks. Deloitte has another study[15] "From e-Learning to Enterprise Learning: Becoming a Strategic Learning Organization," which is another term for innovation. In exploring the relationship between e-learning and shareholder value, the report suggests that many e-learning solutions fall short because they are not developed with a solid business strategy—and a solid learning strategy—in mind.

Deloitte defines the strategic drivers of e-learning investments:

- Aging demographics
- Globalization and decentralization
- Wall Street metrics for the new service economy
- Transformation of traditional roles
- High-velocity business environment
- Legal and regulatory mandates
- The knowledge divide
- Mergers and acquisitions
- Strategic partnering and customer alliances
- Changing expectations of workers.

Cap Gemini/E&Y has issued a Focus E-zine on "Learning to innovate,"[16] which explores networked learning communities as one of "the most remarkable developments of the still-dawning Internet Age." They describe the modern era of corporate learning by providing an evolution from the early training departments in General Motors in the 1920s, the leadership frame of programs of General Electric under the leadership of Jack Welch, the recent studies of the ASTD, and the most recent practices of the Higher Education and Corporate University Xchange. This leads to a description of traditional classroom learning (where technology is an add-on) to first-generation learning (where technology is a constraint) and networked learning (where technology is an enabler). And this is only the beginning.

7.6   ARCHITECTURAL CONSIDERATIONS

1.   Does the program generate connectivity for simultaneous, concurrent, and parallel activities?

2.   Do the processes enable cross-fertilization of useful technical ideas and cross-functional teamwork?

3.   Is there a global sourcing capability to ensure worldwide coverage of potential technological breakthroughs?

4.   Is there a benchmarking initiative to ensure "best-in-class" practices and optimal quality control?

5.   How do the joint planning processes ensure shared vision in formulating strategy?

6.   Does the process enable periodic review and evaluation for necessary project redesign?

7.   Does the communications strategy ensure rapid diffusion of critical information throughout the internal and external research network?

7.7   ACTION STEPS[17]

1.   Make the innovation process explicit and establish guidelines for the acquisition, sharing, and protection of knowledge.

2.   Conduct a knowledge inventory. Build on the tools and techniques of information auditing and information resources management.

3.   Create a focal point, such as a knowledge center, as the hub for knowledge exchange to proactively seek out knowledge that fills vital gaps identified by your inventory.

4.   Map the knowledge domains—both in content and people—in your company into a common schema or thesaurus that make comparisons and knowledge sharing easier.

5. Add contextual information as well as mechanisms to stimulate, monitor, and mine the insights from strategic innovation conversations.[18]

6. Develop "packages" of high-leverage knowledge, in standard formats, for ease of transmission and re-use.

7. Develop measures to assess the use and flow of knowledge through your knowledge databases.

8. Ensure that activities will provide immediate or strategic benefit to the enterprise strategy, producing both incremental and breakthrough returns on innovation—the "new" ROI.

7.8 SUMMARY

Although the concept of a "technopolis" was relatively new in 1987; today it has been accepted as a worldwide phenomenon, albeit under a variety of other names. Countries and regions are seeking ways to link technology—how it is created, produced, and applied—with economic development performance.

The point is that studies are being performed all over the world and reported at an exploding pace—and electronically—in the business and research press, such as *The Economist, Fortune*'s new *Business 2.0*, and the European Union's KnowledgeBoard portal. This is prime evidence that The Innovation Superhighway is in full operation and high gear and that the highway is not about the technology—but about getting the knowledge from the point of origin to the point of need or opportunity, where it may be put to immediate use.

We are learning from the learnings of one another in real time and putting our insights—individually and collectively—into action (i.e., innovating). The quality and scope of what is available as a common knowledge good—increasing with each day—is multiplying by factors we cannot comprehend. It is one of the reasons that the visions articulated by the leadership examples in this book—both people and initiatives—are making a difference; and the transformation is providing a foundation upon which we might be able to build a more sustainable future.

CHAPTER ENDNOTES

[1] *Innovation Strategy for the Knowledge Economy*.Ch. 6.

[2] *Industrial Dynamics* (1985).

[3] *Innovation Strategy for the Knowledge Economy*, Ch. 5.

[4] Brown and Duguid (2000). p 157.

[5] Skyrme (1999), p. 42.

[6] Knowledge networking is a concept developed by Charles Savage in 1992.

[7] Kanter (2001), p. 107.

[8] Note that the objective is "success" and not "satisfaction," for this is the innovation—not the quality—focus. The differentiation is defined in "Customer Innovation" (Amidon, 1997). This maps the quantum difference between "relationships" and "partnering."

[9] Note that the goal is to influence "standards," not exemplify "best practices."

[10] *Creating the Knowledge-Based Business*, p. 176.

[11] Saint-Onge (2001), pp. 296–297.

[12] Trendsetter Barometer (June 17, 2001).

[13] *Gartner Advises on Managing Innovation* (March 25, 2002).

[14] Note that this is consistent with the internal and external assessment outlined in *Innovation Strategy for the Knowledge Economy*. Chs. 7 and 8.

[15] Deloitte Research (2001),

[16] Cothrel et al. (2001).

[17] Adapted from *Creating the Knowledge-Based Business*, Skyrne/Amidon, 1997.

[18] An innovation conversation occurs and involves any one or a combination of the stages of innovation—creation, conversion, and commercialization.

EIGHT
Knowledge-Processing Technology

Now, in the case of satellites,
and with machines
approximating the condition of mind
and minds of humans connecting
across time and space,
the future can and should be more
a matter of choice than destiny.

Derrick de Kerckhove[1]

This fifth element of the management architecture—information science or the technology—has been the primary focus of many knowledge management programs—at least in the United States. It is the culmination of advances in artificial intelligence, computer technology, and communications capability. According to our research, to exploit technology to the fullest, organizations need to give due attention to the human and organizational factors (i.e., the new knowledge value proposition discussed in Chapter 2). This is the area that has experienced the most radical transformation of all as evidenced by the e-commerce and e-learning explosion.

There has been a significant shift—predicted only a few years ago—from information processing to knowledge processing, which includes the concepts of learning tools, intelligent electronic coaching, decision-making systems and more. Artificial intelligence tools, which only two decades ago were shunned, have been embraced as integral to the successful knowledge-intensive business. As the marketplace becomes hyper-competitive, the performance metrics become more complex and intangible, the organization becomes more networked, people become more empowered and energized, and processes become boundaryless, enterprises will become more reliant upon the technology. Competitive positioning becomes a function of the worldwide web.[2]

This book is not intended to describe the evolution of the advancements in technology per se. There are other professionals within the knowledge and innovation communities who are far more expert on this topic than I—and books that would fill a library. Our intent is to illustrate some of the current thinking and some of the themes we've discovered in our research.

8.1   SOME ROOTS

In the early research on the productivity paradox, executives discovered that "IT (information technology) has value only if surrounded by appropriate policy, strategy, methods for measuring results, project controls, talented and committed people, sound organizational relationships, and well-designed information systems."[3]

Technology solutions are used to augment knowledge processes at different stages of knowledge flow. For example, they can support human thinking, facilitate information access, help the human interpretation of complex data, and provide decision support. We have seen the rapid evolution of data warehouses, document databases, discovery tools (e.g., data mining, genetic algorithms, parallel processing systems, neural networks), knowledge-gathering tools (e.g., intelligent agents, text retrieval) thinking and simulation aids, guidance systems (e.g., case-based reasoning, business flight simulators), and collaborative technologies—not to mention the Internet and Intranets.

Modern technological advances are employed to optimize the knowledge flow of the enterprise infrastructure. These processing systems accelerate the development, exchange and application of useful knowledge required for distributed deliberations. They also integrate all business strategies, plans, and operations into a coherent assessment of situational positioning at any point in time.

In *Connected Intelligence: The Arrival of the Web Society*, Derrick de Kerckhove describes the five major shifts in space and time (i.e., warps). These are the fundamental changes that cause quantum leaps in structural economic activity. He suggests that there are commensurate changes in the rate and volume of information processing each time a new medium is invented: speech and writing, the printing press, the telephone, radio and television, computers, and now hypertext, interactivity, and online multimedia. He describes the potential for "new levels of acceleration in the circulation, elaboration, cross-checking and simulation for commercial and scientific, as well as more playful, applications."

There is ample evidence in the media of the blistering pace at which information technology is influencing the process of innovation by providing the electronic infrastructure within which ideas can be created and disseminated. Opportunities seem incalculable. Product life cycles and even industry life cycles are consolidating, merging, and converging. The challenge, of course, is how best to manage this environment in ways that lead to prosperous growth in the enterprise, the nation, and society as a whole.

There have been numerous efforts by experts from different nations who have explored the implications of the global information network—or The Information Superhighway—for their nations. We have illustrated a few on the timeline in Chapter 1, and others have analyzed the GII from the perspective of global networking of R&D and the complex of multi-global network strategies. Akira "Stoney" Ishikawa (Japan) states:

> *The recent rapid development of information processing and network technology is making the following symbolic expressions more real every day: "global village," the concept once used by Marshal McLuhan; and "Space Ship Earth," with the implication that we are inevitably, irrevocably bound to one whole community.*[4]

Under these circumstances, he suggests that it is natural for national and corporate strategies to be directed toward the construction and use of effective communications networks and information systems that function in a global environment, crossing national boundaries.

8.2   COLLABORATIVE TECHNOLOGIES

In addition to the advances in computer technology has come the rapid emergence of the conferencing and communications capability that promoted collaborative initiatives—for the enterprise, for the nation, and across all levels of society. One might begin to differentiate between the various communications mechanisms that can promote both face-to-face as well as electronic conversations across organization boundaries.

Dave Coleman, CEO of Collaborative Strategies, saw the potential for electronic collaboration before many others and has systematically been tracking the evolution, documenting the results and feeding forward the latest collective insights to the larger community via his Web site.[5] Publications include the E-Learning Report 2002—including the Virtual Classroom, Collaborative E-Commerce Report, Real-Time Communication and Collaboration Industry Report, et al.

Coleman also produces an online newsletter—*Inside Collaboration* —that details case study examples, e-community forums, Web/audio/ video–conferencing, and more. This is another good example of contributions being made to The Innovation Superhighway while at the same time contributing significantly to its evolution to realize its potential.

8.3   E-BUSINESS IMPLICATIONS

Once again, there is no way to do justice to the innovation underway electronically. Several authors have been able to keep pace with the developments and help shape adoption and application for individuals and businesses. Dr. David Skyrme (in the UK), for instance, lists the ten Ps of Internet marketing in his recent book[6]:

1. Positioning
2. Packaging—open or closed
3. Portals—gateways to knowledge
4. Pathways
5. Pages—making an impression.
6. Personalization
7. Progression—from free to fee
8. Payments—a virtual necessity
9. Processes
10. Performance—the bottom line.

He suggests that the technology can be viewed as a way to strengthen the one-on-one dialog and increase performance, moving through four customer phases: unaware, aware, interested, and committed. Interestingly enough, these are the same phases that nonprofit organizations use to maintain constructive communication with their constituencies—local, regional, or global.

Brian Davis, at the Kaieteur Institute in Toronto, Canada has initiated a global study[7] of the "enterprise ideas economy." The premise is that in today's knowledge-based economy, ideas are indeed the new currency. They are an integral aspect of the human experience—an amalgam of concepts and intuitions. They can be simple yet complex. Great ideas—regardless of whether they originate in an industrialized or developing nation—can generate immense new value creation and wealth.

The Web site provides an exhaustive and constantly evolving record of relevant quotes, Web sites, and articles on the topic. Davis suggests:

There is a de-facto marketplace for ideas within the enterprise. There are buyers and sellers, demand and supply for good ideas. There are idea merchants and brokers, and trust agents. Ideas can circulate freely or they can be encumbered. There is a payoff for good ideas. And major risks for bad ideas. There is much we do not fully understand about it's dynamics.

Indeed, we have poor metrics for directly measuring the effectiveness of ideas, but the insights provided in Chapter 2 and 4 can provide some guidance.

8.4   EMERGING PRACTICES

Information technology plays an important part in all the cases our research[8] found of best practices in knowledge management. This was most apparent in cases where knowledge databases had already been built. New technology infrastructures, such as intranets, now make it easier to disseminate information around and between organizations, thereby supporting knowledge workers more effectively. Most interviewees were quick to warn that technology should not be viewed as a

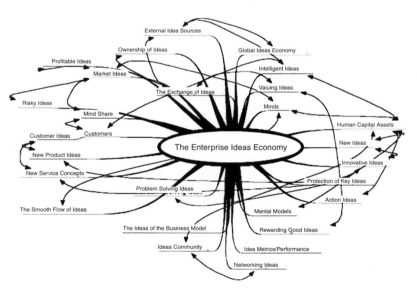

FIGURE 8.1   *The enterprise ideas economy.*

driving force for knowledge management, but simply an important enabler. Several emphasized the dangers of putting technology first. For example, Arian Ward, formerly leader of learning and change at Hughes Space and Communications, writes: "Everybody expects technology to be a silver bullet—it isn't. You cannot ignore technology, but we must remember it is only an enabler. The real value is in linking people together, not in the technology itself."[9]

That said, there appear to be four major trends: a renewed interest in "intelligent solutions;" an infrastructure (as well as a solution) perspective, a growing awareness of the human factors, and a shift toward information (using pull rather than push strategies).

- Knowledge-based companies rely heavily on a good technological infrastructure. Collaborative technologies, such as intranets and groupware, are emerging as the dominant technologies for effective knowledge creation and sharing.
- Knowledge-based systems are not new. After years of steady, but unspectacular, use, expert systems and other systems using artificial intelligent techniques are witnessing a resurgence.
- New technologies and techniques, such as neural networks and data mining, are disclosing new knowledge in corporate data repositories such as data warehouses.
- A technology infrastructure provides facilities at several levels to support personal interaction—physical connections, communications, conversations, and collaboration. Few organizations have fully developed capabilities at the upper levels.
- Technology solutions are used to augment knowledge processes at different stages of knowledge flow. For example, they can support human thinking, facilitate information access, help human interpretation of complex data, and provide decision support.
- To help knowledge workers get just the information they need at the right time, many organizations are emphasizing an

information "pull" strategy, whereby users access information when they need it (e.g., from an intranet or knowledge base). This is complemented by a certain amount of "push" (e.g., via electronic mail), particularly through filtering information and profiling user needs.

- To exploit technology to the full, organizations need to give due attention to human and organization factors. Heavy user involvements, active facilitation of computer conferences, training and coaching are key success factors.

8.5 EVOLUTION OF THE GATEWAY:[10] BRIDGING THE DIGITAL DIVIDE

There were numerous panels at the Global Knowledge Partnership Meeting (Kuala Lumpur) that focused specifically on "Transcending the Divide," Mr. Tengku Mohd Azzman Shariffadeen, Secretary, National Information Technology Council, Malaysia, and President and CEO, MIMOS BERHAD, provided the rationale. He began by defining the quality of life as something that is dynamic (i.e., that changes over time); it is what makes us human, and we all have different perceptions thereof. He suggested that the conventional measurement methods are material and quantitative (e.g., GNP), but there are limits to this extreme materialism, such as the destruction of nature and unfulfilled nonmaterialistic human needs.

After outlining some planning assumptions, he argued for a "perennial perspective" that takes into account the material, intellectual, and spiritual facets of the quality of life and listed the following points:

- Information and knowledge form the basis for decision making and action, particularly in development.
- The quality of decisions depends on the quality and quantity of information.
- Access to information and knowledge enables improvement of quality of life, as long as an enabling framework is in place.

- There will always be inequality in society. However, society has a responsibility to strive to narrow the gap in terms of the social nature of man and as a defense against instability.

Calling for the restructuring of social, economic, and political systems, he illustrated a convergent, integrated Malaysia, one that provides the interface between public, private, and community interest. At the heart was good governance. The key success factor, he suggested was a "mindset" that includes attitudes and values. In summary, he asserted that a knowledge-based development strategy requires:

- Access to the rich diversity of human social and cultural experience in order to build not only an informed or knowledgeable society, but a wise one.
- The capacity and opportunity to participate actively in local, national, and global decision-making processes.
- An institutional governance framework to promote and encourage smart partnerships.

Similarly, getting beyond the rhetoric, there have been numerous articles, conferences, and electronic dialogs on the topic. The Global Knowledge Development (GKD) project most recently maintained a thread for months on "the social capital divide," indicating that the divide was more than technological. This again affirms the need for the knowledge value proposition outlined in Chapter 2 as a foundation for the innovation superhighway to which all might contribute.

Much of the current discussion is politically charged, and current analysis may be based on primarily descriptive statistics and does not take into consideration the multifaceted nature of access; the social, cultural, and psychological causes for lack of access; the need for theory to explain these problems; the policy measures to address them; and the contributions that a communicative or psychological perspective can provide.

The discussion, however did lead to a continuing online dialog that has focused on minimizing the digital divide. In fact, GKD held a consultation on the initiative of the G8 states. At their summit meeting in Genoa, Italy, in July 2001, they addressed the digital divide. Access to the Web site[11] also provides a link to the final 36-point resolution approved by the G8 that included the commitment to reconvene in Alberta, Canada on June 26–28, 2002. What follows is the prime agreement and a list of some of the topical areas included in the resolution:

1. We, the Heads of State and Government of eight major industrialized democracies and the Representatives of the European Union, met in Genoa for the first Summit of the new millennium. In a spirit of co-operation, we discussed the most pressing issues on the international agenda.

2. As democratic leaders, accountable to our citizens, we believe in the fundamental importance of open public debate on the key challenges facing our societies. We will promote innovative solutions based on a broad partnership with civil society and the private sector. We will also seek enhanced co-operation and solidarity with developing countries, based on a mutual responsibility for combating poverty and promoting sustainable development.

3. We are determined to make globalization work for all our citizens and especially the world's poor. Drawing the poorest countries into the global economy is the surest way to address their fundamental aspirations. We concentrated our discussions on a strategy to achieve this.

Specific resolution points included a strategic approach to poverty reduction that includes a pledge for a poverty reduction strategy; debt relief; open trade; assistance with intellectual property rights; building digital opportunities (including the Dot.Force task force); expanded use of information and communications technology (ICT) to train teachers in best practices and strengthen education strategies; and developing initiatives to build agricultural productivity to minimize world hunger.

Others focused on building a legacy for the future with plans for the environment, such as the UN Framework Convention on Climate Change, seeking common agreement on the Kyoto Protocol, and facilitating cooperation between our countries to develop technology transfer[12] and capacity building, and looking toward the World Summit on Sustainable Development (WSSD) scheduled for Johannesburg in 2002—noting the three interdependent dimensions of sustainable development—enhancing economic growth, promoting human and social development, and protecting the environment.

Finally, there was a set of agreements on increasing prosperity in a socially-inclusive society, such as employment initiatives to spur economic performance and social inclusion, as well as plans for combating transnational organized crime and the spread of drugs.

Now, what is interesting is the congruence with these objectives and the new intellectual capital reports[13] outlined in Chapter 4 that have been prepared for several nations (e.g., Sweden, The Netherlands, Denmark and Israel). All are attempts to begin to measure and monitor the intangible metrics that sustain our organizations and nations.

8.6   ARCHITECTURAL CONSIDERATIONS

1.   Does the electronic infrastructure provide for optimal technical interchange of university scientists with industrial engineering managers?

2.   Is there a competitive intelligence system that gathers, synthesizes, and feeds critical data forward for planning analysis?

3.   Are there new service delivery techniques that would accelerate the flow of information to those who might need to know?

4. Are technology innovations (e.g., e-mail, conferencing, fax, bulletin boards, videos) used to improve efficiency and effectiveness?

5. Is the technology used (beyond automation and information) for transformation purposes?

6. Is there a way to provide optimal utilization of shared technology resources across sector or organization boundaries?

7. Are there network management tools that might enable the "intelligent" flow of knowledge—creation, exchange, evolution, and application?

8.7   ACTION STEPS

1. Understand the nature of the technology investment that supports your knowledge program.

2. Review your use of advanced technologies, (e.g., intelligent, case-based reasoning, multimedia, video- and collaborative conferencing) seeking to increase the flow of knowledge (i.e., its creation, exchange, and application) rather than transaction efficiencies.

3. Set standards and review the performance of key levels of a technology-supported knowledge infrastructure—connectivity, communications, conversations, and collaboration.

4. Create appropriate access to external stakeholders who might be considered as sources of knowledge and engage them actively in the innovation process.

5. Give due attention to human factors, such as the psychological dynamics of groupware and the characteristics of "usability."

6. Provide for the necessary training, mentoring, and incentives that will catalyze the use and usefulness of your technology.

7. Ensure that your enterprise is tapping into the dynamic evolution of the networks externally as your own intranets are developed and maintained.

8. Consider your own infrastructure—both human and technical—as an integral node in the innovation superhighway.

8.8 SUMMARY

A new electronic era is coming; and it is just around the bend.

During the past few years, the development of e-learning, e-commerce, and societal connectivity for ICT projects has been accelerating at warp speed, and social problems such as the digital divide are being addressed. There is a need to put all of these developments into a frame for understanding and, if possible, to increase the potential for profitable and prosperous impact. This is the essence of the innovation superhighway that can, like a magnet, coalesce these seemingly fragmented initiatives into a coherent infrastructure to sustain us as individuals, enterprises, and nations.

The implications for innovation infrastructures are enormous—equivalent to the projections of increased usability and relevance. Our challenge is to be able to manage the behavioral progress in consort so we are able to take full advantage of the technology that enables us to innovate our future together.

CHAPTER ENDNOTES

[1] *Connected Intelligence* (1997) p. xxxi.

[2] See *Innovation Strategy for the Knowledge Economy*, Ch. 6.

[3] *Information Technology in the Services Sector* (1994).

[4] Ishikawa (1995).

[5] For further information, visit: http://www.collaborate.com/

[6] Skyrme (2001), pp. 196–224.

[7] For further information, visit http://www.kikm.org/Ideas%20Economy.htm

[8] *Creating the Knowledge Based Business* (Skyrme and Amidon, 1997), Ch. 8, pp. 383–384.

[9] Ward (1996).

[10] For a description of The Development Gateway project itself, see Chapter 14.

[11] For further information, visit
http://www.genoa-g8.it/eng/attualita/primo_piano/primo_piano_13.html

[12] We would suggest a review of the technology transfer evolution into a knowledge innovation systems thinking as detailed in Chapter 2.

[13] See Chapter 13 for profiles of some of the principals involved.

PART III

~

The Globe as a Network

NINE
ENTOVATION®: A Case Story

Now I can see more clearly that
the game I am playing has no special or numerical boundaries.
The outcome is less related to whether the change idea is accepted,
as though I am participating in a game that can be won or lost.
The game is much broader and more open-ended.
Now winning is insufficient as it is irrelevant.
Instead, the game entails continuing to play evolve and grow,

Recounted by Stephen Denning in *The Springboard* and
based upon Carse's *Finite and Infinite Games*.

The challenge sounded fine in theory; but how might it operate in real life?

It was 1983. A $13.2B Fortune 50 company with 120,000 employees had asked us to scout, finance, and transfer worldwide knowledge into the organization to yield new products and services in the marketplace in advance of the competition. We accomplished this through the Office of Sponsored Research, which funded 240 projects in 100 worldwide universities. We managed liaison relationships with over 50 research consortia, ranging from a $10,000 research center affiliation to the multimillion dollar investment in the Microelectronics and Computer Technology Corporation (MCC) in Austin, Texas. The business agenda was one of organizational learning, not technology development. The skills required for success were based on relationships, partnering. and strategic conversations. We called it "Virtual Research & Development," our global network of expertise.

Even then, we realized that the base of knowledge did not reside inside the firm. Creativity and new ideas often came from alliance partners, customers, and even competitors. We knew that there were connections that needed to be managed and not left to serendipity. We used the term "virtual" to capture the essence of our objective: an international innovation infrastructure within which ideas were created and put into action to produce marketable products and services in advance of the competition. This was our innovation strategy. In organizing the staff, we made several planning assumptions, one of which was that networks would link science and society in ways yet unimaginable.

9.1   THE FOUNDING OF THE NETWORK[1]

ENTOVATION®[2] (derived from ENTerprise innOVATION) International, Ltd. was originally designed as an informal Rolodex of 400 contacts from 20 countries. By hooking into the values and vision of one another, we were able to link in ways we never could before. Synergies occurred that heretofore would not have seemed possible. The growth occurred in five stages, from defining distinctive competencies and providing structure to the Network to eventually operating as a fully functioning Knowledge Innovation® system. The five stages are detailed in Figure 9.1.

1.   *Defining distinctive competencies (1993–1994).* We defined distinctive competencies and made the network international in scope. We established a Web site, and our list of e-mail addresses was converted into an electronic dialogue one of the first in the knowledge field. Here the role of the Virtual Chief Knowledge Officer (CKO) was one of research and crystallizing the various facets of the evolving knowledge profession.

2.   *Structuring the network (1995–1997).* We realized we needed to better structure the network, as a holonomy,[3] and define its pur-

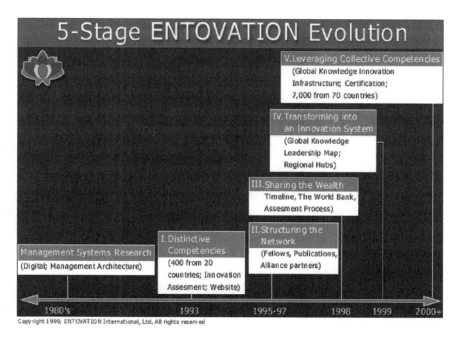

FIGURE 9.1   *Evolution of the ENTOVATION network.*

pose along with a set of principles to guide our actions. By 1997 the network had expanded to 2,500 people in forty countries. The CKO's role now was to identify pockets of expertise from around the world where scholars were researching progressive methods and practitioners were practicing knowledge techniques with significant bottom-line results.

3. *Sharing the wealth (1998).* Now we sought to share the wealth, position our view of the knowledge economy in a way to promote further dialogue, and enhance visibility through the Network and the knowledge press. The CKO's role was essentially that of a managerial architect, charged with articulating the evolving vision and framing the dialogue both electronically and face-to-face. The CKO also served as the community conscience to maintain a code of values, ethics, and standards to be emulated.

4. *Transforming into an innovation system (1999).* We've sought to transform the innovation system, by featuring top colleagues on the Web site, overhauling the Web site, and serving in an advisory capacity to The World Bank. Again, the role of the CKO was to maintain the expansion process into countries not yet represented on the organization's map. There was significant interest from Latin America, Asia, and the Middle Eastern developing nations.

5. *Leveraging collective competence (2000 and beyond).* As we look to the future we will be hosting a global knowledge management roundtable and participating in research on using the architectures, methodologies, and research to date from participants in the Network. The role of the CKO will be to shift to one of training and mentoring the trainers, developing the standards for a certification program, and assisting nations transforming into knowledge economies.

9.2   THE ENGAGEMENT PROCESS

The Network has grown to about 9,000 theorists and practitioners from 90 countries. The Web site experiences 210K hits from 6,000 unique visitors each month. The articles and books are translated into a dozen languages. The Network operates as a holonomy—a nesting of networks—with a core group of individuals that serve as intimate advisors, a group of Entovation Fellows who represent expertise in each of the ten dimensions of innovation and global liaisons who have varying degrees of relationship from passive recipients of our monthly newsletter, *I³ Update/ENTOVATION News*[4], to instrumental architects of knowledge strategy for their countries.

Regardless of the degree of Entovation intimacy, all relationships are treated as an opportunity to build intellectual capital and to establish credibility and brand credibility while constantly building competencies by learning from the successes of clients and other stakeholder relationships. In this regard, collaboration among parties is essential and the collective wisdom is the only way to create new standards rather than following best practices—a prescription for mediocrity or failure. Recently, we embarked on a technology platform to manage an international intranet among select members of the Network; and the Roundtable—'Building Collaborative Advantage' in New York in 2002 was met with great success having 17 countries represented and bestowing the award KEN Practitioner of the Year to Admiral Bobby Ray Inman (see Chapter 13).

9.3   PROOF OF CONCEPT

All this still may still sound theoretical; but on Global Learn Day (October 2000), participants in the ENTOVATION 100 (E100) who are featured on the Global Knowledge Leadership Map[5] were facilitated in a 24-hour dialog around the world, beginning with the Far East (Malaysia, China, Japan) and ending with the research agenda based at the Banff Centre for Management (Calgary, Canada).

It was the equivalent of an international intellectual marathon —broadcast live on the Internet and was described as a "sparkling" event. Most participants experienced a new level of understanding of the potential power of the technology and the value of a solid professional network with a purpose. In the published summary there are seven vignettes of colleagues discovering one another—some for the first time.

Perhaps it was Dr. Tom Malone, formerly professor at MIT and now distinguished scholar at North Carolina State, who summed up the real opportunity as a defining moment in our history.

> *I believe we are at a historical choice point in determining the kind of world our children's children will inherit. If we make these choices based only on the models of our industrial-age past, we will almost certainly miss the true opportunities before us. Knowledge does have the potential to create economic sustainability in our society*

There were some real lessons learned: Members of the Entovation Network have a great deal of expertise to offer one another, and the connections happened in unexpected ways. The combination of audio and text interaction facilitated the real- time worldwide dialog. Video would have been nice; but it was not necessary. Advance preparation (i.e., photographs, biographical information, career highlights, and suggested URLs) provides a succinct way to profile the talent and current projects.

The dialog must—at least initially—be structured so as to illuminate the aspects and attitudes of participants that might be useful to one another. In spite of the available technology, most people are resistant to (and some are unable to afford) taking advantage of the new technology, such as the audio clips. Like a kaleidoscope, there is no turning back. Once participants realize the value of the interaction and their potential contribution, there is no alternative but to build on the competencies of one another. The GLD IV Archives provide those listeners worldwide an experience—especially those interested in elevating the distance-learning agenda as the integral vehicle for innovation in the Knowledge Economy.

As Stephen Denning, former CKO of The World Bank and author of *The Springboard* suggests,

> *Storytelling gets inside the minds of the individuals who collectively make up the organization and affects how they think. They worry, wonder, agonize, and dream about themselves and in the process re-create their organization. Storytelling enables the individuals in an organization to see themselves and the organization in a different light, and accordingly to make decisions and change their behavior in accordance with these new perceptions and insights.*

Now, Entovation is a virtual organization. Through the telephone conversations over the course of the 24-hour period, members were recounting stories about their roots and aspirations. Moreover, they were—from different cultures of the world—able to learn from and contribute to the "real-time" knowledge creation of others. It was a prime example of what The Innovation Superhighway has to offer us as individuals, as enterprises, and as ambassadors of our respective nations. What follows is a glimpse at seven of those strategic conversations.

Vignette 1: Customer Success

It was the story recounted by Gulgun Kayakutlu, an expert on small and medium-sized businesses, about the aftermath of the recent earthquake in Turkey that sparked an intensive online dialog about customer relationship management (CRM). How? She described how in only fifty-two seconds, 80 percent of the manufacturing base was destroyed. How does one go about recovering customer information? The rebuilding began with a systematic study of customer knowledge (i.e., interacting with and learning from customers)!

As Gulgun was describing the knowledge processes required for the successful reconstruction via the telephone, a lively discussion among other Entovation colleagues—Pat Parker-Roach (Bolton, Massachusetts) and Yvonne Buma (The Netherlands)—was happening in the chat room. Pat suggested the problem with implementing such programs is a matter of the dialogue skills required in the bi-directional flow of knowledge. Lynne Schneider (USA) suggested that most CRM programs are dropped at the front or back office with little or no understanding of what constitutes customer success. Philip Maciejewski (Poland) added that they always have a relationship between the customers; but that there is nothing new in CRM but some technology. Lynne offered the Entovation concept of "innovating with the customer." Pat announced the new CRM consortium as part of the Society of Learning (SoL) based at MIT. They all were eager to hear about Gulgun's real-time customer success. Gulgun was also responsible for the Turkish translation of the "Momentum of Knowledge Strategy." The Network is in operation.

Vignette 2: Global Knowledge

Chin Hoon Lau, the representative from Malaysia, hosted activities in conjunction with the Global Knowledge Partnership sponsored by the World Bank in March 2000. Throughout the twenty-four hours, this molecular geneticist described his Lagenda Knowledge Systems business as well as his initiatives in virtual collaboration as a way to transform voluntary groups into viable entities. Chin Hoon is responsible for the Chinese translation of the "Momentum of Knowledge Strategy." While he was on the air, we also visited other experts in the region (e.g., Jin Zhouying from China, Karl-Erik Sveiby and Sante Delle Vergini from Australia, and Stoney Ishikawa from Japan.).

But Chin Hoon's comments were not limited to the Asia-Australia region; he held conversations with other colleagues from all the other regions on a variety of topics. Similarly, Sante's discussion of intellectual property (IP) in the Knowledge Economy sparked a continuing debate on what can be protected and how, as well as comments on the IP Committee of the World Trade Organization (WTO). Although there were no conclusions reached, all participating gained a better understanding of the issue and implications for various parts of the world.

Vignette 3: Old Mother Europe

The virtual visit to Europe and Africa prompted a robust three-hour conversation about "innovating Old Mother Europe." Gulgun (Turkey) talked about the "mind-tuning" necessary. Lynne (USA) described the EU Knowledge Councils but added that the change in attitudes was essential. Philip (Poland) queried, "Can we really see the power of Intellectual Capital?" Another colleague from Poland, Volker Rohde described the potential for "building the capacity to create within the next 10–20 years a platform for people around the world—beyond CNN." This is precisely the foundation of the Global Knowledge Innovation® Infrastructure sponsored by The Banff Centre and the new EU-sponsored KALiF Project described by Michael Kelleher (Wales).

Other progressive initiatives were described by Charles Savage and Elizabeth Sundrum speaking of their new e-culture initiatives and values technologies. Joachim Doering, VP Siemens (Germany), was visible during the day describing how to implement a global knowledge-sharing network as was done within his firm's ICN business (see Sharnet description in Chapter 14). There were questions about the unnecessary duplication of effort and a debate about whether reinventing was a viable strategy (and whether it did lead to innovation). There seemed to be some consensus that business transformation was a matter of innovation (e.g., rethinking). In fact, Siemens was responsible for the trend analysis performed by Jan Wyllie in Trend Monitor International, published by ENTOVATION as the "Knowledge Millennium Generation (see Chapter 15). Such a discussion cut to the heart of the real meaning of innovation—capitalizing on the best of the past and realigning the rest for future opportunities. As Henry Thoreau wrote in *Walden*, "If you have built castles in the air, that is where they belong. Now build the foundations under them."

Vignette 4: Entrepreneurialism

Piero Formica (Italy), during a coffee break at a conference he was chairing, described the Entrepreneurial University he has been innovating with faculty from multiple universities and focused on "real" business projects. Piero was discovered by Entovation in the EU meeting in Utrecht hosted by CIBIT, another alliance partner of Kelleher's. He is a leader in the International Assembly Association of Science Parks and was speaking from Birmingham, England, which was the location of my own first international keynote presentation in 1988. Jean Marc Le Duc, Ministry of Research (France), had convened the Grande Colloque de Perspective in 1989, also hosted with Eunika Mercier-Laurent. This was the time of the launch of Innovation Strategy for the Knowledge Economy, the French edition released in 2001.

He joined the discussion with a perspective from a national government and his new project of cinecities. Lars Kolind (Denmark) was featured as guiding the Intellectual Capital (IC) indicators for the nation.

Esko Kilpi (Finland) has been a similar leader in his own country and was also at the Utrecht meeting. Like Karl-Erik Sveiby (Australia), Ante Pulic (representing his homeland of Croatia, but on the faculty in Austria) has been a leading light in the measurement of the IC field. A fellow Austrian, Manfred Bornmann, was responsible for the German translations of the book and the Web site. And from Africa—although he is currently resident in Saudi Arabia—Ali Liban (Somalia) was discussing the practical applications of patents and the environmental implications and concerns about the development and visibility of other African nations. These are long-term learning connections that have helped to fuel the progress within companies, academia, and government. These national and/or regional learnings have shadow influence around the world thanks to the technology and human commitment by GLD active participants.

Vignette 5: Knowledge-Sharing

It was 1994 when we first discovered Ted Lumley (Montreal, Canada), one of the leading knowledge practitioners from Mobil Oil Corporation. Together we orchestrated the first Knowledge Management Conferences for the oil and gas industry. Along with Ed Witterholt (U.S.) from British Petroleum, we developed a timeline of activities to put into perspective the new knowledge focus. Around the same time, Dr. David Skyrme (U.K.)—like Witterholt from the UK—introduced us to Jan Wyllie (U.K). We commissioned some trend analysis for the publication, *Collaborative Innovation and the Knowledge Economy*, in which we included the "Economics of Intangible Value."

Shortly thereafter, we served on the advisory team for the World Development Report—"Knowledge for Development"—and began to work with Stephen Denning, the CKO of The World Bank. All of this is to preface how three talented individuals were brought together through Entovation linkages; now, the three are working collaboratively on "The Springboard" and "Sweat Lodge"—an experiment beyond tacit knowledge. Jan shared the story on the air during the broadcast as he defined "real knowledge" as including feelings, actions, social relationships, sense of purpose, and spiritual well being. The nature of such knowledge cannot really be "captured"; it is best conveyed through story-telling (the topic of Denning's new book), which offers a deeper level of mutual understanding. This is the essence of the real nature of change in absolute time. It is also the story of the interweaving of expertise and aspirations that occurred throughout the 24-hour GLD dialog

Vignette 6: Latin-American Learning

Since the European meeting in Utrecht, we have been working with representatives from Central and South American to convene the Latin America Roundtable on the Implications of the Knowledge Economy. Lynne Schneider (USA) had just returned from Argentina, Brazil, and Mexico, where the political leaders are recognizing the potential of such a regional effort. Discussions originated with Dr. Javier Carrillo, Director of the Knowledge Systems Research Center of ITESM—notably the MIT of Mexico. As the creator of the Knowledge-Based Value Model and graduate KM curriculum, he also architected the KMMetaSite, which captured the interest of most GLD participants. It is a masterful compilation of the worldwide knowledge resources and Web sites. His leadership in relevant knowledge and innovation journals as well as consortia is admirable; but his work with the International Center for Sustainable Development, the Club of Budapest, is what places his talent on the world stage.

A variety of others were featured in the region. Gerardo Calderon (Mexico), formerly CEO of Intracorp, has provided for the Spanish translations of the book and articles. Alejandro Fernandez, former VP of Human Resources for PDVSA (Venezuela) was a Sloan Fellow with me in 1989. He was the host for Global HR 1999—a federation of seven human resource professional organizations. In 2000, Leif Edvinsson and I were featured at Global HR 2000 in Paris. Next year, it was in Switzerland, and in the year 2002 it comes to Mexico City. Alejandro described the role of PDVSA as a government-funded corporation as well as the organization's in-house knowledge symposium for 450 top executives—a model for large-scale institutions worldwide. Our recent meetings with Banamex—thanks to the introduction by John Hibbs (U.S.)—provide another corporate example of IC leadership to be harnessed. Vidyartha Kissoon (Guyana) described the knowledge-sharing opportunities in the Caribbean. Through the Sustainable Development Networking Programme (SDNP), they determine agencies that are duplicating work across the region and promote the sharing on all social issues. Vidyartha was discovered during the Global Knowledge Development (GKD) in conjunction with the Malaysia GKII conference referenced in Vignette 1! This is a prime example of how insights can be spread within a region and around the world in lightning speed with the power of communications technology and the sharing of intellectual wealth.

Vignette 7: Executive Leadership

Throughout the day, the symbiosis was evident. Experts were building on the ideas of one another and meeting—albeit virtually—contacts that were previously only names on the Internet. The names became faces and backgrounds of expertise as the biographic forms were completed for GLD. For many, this was the first time they were in conversation. Doug Macnamara, then VP of The Banff Centre, and Andre Mamprin, his assistant, initiated the program for the North American region. Describing the Global Knowledge Innovation Infrastructure (GKII)—now relabeled The Innovation Superhighway —and the unique executive management program on knowledge and innovation, they described the competency-based models they have researched, as published in "Leadership @ Internet Speed" and the recent article on the "7Cs of Knowledge Leadership", published in the *Handbook of Business Strategy*. Lynne Schneider (USA) described the success of the enterprise model and holonic networks as an exercise in knowledge management systems. We featured Dr. Clint Ackerman (USA) and the new Knowledge Jobs search firm; and Bryan Davis (Canada) of The Kaieteur Institute and his focus on e-Knowledge. Charles Armstrong, CEO of Armstrong Industries and Know, Inc., outlined his KnowledgeShop (one of the new knowledge trading systems) and Knetus—a Knowledge Networking program for competitive advantage.

The Banff Programme on Aboriginal Management was tied to the opening remarks of Navajo Elder Katherine Smith and plans for a book by Ali Liban (Somalia). Thus, the search for an understanding of knowledge, learning, and innovation returns to the opening remarks. As Cindy Gordon (Canada) says, "The journey is a long one and involves the understanding that different cultures attach different meanings and interpretations. To achieve our desired state of a global knowledge economy, we must not forget who we are and what we want to leave behind for future generations to carry forth."

Participation in the GLD was an experiment for Entovation —an initial introduction of the Entovation 100 to one another. It is the beginning of what will evolve into a monthly dialog on al ten dimensions of innovation strategy, the findings of which will be published as a new Intelligence Service. What we learned is summed up in the following:

1. Members of the Entovation Network have a great deal of expertise to offer one another; and the connections happened in unexpected ways.

2. The combination of audio and text interaction facilitated the real-time worldwide dialog. Video would have been nice; but it was not necessary.

3.   Advance preparation in the form of the background information (i.e., photographs, biographical information, career highlights and suggested URLs) provides a succinct way to profile the talent and the current projects.

4.   The dialog must—at least initially—be structured so as to illuminate the aspects and attitudes of participants that might be useful to one another.

5.   In spite of the available technology, most people are resistant to (and some are unable to afford) taking advantage of the new technology, such as the audio clips.

6.   There is no turning back. Once participants realize the value of the interaction and their potential contributions, there is no alternative but to build on the competencies of one another.

7.   The GLD IV Archives provide those listeners worldwide an invaluable experience, especially those interested in elevating the distance-learning agenda as the integral vehicle for innovation in the knowledge economy.

9.4   BUILDING THE SOCIAL CAPITAL

In a recent article (2002),[6] Xenia Stanford, editor of *KnowMap*, performed a social capital and innovation analysis of the ENTOVATION 100. She described social capital as much more than the sharing of information and the growth of knowledge, saying

> *Social capital encompasses not only shared access to vast amounts of timely information but many positive properties of interdependence: shared values, goals, and objectives; shared expertise and knowledge; sharing of work, decision making, and prioritization; shared risk, accountability, and trust; and shared rewards. (Fountain, 1997)*

Benefits of collaborative and well-functioning social networks include understanding who has specific knowledge and who will benefit from that particular knowledge. Stanford explored how social capital enables innovation. It can do so through one of these means but only if the social network is working well, as shown by the following elements:

- *Leadership*—clear, visible and shared leadership with little hierarchy—allows sharing of ideas throughout the organization and encourages innovation.
- *Participation*—shared participation in decision making, willing contributions made by and accepted from every member with support throughout allows innovation on what has been called "the shop floor" (i.e., those who implement and use the designs).
- *Culture*—the group has rules, norms, and fulfillment of obligations whereby risk-taking behavior is encouraged, which can drive innovation, while socially destructive actions are handled swiftly though fairly.
- *Sustainability*—specific capacities of the organization for the formulation and handling of demands enable the network to work through issues, build a cooperative group, develop an organizational memory, and create a future vision empowering the network to survive and thrive beyond the ups and downs that are natural in any social group.

Stanford concludes that to turn the social network into innovation capital, it must remain leading edge. It should not emulate best practices but should reach beyond to new and better ones.

The mere existence of a network does not immediately guarantee success. Many participants are embroiled in disputes, lack visible leadership, do not collaborate, and have no empowering means of decision making. Further, teams must have methods to encourage successful behaviors while reducing sabotage and promote risk taking with necessary controls to avoid destructive actions.

To assess with empirical measures whether or not the E100 measures up to this challenge, Stanford used the critical success factors that,

Fountain notes, are needed for networks to build social capital and lead to innovation. These were built into a social capital assessment tool (SCAT) adapted from one developed by Krishna and Shrader. Although the population polled was small, trends can be seen according to the four categories presented above. The results are shown in Table 9.1.

All of the categories demonstrate a higher than 50 percent score for the E100 network. This means it is already succeeding as a social capital network and, with the lessons learned from the study, it has the ability to work toward even more collective innovative advantage. The strongest score for subsets of these categories was in the Sustainability area, labeled Formulation of Demands. This rated 80 percent, while the other subset of this same category, Specific Capacities, ranged from very high to adequate.

Other high scores were found in participatory decision making where involvement of members and use of viable processes scored 75 percent. This can be attributed to the Virtual CKO, as decision making is delegated to members and methods are used to make for solid and supported decisions.

Inclusion of women in the membership ranked very high, while involvement of members from more impoverished economies rated as average. The average rating for those from impoverished countries is not only very understandable, it is very commendable in consideration of their lower access to computer and communications technology.

TABLE 9.1   *Results of Social Capital Survey*

CATEGORY	E100 SCORE
I. Leadership	61%
II. Participation	63%
III. Culture	60%
IV. Sustainability	59%
Overall Score	61%

What was disappointing is that the lowest score (40 percent) for participation was found among the more elite (those highly successful in business) members of the network.

Since the network is still fairly new and constantly innovating itself with the addition of new members and new joint projects, it is not surprising the scores in some areas are not higher. However, the E100 has proven that it has the structure and credibility to become even stronger, to build more social capital, and to increase innovative capacity for reaching the marketplace.

9.5   LESSONS LEARNED: THE NETWORK IN RETROSPECT

In a recent professional meeting, a newcomer in the knowledge field asks, "Are you based in the United States, the United Kingdom, or Canada?" The confusion is understandable since the headquarters are in Massachusetts, the Web site—until recently—was based in England, and the Banff Centre in Calgary, Canada was designated to host our research agenda.

Our experts come from all over the world. Therefore, it matters not the site of the operating base of the chief knowledge officer for such a worldwide virtual laboratory of ideas. With such advancements in computer and communications technology and given that quality expertise has no boundaries of national origin, the network can function quite well wherever there is a phone jack. On the other hand, one of our primary assumptions is that the network is both technical and human.

One cannot underestimate the value of face-to-face communications, even brief interactions. There have been numerous occasions when presentations and even entire conferences have been planned without the principals meeting one another except by phone or e-mail. However, relationship or social capital, which may be the linchpin to a successful future, is enhanced when people are afforded the time to share, without technical limitations, their values, operational standards, and aspirations. We can take a look at the evolution of the

Network and evaluate some of the forces that were enabling growth and those resisting factors that were inhibiting progress.

9.6   WHAT WENT RIGHT?

- People were ready for a positive, constructive change beyond downsizing. People know intuitively there is a better way to operate, even if they cannot define it precisely.
- There was an increasing receptivity to advancements of and experimentation with technology.
- The quality of the intellectual capital—especially the collective wisdom—was unsurpassed. There are many people entering the field.
- However, much of the material in publications and on the Web is not of much value. Sifting the chaff from the wheat is essential. "Knowledge about knowledge" may be the most valuable expertise of all.
- There ensued an inevitable realization in the value of knowledge innovation. To date there have been two distinct communities: the innovation community and the knowledge management community. Most major research efforts are discovering that the focus must on be the innovation process.
- Good people surround themselves with other good people, so the referral network was exceptional.

9.7   WHAT WENT WRONG?

- Articulating progressive concepts is the easy step, but having managers put the concepts into action is another. Many decisions were made on moving the mission versus making a profit. Sometimes, it may have been the wrong decision.
- Volume of activity on the Web site and e-mail was unexpected. This is in terms of the activity on our own site as well as the

increase in sites that provided competition. We also underestimated the degree of innovation in the Internet, requiring significant investments to improve market image and services.

- Building credibility as a virtual network is difficult in contrast with the established major consulting firms.
- Managers are still seeking the quick fix and best practices rather than understanding the fundamental changes required and the need to establish standards.
- Reciprocity doesn't come easy, because of a basic competitive work ethic. Virtual reliance on others for building substance is risky to say the least. One is always subject to their priorities. Worst, one is vulnerable to others taking your ideas and moving them into competitive products and services if proper legal agreements are not in place.

In the beginning, we wondered how to tap into the combined insights of worldwide experts from diverse backgrounds. The answer was simple—let's query them. The Entovation Network is one example of how a community of experts can respect the competencies of each another, learn from a diverse set of perspectives, and contribute to a common language and a shared vision. It is not perfect, but few enterprises are.

The Network capitalizes on the best of what a knowledge economy will afford: flexible, fluid relationships, contributing to the common good.

9.8 Summary

Amidst the complexity of the knowledge era, we must both simplify and magnify our relationships. No longer are finances the scarce resource to be managed. It is how we choose to spend our time, in communication with whom and to what end. If a virtual chief knowledge officer (CKO) is the one who exercises leadership without authority;

then the onus is upon each of us to architect our time with one another, face to face as well as remotely, with meaningful dialog.

The Entovation Network has evolved as just one international example of The Innovation Superhighway. It has been designed with a combination of architecting and self-evolving mechanisms. It has the potential to enjoy a broad sphere of influence and to serve as a timely learning and intelligence system for all those involved. It's potential global reach has yet to be realized.

CHAPTER ENDNOTES

[1] The story of the evolution of Entovation—"The Virtual CKO: Leading Strategic Conversations" was originally submitted for an ASTD Action Series publication (2000). Abstracts here are reprinted with permission.

[2] Entovation® is a registered trademark of Entovation International, Ltd.

[3] Holonomy is a concept of nesting of networks, best popularized by Jessica Lipnack and Jeffrey Stamps in *The Age of the Network*.

[4] To visit the archive of articles, see http://www.skyrme.com/updates/archives.htm

[5] To visit the Global Knowledge Leadership Map, see http://www.entovation.com/kleadmap/index.htm

[6] This article by Xenia Stanford (2002) is excerpted with permission.

TEN

Global Momentum of Knowledge Strategy

The bigger the world economy,
the more powerful its smallest players.
The study of the smallest economic player,
the entrepreneur,
will merge with the study of
how the big bang global economy works."

John Naisbitt,
Global Paradox

Ultimately, the new economy will evolve based on the knowledge and actions of individuals within whom lies knowledge or meaningful, actionable information. Who are some of these new players on the world stage? What are their roots and aspirations?

In my own quest for these knowledge leaders, I realize there are now hundreds of conferences featuring aspects of the knowledge economy in every corner of the globe. What began in 1987 as an initiative to harness the intellectual capital of a nation has been embraced as a global agenda of international collaboration. The management technology is universal and can be applied to small, medium, and large-scale enterprises. The focus on knowledge applies to both profit and nonprofit organizations. It provides a shared purpose among all levels of the economy, from the individual to the societal. In ten short years, the Entovation Network has grown to include professionals linking across functions, industries, and regions of the world. And the benefits are just beginning.

There is hardly a company that hasn't dedicated resources to task. There are numerous courses, degree programs, post-doctoral studies, and e-learning opportunities in most cultures of the world. Governments have recognized that managing their knowledge capabilities on behalf of their constituency is essential to maintaining relevance and sustainability. E-government initiatives flourish; and policies to enhance computer and communications are commonplace in local, federal, and societal agencies. A new knowledge leadership has emerged and with the new leaders an opportunity to influence progress in ways previously unthinkable. The technical and human connectivity is creating a management modus operandi that requires one to innovate or perish.

In 1996, we published "The Momentum of Knowledge Management," (see Appendix E)[1] which has now been translated into a dozen languages. As I have traveled around the world being shown how people and organizations are implementing these knowledge concepts, I have been heartened by the degree of ingenuity and sense of purpose I have discovered. I've learned that the European countries—Eastern and Western alike—have collaborated to create a regional approach to manage their resources—financial, human and technical, and that all has been done without individual countries losing any of their precious cultural heritages. I've learned that developing nations of the world want to leverage their own diversity rather than assume the values and practices of the industrialized world. I have learned that people representing countries on the Pacific Rim have a dedication to ensure the prominence of their country or region in the new millennium. And I have also learned from them the value of Tao—the necessary balances required of individuals as responsible executives and as nations—including East meeting West and North meeting South in the Knowledge Society.

I have learned how intricately interlaced is the transformation underway with the environment as well as the cultural and performing arts. I have been taught the value of knowledge visualization; and how people learn differently—some from the printed word, others from surfing the Internet. There are people of certain cultures known for the brevity and poignancy of their words; and there are others that document volumes. There is innovation and early adoption of the technology coming from unexpected places; and the governments of some nations—not well known for their progressive practices—are taking the lead to ensure that their constituency benefits from the opportunities afforded a knowledge economy.

Of course, I have also learned the downside. There are people and nations that are still locked into their traditional, quality methodologies and—worse—still victims of the reengineering and downsizing rage. I have met many who are still skeptical of the value of a new view of their work and their world. There are those who are resistant to any form of change; and there are those who still suffer from the not-invented here (NIH) Syndrome. For them, they must be perceived as the originator of (the best) concept or label.

Theft of intellectual property—to a large extent due to the accessibility provided on the Internet—has run rampant, because the legal profession has not yet comprehended how to protect a resource that multiplies as it is shared. There are many—even within what we might consider now the knowledge profession—who compete far more than they collaborate and promote themselves, often at the expense of leveraging others. And there are many research, technology, and consulting firms who have picked up the knowledge—and now the innovation—banner without having a notion of the purpose and promise of the real knowledge agenda.

10.1   THE ENTOVATION 100

In order to give visibility to those who might have the values and vision of a knowledge economy, we created a graphic representation of the world showing the one hundred or so theorists and practitioners now representing diverse countries. What appears on the map[2] in

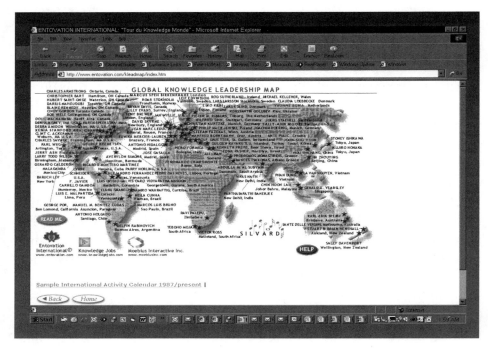

FIGURE 10.1   *The global knowledge leadership map.*

Figure 10.1 is a diagonal slice of this network, and their names and vision statements can be seen on the website.

They come from a variety of disciplines, a wide range of functional responsibilities, and they represent 50 nations. There are some recognized intellectual leaders (e.g., Edvinsson, Nonaka, Pasher, Sveiby, Saint-Onge) as well as newcomers, some of whom just graduated from Ph.D. programs. Some are CEOs or senior managers; others are government officials or academic researchers. There are experts in performance measurement, competitive analysis, and alliance strategy as well as computer/ communications technology. They are all playing a role in shaping our new economy.

What these individuals seem to share is a sense of values, a compelling vision, and standards of operational excellence to emulate. This is the reason they have been featured. They are not *all* the experts; the experts have their own forums. They are not *all* the students; they have their internal academic networks. They *do* represent a cross-section of expertise that promises to provide robust fodder for the implications of the knowledge economy. In short, I believe they are a virtual community of collaborators working for the common good—a new economic world order based upon knowledge. Using this network as an innovation superhighway should result in profitable growth for their enterprises and assure the vitality of their national economies and the advancement of society—industrialized and developing nations alike.

To participate, each provided answers to the following questions via an electronic interview:

- What are your roots in the knowledge field?
- Who has influenced you and why?
- What have you been able to accomplish?
- What still needs to be done?
- What is your vision of a knowledge economy?

Results of the interviewed were initially premiered at the 20th Annual McMaster Business Conference (January 20, 1999) in Hamilton, Ontario, Canada, as part of the presentation "Tour de Knowledge Monde" in a knowledge concert—a form of knowledge entertainment, if you will. As we visited the various knowledge professionals in different corners of the world, Dr. Silvard Kool, a professor of Marine Biology at Boston College—and also an internationally acclaimed concert pianist—accompanied the presentation with music indigenous to the relevant part of the world. These tours have since traveled through North and South America and to Sweden where the program was Webcast live on the Internet.

We featured representatives from several countries who had responded with their reflections and aspirations. Their messages document the multiple facets of expertise of knowledge professionals as well as their broad geographic reach in both industrialized and developing nations. Readers will begin to see the emergence of a common language and a shared vision.

10.2   GLOBAL RESPONSES: SIMILAR YET VARIED

Professionals from the following countries offered their comments: Argentina, Australia, Austria, Belgium, Bermuda, Brazil, Canada, Chile, China, Colombia, Croatia, Cuba, Denmark, England, Finland, France, Germany, Greece, Guyana, India, Indonesia, Italy, Israel, Japan, Korea, Latvia, Malaysia, Mexico, New Zealand, Nigeria, Norway, Paraguay, Peru, the Philippines, Poland, Portugal, Saudi Arabia, Singapore, Somalia, South Africa, Spain, Sweden, Switzerland, The Netherlands, Turkey, United States, Ukraine, Venezuela, Vietnam, Wales and Zimbabwe.

There are some startling similarities in the way in which problems, issues, and solutions were characterized. On the other hand, there were also several counterpoint positions on the topics, which leads us to believe that the knowledge field is beginning to mature in ways that concepts and practices can be debated—quite a stretch from only a few years ago when they could hardly be discussed.

For instance, some believe that the knowledge economy is a matter of philosophy and have been influenced by historic and modern philosophers. Others believe that the field of knowledge management attracts philosophers and beware! One respondent believed that there was a need to influence middle managers, while others thought it was essential to have a senior management agenda. Still others believed that this is a revolution, a grass-roots movement causing fundamental transformations. Many described how extremely complex is the subject —all-encompassing, global, multidisciplinary; and multi-dimensional; others felt it was not rocket science but more a matter of good common sense.

Some felt that they were wrestling with new concepts and language; others say that the focus is as old as the beginning of time when humans began to communicate. Several had come from the fields of quality or reengineering; but they all considered that this new direction would provide far more sustainable results. The leadership required was described as "courageous," "inspiring," and "visual/visible." Some described it as the shift from the micro to the macro perspective of the world. Others felt that it was a matter of making the macro level more operational. The most compelling observation is that one cannot tell who is a theorist and who is a practitioner. There were many surprises!

Three things were very clear. First, the transformation is more a function of behavior and culture change than technology. Second, these changes are difficult, but well worth the effort. Third, all seem to feel that we are on the right path toward a more prosperous future.

10.3   RESPONSES BY QUESTION

10.3.1   What Are the Roots Of Your Interest In The Knowledge Field?

Knowledge professionals come from a variety of disciplines and backgrounds: physics, chemistry, medicine, S&T policy, technology development, business administration, psychology, manufacturing, accounting, telecommunications, software development, information systems, economics, and more.

Their professional responsibilities included technology transfer, licensing, HR management, business process reengineering, strategic alliances, quality, communications, knowledge processing, stress management, systems dynamics, knowledge elicitation, mapping and modeling, and more.

The scope of current work varied: bridging between technology strategy and planning, organizational transformation, scientific method development for knowledge leadership, government intervention, and creating a general understanding of the future.

10.3.2   Who has Influenced You And Why?

Managers, parents, family, friends, peers, clients and spiritual leaders have influenced many respondents in personal ways. They learned from those who were competent and those who were not. Many professors were named that represent a cross-section from the hard and soft sciences.

Several authors had provided direction, either through books and/ or research reports (e.g., Nonaka, Amidon, Sveiby, Skyrme, Senge, Stewart, Edvinsson, Savage, Davenport, Peters, Kogut, and Ackoff); but none provided as much impact as Peter F. Drucker. Of course, there were numerous others who were referenced, such as Argyris, Effendi, Marcic, Davis, Bacon, Hume, Shein, Kantor, Kofman, Dodgson, Zohar, Lev, Hall, Husserl, Hegel, the young Marx, Masuda, McLuhan, Polyani, Wittgentein, Shannon, Simon, and March, among others. Some are well known in the knowledge field while others represent the influence of other communities.

Interestingly enough, there were some former CEOs referenced, such as George Kozmetsky (also featured on the Map), Regis McKenna, and Arie de Geus who are also well-known authors. There were other management practitioners, such as Andy Law (Fast Company), Keith Davies (Institute for Life-Long Learning) and Norman Strauss (Ethos Metasystems). Still others reference "clusters of people and networks," more on the idea of "communities of practice"—both human and technical.

10.3.3   What are the greatest challenges you have faced?

Everyone seems to be gaining knowledge of the concepts. Of course, such understanding leads only to the need for further understanding! Others have clearly been putting the concepts into practice and are much more concerned with implementation strategy, communicating the mission, creating the value proposition, and maintaining the momentum.

First, there is a need for understanding the real value of knowledge. We cannot get lost in the buzzwords. There are new definitions of terms that are often confusing. There are disparate perspectives in the field, which need to be rationalized. This applies to philosophy as well as practice. There is a need to connect the notions of human potential to economic results.

The value proposition has shifted from one of cost quality and time to one of economics, behavior, and technology as described in Chapter 2. In short, people are searching for ways to go beyond the deep emotional commitment to the mission and arrive at more rational thinking about the relevant tools and techniques. It was characterized as being on the "leading" as opposed to the "bleeding" edge. How might we articulate the knowledge agenda in pragmatic management terms rather than academic philosophy?

Second, there is a need for change within enterprises, in national policy and society at large. The old rules just do not apply to the new economic realities. In some respects, we are living in fifth-generation change dynamics and operating with second- and third-generation management technology. Several described new organization forms: self-directed, networked, and purposeful. We may even be innovating the whole art of leadership that is more suitable for twenty-first century management. It requires those comfortable with adapting to new mechanisms (e.g., the balanced scorecard, visualization of Intellectual Capital). How might we shift from classical and traditional thinking to a more flexible modus operandi to be able to take full advantage of this emerging field? How can we prepare people and organizations to act more intelligently? How can we make knowledge just as important and measurable as cycle time, process yield, cost reduction, and productivity.

Third, there is a need for supporting mechanisms for practitioners to put the concepts into practice. It seems that the technical support is more widely available than we would have thought, although admittedly the technology is often misused. The potential has yet to be realized. Although intranets have been effective in promoting internal conferencing and the Internet has enabled global networking, it is clear that we need a new class of tools to effectively create, codify, exchange, and apply new knowledge effectively and efficiently. Much of the visualization and modeling research is moving swiftly to that end.

We need to challenge traditional thinking. To create entirely new management philosophy, standards, and practice, we also need new models of success, complete with case study examples. Experts from multiple countries need powerful messages to convince their business communities and government officials to take action. Many have accepted the rationale; they have even articulated their intent to become a knowledge-based enterprise or a knowledge-based nation and are now seeking options for implementation. There is probably some mapping "of an international order" to be done so that we can learn from the learnings of one another.

10.3.4 What have you been able to accomplish?

Responses varied from those who felt they had accomplished "little" to those who reported having made "significant progress."

There were, of course, many who had research results to report. The research was not always done in the academic laboratories, however. In many instances, results were from action research and collaborative learning where people were able to explore the connections between the disciplines and across functional and even industry boundaries. Most responses, however, were quite nationalistic in spirit, with the exception of the activity in Europe now promoting a more regional geographic approach for economic wealth.

Some had made the connection between mission and performance. Others had influenced language and cross-boundary processes. Several were practicing what they preach by initiating and participating in a variety of teams, networks, and special interest groups dedicated to the focus of knowledge and/or innovation. Some had even bridged the two!

For some, they progress was due to their own initiative, crystallizing the agenda in terms that they could formalize in a research institute, a futures center, a survey, a degree program, a start-up firm, or a specific product or service. Many have authored their own books and articles and are active in the "community of knowledge practice." All considered themselves more learners than leaders per se, but each is making a significant contribution to the field.

Many commented that this was a never-ending work, a "work-in-progress" so to speak. They'd been able to accomplish bits and pieces, but had not been able to realize the potential of the broad overarching goals and potential this economy brings. One thing most respondents shared was that they did understand the total picture and the value of viewing the opportunity in holistic terms.

10.3.5   What Still Needs To Be Done?

Simply stated, there is agreement that there is a lot to be accomplished, almost everything. Most realize that we are only at the beginning of a major transformation that will take decades. We have only scratched the surface of the real impact of this new economy. It will take several years for the common language to emerge. We need to reconnect the roots of heritage with the vision of what we might become (i.e., recover from the downside effects of downsizing and reengineering).

First, we need new concepts, articulated in words that are easy to understand and even easier to implement. They must be easy for managers to consider without being simplistic. Knowledge must be seen as a resource—in some instances, as the raw material from which products and services are developed. We need to document the importance of this "knowledge capital" as a precious asset to be managed for the benefit of an organization as well as the sustainability of mankind. We need an economic theory of knowledge!

Second, we must create awareness—focus attention and make the opportunity more public. The vision must be visible. We must overcome the traditional paradigm of "knowledge hoarding" and create new methods and incentives for knowledge sharing. We must capture the attention of senior management, middle management, and newcomers to the field. Move the debate "from technology to content" says one respondent. Another says move the debate "from content to process, the innovation process."

Third, we must create the environment to manage collective intelligence and an innovation culture that values new ideas and responsible risk taking. Academics, industry leaders, and government officials all have something to contribute, and even more to learn. Focus must be on interaction, interdependence, and collaboration, not competition. We need to bring together East and West in ways that support and leverage the creativity of one another.

Fourth, we need practical and acceptable methods for the measurement of intellectual capital as well as the effective deployment of knowledge management technology. The supply chain needs to be redesigned as an innovation value system. We need more systematic methods of evaluation and institutional frameworks conducive to these modern methods. We need more effective training methods for both business and technology managers. We need more stories of successes and failures, with story telling becoming an art of the knowledge economy. We need more intelligent ways to dialog, both electronic and face-to-face. We need to make the virtual community manageable through such structures as "knowledge cells." We need a new value system based on collaborative work.

10.3.6 What is the Vision That You Hold For A Knowledge Economy?

There is no way to do justice to the power of the multiple visions shared. Clearly, knowledge is seen as the engine for value creation. What lies in the future must be grounded in values, competencies, and the quality of relationships. It is an economy of open access rather than knowledge being perceived and managed as a "private good." The reasons are because of the bountiful nature of the resource and its quality to multiply as it is shared with others.

A new economic world order based upon knowledge, not technology, innovation, not solutions, value-systems, not value chains, customer success, not satisfaction, and international collaboration, not competition." (Amidon. 1999)[3]

This new economy we are innovating works for the people creating a world free of poverty, disease, and violence. It is an economy directed toward sustainable development placing knowledge at the point of need or opportunity. It is an economy that is transnational in scope, balancing the local and national needs with a global scope. The driving mandate is one of creating a society with a better quality of life and increased standard of living worldwide. And the initiative begins with the individual, where knowledge resides!

10.4 What They Said

What follows are sample comments provided by individuals who are featured on the Map:

- "Unlimited opportunity to make a difference." (Ackerman)
- "Knowledge is more important than raw material." (Al Subyani)
- "A world full of satisfied stakeholders." (Bart)
- "An economy grounded solidly in moral and ethical standards." (Benítez)
- "The vacuum of ignorance is filled with understanding, the world is freed from poverty, disease and violence, people are stimulated and satisfied by learning and innovation." (Brewer)
- "Future work is more abstract—turn the world of ideas into rapid development of goods." (Bruno)
- "A world without nations, just human beings working for the common good." (Calderon)
- "The emergence of a global consciousness, a critical mass of individuals realizing the potential of knowledge to leverage a universal process of sustainable development." (Carrillo)

- "Knowledge is shared all along the value and supply chain, using stakeholders as a source of knowledge." (Chiaromonte)
- "The government can act as an articulator and promoter of the interaction process (across government, companies and universities), aiming at the generation of innovation." (Cunha)
- "New meaning to the importance of combining human capital and structural capital." (Edvinsson)
- "Knowledge Economy, in a paradoxical way, is becoming the most equalizing force in the world/the West acquiring a humility which helps us become better citizens of the earth." (Evans)
- "Multinational groups with members out of different disciplines, forming and disbanding around their subjects of interest, enabling collaboration and innovation, both international and national/local, where valued intangibles materialize in increased quantity." (Fazekas)
- "I have a dream—technology will be our first resource to reach vast amounts of our population to allow them to access qualified knowledge without current limitations they are now facing." (Fernandez)
- "The more I give you, the more I have. The more I change, the more I have to change; I do not negotiate a contract, I negotiate a relationship. Thus, the invisible hand of the market must be accompanied by an invisible handshake." (Formica)
- "Knowledge is the unique resource for enterprises and individuals to live in a good manner in the New World." (Gasalla)
- "A shared virtual memory storing networked pieces of knowledge and automating the knowledge creation circle at the global scientific community level." (Gruetter)
- "Pay special attention and focus to solve the world development problems from a knowledge perspective and to get a consumer 'economically cultivated'." (Hidalgo)

- "Will give more value to people and use technology to better understand how to manipulate the knowledge hidden in people." (Kayakutlu)
- "A civil society in which noble managers of all types collaborate to produce the best goods and services. A society which respects, values, and uses the tolerant, equitable aspects of our heritage organizations in which smooth-talking, self-aggrandizing, exploitive managers are not successful." (Kennedy)
- "Real knowledge management is about the flow of meaning." (Kilpi)
- "The rise of newer kinds of economic goods and services that are digital in form, heavily dependent on knowledge and, in many respects, will transform today's technology information society into a digital/knowledge-based economy." (Kozmetsky)
- "Getting beyond the zero-sum game." (Kurtzke)
- "With knowledge being a universal language, this is a form of economy which will promote collaboration rather than competition or conflict, and one that promotes a business environment that reduces wastage of earth resources and human years due to replication and re-inventing wheels, insecurity and isolation." (Lau)
- "We will learn that there is nothing to hold, when we have the knowledge and we can (use) manage it, so we can do anything we think. We have to work on the borders of our mind to see the full potential." (Maciejewski)
- "Individuals, organizations and nations alike must reestablish their 'Value Quotient' based upon knowledge-driven innovation. Entitlement is dead. Exploitation of non-renewable natural resources is not sustainable, use knowledge and experience to create a new balance between need and resources on a global scale." (Macnamara)

- "Knowledge is comparable (but not identical or similar) with 'material' and 'energy'. Economy is always based upon knowledge." (Mahdjoubi)
- "A world in which you can access knowledge and use it to create value without restrictions." (Malpartida)
- "A new value-system in which people are motivated to exchange knowledge and do collaborative work." (Mercier-Laurent)
- "A World in which man would be at the service of man and not using him for his own benefit." (Montero)
- "The future of a World Economy." (Nguyen)
- "An economy that works for the people, by the people, and of the people. An economy that is not controlled or led, but supports a decent living for all." (Preiss)
- "Knowledge does not follow the rules of all economic resources; it is not scarce! It is not subject to the laws of diminishing returns! If we can find the way to leverage the intellectual capital of ourselves, of our firms and our communities, we can create a better future for us all." (Rabinovich)
- "Knowledge becomes the main engine of value-creation. Human beings and the quality of their relationships becomes the key determinant of success in this economy." (Saint-Onge)
- "When we discover the creative energy in one another's souls, then we have unlimited fuel for the Knowledge Economy. The real frontiers are within us as we learn to appreciate and value differences, unique differences, and learn that as we become energized as individuals, our Knowledge Economy will gain energy in new ways." (Savage)
- "Technological solutions for knowledge management, especially multimedia and 3D/VR." (Sihn)
- "Stop. Think. Listen. Learn. Understand what motivates other people, so that you can share your knowledge in a way that builds a truly collaborative win-win relationship." (Skyrme)

- "Big improvements for companies that structure and manage the strategic importance of knowledge." (Stokholm)
- "An Economy managed as if people matter." (Sveiby)
- "The Knowledge Economy will become the great equalizer between the haves and have-nots. People's mental machinery, their intelligence and attitude, is a greater resource than what they know or understand. Given that, and the increasing levels of education in many developing nations, we have the potential that people everywhere can participate in the knowledge economy on more equal terms than before." (Wiig)
- "A structure where innovation and sharing is facilitated and not left to chance, where individuals can obtain added knowledge by building on their competencies (converting training to a 'pull-system')" (Yearsley)
- "Society in which the knowledge assets become the core competitive power and creates value, the direction toward the new millennium." (Youn)
- "The Future is an 'Intellect Economy,' related to practice and action. Intellect integrates knowledge with capabilities. It's where the East and the West come together for mutual gain." (Zhouying)

Responses have also been synthesized to identify the trends of the new economy. In the next chapter, you will see the results that these interviews revealed and the cause for appreciation of the potential merits of this evolving superhighway as an innovation system. With the available technology, we have had a chance to put these experts in real-time dialog with one another.

10.5   TESTIMONY: VALUE OF THE GLOBAL NETWORK

Of course a collection of people—even organized according to various competencies and levels of affiliation does not a "network" make. People must take advantage of the affiliation with others on a local and global level. To structure the connections, we have analyzed the interview responses with source quotes according to the ten dimensions of innovation described in Chapter 11. In this way and through several months of electronic dialog, members have been exploring their relative interests and insights. In this way, the network becomes a business intelligence system for global learning.

In March 2002, the Network was selected as a finalist for the Competia Award[4] as Competitive Intelligence (CI) Champion of the Year. To participate, several members of the E100 document what they have observed and/or gained from affiliation:

- "The Entovation 100 is the most unique global and cross-organizational place where people in the Knowledge Management arena can be found." (Dr. Joerg Staeheli, Switzerland)
- "The methodologies—as well as networking brought forward by her work—are a true global entrepreneurial spirit for nourishing intellectual capital." (Leif Edvinsson, Sweden)
- "Entovation for me is a source of energy, passion, persistence, entrepreneurship, innovation, friendship and fun." (Dr Edna Pasher, Israel)
- "The Entovation network provides the best source of thinking and practice on knowledge innovation" (Chin Hoon Lau, Malaysia)
- "The Entovation Network addresses the essence of the key challenge we face in the knowledge era: the constant need to innovate for individuals, organizations and societies." (Hubert Saint-Onge, Canada)
- "Being part of the Entovation Network has helped us expand our readership to 6 continents, over 32 countries and more than 38 states and provinces in North America." (Zenia Stanford, Canada)
- "Thanks to the Entovation network, they can cohere in new intercultural groups for common purposes, whether for col-

laborative business projects or for sharing knowledge and creating new intangible values both in the business community and in the society." (Dr. Piero Formica, Italy)

- "We have been inspired by the depth and range of contacts—valuable perspectives from other countries—within the Entovation Network that have greatly enriched our work. (Dr. Charles Savage and Elisabeth Sundrum, Germany)

- "More deep knowledge sharing cannot be accomplished without this kind of network. Preventive-action meetings can most effectively be achieved through deep and well-thought collaboration of the individuals represented in the Entovation Network" (Dr. Akira "Stoney" Ishikawa, Japan)

- "The Entovation Network has provided a constant source of incredibly valuable, instant access to intellectual capital, and grow trusted personal networks for opportunities to connect, share, innovate, and add positive exponential value to initiatives and self-knowledge that otherwise would not be available individually or through any other resource." (Lynne Schneider, USA)

- "It has been a pleasure and an honor to be part of the Entovation Network. I've received many benefits from your personal competence and strong expertise, and from many network connections very useful to me both in my government job (managing knowledge workers) and in my non profit institution." (Dr. Jean Marc LeDuc, France)

- "The knowledge and insights brought through membership of the Entovation Knowledge Leadership Network have provided new ideas for contexts, concepts and processes necessary to embed knowledge as THE 21st century currency for economic and social prosperity." (Dr. Michael Kelleher, Wales)

- "I had not discovered knowledge innovation until later even though I have been working in this field for many years. Entovation has helped me put the work I have been doing into a proper context and system." (Ali Liban, Somalia)

- "Through the Entovation Network, Debra has been exceptionally skilled in building consensus and working complex issues that require collaboration—with sensitivity and resoluteness" (Dr. George Kozmetsky, USA)
- "Through Entovation, I have been involved in groundbreaking innovative research. The main challenge has been that our findings were ahead of their time. Now the world is catching up." (Jan Wyllie, UK)
- "The idea of new economy is coming through—more and more people start to understand the way of innovation and intellect power—the vision of global Entovation Network since my participation in 1995. It is interesting how the view has changed—from ambitious global visionary—to simple worker on the global vision." (Thomas Philip Maciejewski, Poland)
- "Through the Entovation contacts, we've opened the minds of colleagues; now we must do the same for policy makers in order to influence the kind of world we want our children to inherit." (Dr. Tom Malone, USA)
- "The Entovation 100, and the 10 Fellows represent the most knowledgeable and applied practitioners in the world when it comes to innovation, knowledge and leadership." (Doug Macnamara, Canada)
- "Thanks to Entovation that all the academicians working on the subjects have found each other. And thanks to all our virtual team that I have learned so much and become one a pioneer in my country." (Gulgun Kayakutlu, Turkey)
- "The Entovation Network helps me understand better the global development of economic systems and innovation as a part of them—innovation not only in business but in human relations as well. Building our National Innovation Programme." (Janis Stabulnieks, Latvia)

- "The Entovation Network brings real meaning in the concept of sharing knowledge and connecting people—where the focus truly is primarily on people and their collective know how. There is no restriction for innovative and entrepreneurial ideas to expose, which makes this a special place to me." (Dr. Manfred Bornemann, Austria)
- "Entovation is designed to put people and ideas in direct communication with each other and is build on trust and the willingness to share knowledge. A perfect example of the possibilities of this network was exhibited during Global Learn Day 2000 when some 60 members of the network in all the corners of the world met each other (sometimes for the first time) and shared their learning with each other and the audience." (Yvonne Buma, The Netherlands)
- "The dedication, as much as knowledge, kept me on track to a destination I only now realize—the birth of the Association of Knowledgework. How many more success stories can be told based on the wisdom and leadership of the Entovation Network?" (Jerry Ash, USA)
- "Knowledge involves scrutiny and dialogue. Knowledge involves not just retention through existing practices but also creatively disseminating that across the boundaries of organizations. This Entovation Network brought us together and more than that instilled in us a confidence that KM was not just a dry activity." (Dr. Parthasarathi Banerjee, India)
- "The Entovation Network is really unique experience promoting transformation of our Earth into one living intelligent community. (Konstantin M. Golubev, Ukraine)
- "In order to grow fruit we need a pip. In order to get a reaction we need a critical mass to produce it. Entovation acts both ways: as the nucleus of knowledge economy and the creator of the critical mass for its diffusion." (Dr. Ante Pulic, Austria)

- "With the cooperation of the whole Entovation network we hope to keep our leadership here in my country." (Luis Ovidio Galvis Caro, Columbia)
- "To my knowledge, Entovation is a first planetary Network of specialists coming from different domains and having common goal—to introduce a new way of thinking—with a collective intelligence. We learn from each other, share our experiences and innovate the future together." (Dr. Eunika Mercier-Laurent, France)
- "Amidst the twilight of transition, the role of working models and successful practices are immense. The Entovation Network has pioneered visionary practices in networking that sheds light and nurtures hopes in what a knowledge-based world might be like. This is one of the most concrete cases in virtual community making that we can identify as prototypes of the new paradigms." (Dr. F. Javier Carrillo Gamboa, Mexico)
- "The Entovation concept and implementation is a unique resource for KM professionals around the world and a unique community of brilliant and pioneering people." (Sally-Ann Moore, Switzerland)
- "We've been taught: Either Network or Not Work (thanks Stephen Rosen). The Entovation network has put the teaching into practice with dramatic clarity." (Dr. Parry Norling, USA)
- "The Entovation network is the cutting edge of where the world needs to go—they got there before anyone else." (Larraine Segil, USA)
- "The Entovation Network—especially the I3 Update/Entovation News is good resource for those creative people as a platform to exchange opinions, get some new ideas and cause new insights." (Jin ZhouYing, China)
- "The Entovation Network is more than a source of intelligence. It connects people to people, enabling analysts and innovators to tap into a highly talented global network of inno-

vation and knowledge leaders of various forward-looking communities around the world—a network of knowledge networks." (Dr. David J. Skyrme, UK)

- "Entovation—perhaps one of greatest intangible assets on the face of the planet—is a global community of organic knowledge and innovation that will help to shape a new world social currency." (Sante Delle Vergini, Australia)
- "Always in the network since almost 10 years—sharing, translating and (the attempt to) applying the concepts have made Entovation a permanent part of my life." (Stefan Fazekas, Austria)

10.6 SUMMARY

Knowledge resides in the minds and hearts of individuals who are called to action. This is one of the reasons that the knowledge—as opposed to the information or digital—economy provides a human and humane agenda. The challenge is to connect—with the support of a global technology infrastructure—the capacity to evolve a common language and create a shared vision of what the future might be and then act on it.

The Entovation Network has become a robust source of insight, which, when harnessed, has the capacity to impact multiple spheres of influence around the world—across functions, industries, and nations. It is an example of an integral facet of the innovation superhighway—a work in progress.

CHAPTER ENDNOTES

[1] The original article appears in Appendix E; for the translated versions, visit http://www.entovation.com/momentum/momentum.htm

[2] For access to the electronic version of the Map to visit members of the E100, see http://www.entovation.com/kleadmap/index.htm

[3] This is the conclusion first published in the Global Momentum of Knowledge Strategy in 1999. For translated versions of the original article, visit http://www.entovation.com/momentum/globalmn.htm

[4] Competia Inc. is a Canada-based company dedicated to competitive intelligence and strategic planning professionals worldwide. Visit http://www.competia.com

ELEVEN
Trends of Innovation Strategy

An idea can mobilize individuals
into a crusade in search of an ideal.
It can induce them to undo and redo
what they have done wittingly or unwittingly,
and to regain control over the whole
of what they are a part
and more importantly,
of themselves.

Russell L. Ackoff
Redesigning the Future

It was August 2000, and the conference was designed as a Davos-like meeting of the minds, but for the leaders of Austria. This annual meeting of Alpbach[1]—co-sponsored by the Austria Research Centers, the Federation of Austria Industry, and the Austrian Broadcasting Corporation—was a week-long activity dedicated to "Knowledge as a Production Factor." Hundreds were in attendance, with sessions ranging from Nobel laureates to children (ages 8 to 18) who participated in Junior Alpbach.

Perhaps Albert Hochleitner, Director General, Siemens Österrich, Vienna, and President of the Board, Austrian Research Centers, delivered one of the most telling presentations. He suggested that the world barriers are transparent. Achievements of the past are losing value. Today, we buy, sell, and use knowledge. Knowledge—and how to deal with it—is critical to surviving nations. There is a doubling of knowledge every five years. Size alone is no longer the yardstick for achievement. Along with suppliers, markets have grown. Customers used to rely on resource-based production; today, they can pick from many things. The focus on knowledge and the knowledge society is beyond the level of talk. Companies only use 40 percent of the knowledge of their staff[2]. This is reason for alarm.

Hochleitner provided three examples of why knowledge as a production factor has not been understood.

1. *Time.* There is little time allotted to deal with strategic planning. Less that 2 percent is spent on the future perspective. Some companies allow even less than 1 percent! Although the urgent business of everyday life is important, it is not as important as the future.

2. *Language.* When we deal with knowledge, there are few common terms and a lack of common instruments for implementation. Standard accounting is based on double-entry bookkeeping principles that remain unchanged. We cannot manage what we cannot measure; what we cannot count counts!

3. *Process of innovation.* There is a plethora of terms and terminology. Product innovation ignores process and social innovation. Innovation is often mixed up with invention! People can be creative only when they have "know-how." Gurus in the tower are obsolete as well as being wrong. There needs to be a visionary force as well as sober work and an adequate mindset that appreciates curiosity and an opportunity to shape the world. Therefore, it is not the facts, but our attitude toward innovation that matters. We must not underestimate.

When we are filled with fear in the new millennium, knowledge will not be disseminated automatically. It must be managed—mined, monitored, and sold. Hochleitner had several recommendations:

Knowledge has to be identified, knowledge must be distributed, and new knowledge must be acquired. He concluded, "Doubt may grow with the new knowledge economy; only those will survive who have an awareness of the enormous potential and are harnessing it. It is not enough to know, we must apply knowledge—we must do!"

11.1   META-VIEWS OF THE E100

Overall, progressive knowledge leaders see a shift from the focus on limited resources—financial, human, and technological—that pervaded the industrial age. With a grant from Siemens AG, we asked Jan Wyllie, CEO of Trend Monitor International,[3] to provide an in-depth analysis (below) of the fundamental trends synthesized from the course quotes of the E100 interviews. By determining key patterns, we have discovered the scope of collective findings among this diverse group of knowledge professionals. What follows are the five meta-views that arise from his process of concept mapping. Their comments have also been categorized according to the ten dimensions of innovation strategy (which appear later in this chapter) and will soon serve as the foundation of an electronic dialog on the topics individually and the methodology as a whole. The collective insights may be available in a new forthcoming intelligence service.

In the meantime, enjoy the identification of the trends below as a prospectus on the future we are innovating! At first blush, these identified trends might seem as though they come from Pollyanna. On the other hand, if these are legitimate, relevant observations of the shifts in our society, perhaps they do point a direction that can be embraced by veteran and new knowledge managers alike. The five meta-view developed at the conference, along with comments and questions, are summarized in Table 11.1.

TABLE 11.1   *The Five Meta-Views*

Meta-view 1: Economy to holonomy

A multifaceted conception of a world knowledge commonwealth replacing the world of nations is proposed as a means of going beyond the one-dimensional, zero-sum game of economics and interest-driven money. The knowledge commonwealth, which includes what we now classify as social and moral issues, could not be controlled or even led, although it might be balanced. In this new Eden, the Tree of Knowledge and the Tree of Life grow together "into one tree," as thinking about knowledge becomes less abstract and more conscious, more concerned with diversity and wisdom, than the struggle between right and wrong.

Comments

If the validity of both nations and companies is being questioned, the key drivers and supports for the Western consumer economy are likely to be rethought out of existence. A new, much more holistic concept of wealth is implied in which the importance of money as the measure of all things necessarily becomes diminished. One of the original reasons for forming nation-states was to curb human greed and aggression. It is ironic but hardly surprising that this artifice has had the opposite effect.

Question

Without the national state and corporate players as the main economic actors, who would the players be in a knowledge commonwealth?

Meta-view 2: Control to humility

The illusion that we can control the world using knowledge instruments, such as policy and the scientific method is being questioned. This new knowledge of ignorance concerning the ecology of which humans are merely a part, along with the Uncertainty Principle at its center, is more reminiscent of the nature of ancient knowledge in which humans were the humble subjects of nature rather than trying to be its masters.

TABLE 11.1 (continued)

Comments

This kind of ancient knowledge is illustrated by a recent quote from Hopi Indian Elders who have preserved this kind of ancient knowledge and applied it to our time. "There is a river flowing now very fast. It is so great and swift that there are those who will be afraid. They will try to hold on to the shore. They will feel they are being torn apart and will suffer greatly. Know that the river has its destination. The elders say we must let go of the shore, push off into the middle of the river, keep our eyes open, and our heads above the water. And I say, see who is in there with you and celebrate. At this time in history, we are to take nothing personally—least of all, ourselves. For the moment that we do, our spiritual growth and journey comes to a halt. The time of the lone wolf is over. Gather yourselves! Banish the word struggle from your attitude and your vocabulary. All that we do now must be done in a sacred manner and in celebration. We are the ones we have been waiting for."

Questions

From where does wisdom come? Does it come from possessing good knowledge? Or is it the source of good knowledge?

Meta-view 3: Knowing to imagining

It is suggested that imagination might be more valuable than knowledge.

Comments

When all is certain and understood, there is little need for imagination. When all is doubt and uncertainty, the imagination becomes a key survival tool. Without imagination it is impossible to consider and think about the unknown. Without imagination, there can be no living stories, only dead information. Innovation is the product of imagination, and so is adaptation.

Question

If imagination is at the root of all knowledge why do different forms of knowledge, such as arts and sciences, seem to pull in such different directions?

Table 11.1 (continued)

Meta-view 4: Limited to unlimited

The knowledge economy is seen as "fueled by creative energy" and a "well spring of limitless resources," because knowledge can grow exponentially as it is created and shared. With knowledge, people can learn to do what they think. Intangible knowledge assets are reported becoming more valuable than tangible assets.

Comments

The problem with concepts, such as exponential growth in a knowledge economy is that they try to put a quantitative value on qualitative change. Indeed part of the qualitative change may be to stop trying to put a quantitative value on intangible assets, such as knowledge.

Question

Is it meaningful to talk about an economy without modes of measurement?

Meta-view 5: Goals to aspirations

It appears that the goal is no less than the "redefinition" of the whole field of management in response to "kaleidoscopic change" which demands "new forms of measurement, learning strategies, leveraging of technology, and new modes of interaction, both inside and external to the organization." Other Entovation Fellows feel that organizations should be mission oriented, self-directed—and happy—in order to be productive and to "replicate opportunities,." Managing intellectual capital is seen as a way of giving more value to customers than managing products and services. The goal of knowledge, which is conceived as multicultural and multidisciplinary, is to transform people and organizations "from within." More emphasis needs to be given to practice and information than to theory and technology. Both technical knowledge and information—both for and about customers—are necessary for "world development" and the "economically cultivated" consumer.

TABLE 11.1 (continued)

Comments

Until quite recently, an organization's main challenges were to chart a course using strategic planning, for example, and then to stay on course despite being buffeted by the waves of change. The core assumption was that the co-ordinates of direction—North/South, profitable/unprofitable, right/wrong, progress/regress—remained constant like latitude and longitude on the map. Organizations could be blown off course, they could even change course, but at least they would know where they were. Now the challenge is to thrive in a chaotic, complex, and unpredictable—kaleidoscopic—flow of opportunities and dangers in which an organization's habitual coordinates no longer seem to apply.

Questions

If the goal is to look for new coordinates—new values—to guide our perceptions and decisions, in which direction should we look? How might we navigate?

11.2   TEN DIMENSIONS OF INNOVATION STRATEGY[4]

These interviews provided rich source quotes to identify the emerging trends according to the ten dimensions of innovation strategy (see Figure 3.2). Of course, what is represented below was limited to the questions of the interview: "What are your roots in the knowledge field? Who has influenced you and why? What have you been able to accomplish? What still needs to be done? What is your vision of a knowledge economy?"

The results are also constrained by the backgrounds and perspectives of the participants. Every effort was made to include a diversity of functions, sectors, industries, and nations, both developing and industrialized nations. What follows should be a good beginning, however, for what might constitute part of the research effort outlined in the final chapter of this book to create The Innovation Superhighway.

What follows have been synthesized into a series of documents entitled *Voice of the Entovation 100* (Amidon and Wyllie, 2002). They are detailed according to the interdependent facets of knowledge strategy outlined in Figure 11.1 below.

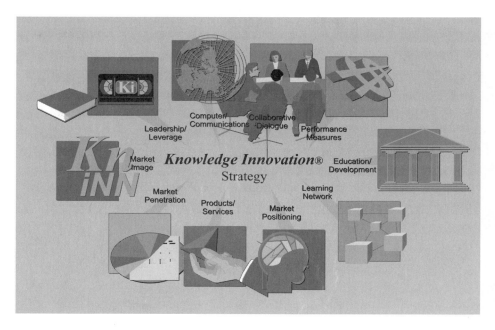

FIGURE 11.1:   *Dimensions of knowledge innovation strategy.*

1.   Focus on Collaborative Process

During the past few years, we have seen a dramatic shift from competitive strategies to the value of collaboration. This modern management modus operandi comes from an explosion in virtual networks, cross-boundary interaction, and the development of shared purpose. Many progressive enterprises—private and public—are realizing that managing the process explicitly is a path toward more sustainable innovation. Knowledge leadership has become a matter of being able to create value through collective competencies often harnessed through vertical and diagonal initiatives versus the traditional hierarchical management techniques.

1.   *Company to community.* The validity of the current concepts of abstract corporate legal entities is being questioned as being part of the discredited rationalist doctrine, which separates

mind and body and thoughts and emotions. A new community value system based on compassion is advocated.

2. *Collaboration to cohesion.* It now almost goes without saying that collaborative relationships are being increasingly emphasized at the corporate level. Competition remains the dominant paradigm at the level of the nation state. Here is the first indication that beyond collaboration, there exists another, more intense, relationship, called cohesion.

3. *Communities of practice to shared meaning.* When the certainties of our era dissolve before our eyes into chaos, the time has come to make new meanings. Sharing best practice is not about asking the question "why"; sharing meaning is.

4. *Security to trust.* Cheating in an open knowledge-trading environment is not sustainable, since it would quickly lead to exclusion. Trust and reliability are seen as becoming more important, as security and contractual enforcement become less certain.

2. Focus on Performance Measures

Perhaps the most dramatic changes as a result of this new knowledge economy has been in performance measures—a new form of knowledge economics if you will. The primary resource to be monitored —and even measured, as many would suggest—is the intangible value of an organization. It is no longer sufficient to measure only financial indicators of an enterprise, a nation, or a global economy for that matter, for there are too many other significant variables contributing to sustainability or prosperity. The traditional balance sheet measures the past, but indicators for the future are needed. The accounting profession has aggressive plans for guidelines and several companies—and countries—have come forth with their own methods for intellectual capital reporting.

1. *Realizing value to creating value.* That knowledge can create an explosion in value without using physical resources is now held to be self-evident. In the world of physical things knowledge is also universally credited with enabling people to produce more with less. So intangible assets are seen as being more valuable than tangible assets, while stories are portrayed as being more valuable than theories. Physical things are seen as losing their intrinsic value and are valued according to their role in an active process.

2. *Single measure to multiple measures.* "The financials" are increasingly portrayed as taking the back seat to other values (e.g., relationships, people, and image) as a result of the need for new performance measures beyond mere cost efficiency. Knowledge is seen as needing to be managed and evaluated in terms of its contribution to competitive advantage and recorded on company balance sheets as "intangible assets" or "intellectual capital." New performance indicators listed by participants include the quality of company mission statements, the "balance scorecard," capacity for knowledge re-use, national accounts on knowledge competence, staff turnover, and customer loyalty.

3. *Dis-alignment to re-alignment.* The knowledge agenda in organizations has been traditionally blocked by business and financial practices that were set up to deal with a reality in which the name of the additive game is acquiring more. At best, knowledge serves as a means to this end. It is being discovered that knowledge can be neither counted nor managed according to these precepts. It cannot be added, although it can be combined in mysterious ways. As the role of knowledge in the pursuit of purpose becomes better understood, organizations that manage their assets according to traditional financial values are seen as being dysfunctional in that knowledge and

purpose—accountability and responsibility—are seriously out of alignment.

In countries that do not have the Western financial traditions, the trouble is seen as replacing family and community "cronyism" with Western-style financial discipline. At the same time, the knowledge movement is bringing the self-same financial system into question.

The meaning of trust in the non-Western financial context is much less abstract, more concrete, and much more complex. Ironically, the focus on knowledge is making the abstract trust of the financial transaction insufficient as the binding agent of the knowledge economy.

4. *Get-rich-quick to perseverance.* Perseverance furthers in the knowledge field that is definitely not a get-rich-quick option. Time is the most essential value.

3.   Focus on Education And Training

The focus on knowledge and innovation (i.e., how to put knowledge into action) has provided a common language across functions, sectors, stakeholders, and nations. Education–based strategies are seen as an equalizer between industrialized and developing nations. There is evidence of a major shift from teacher-oriented to learning-centered education strategies enabled by advanced technologies and the explosion of Internet and intranet communications. Learning occurs throughout all activities of the enterprise, not just the classroom. Progressive approaches are designed to be more "pragmatic," yielding performance results, but a balance is needed between the traditional academic approaches and the practical, "real-time" application of learnings, such as industrial incubators, lessons-learned initiatives, and the like. Story telling as a documentation and deployment mechanism has enabled very complex concepts and results to be transferred readily. Since the 1980s, learning has been the path to developing "competitive advantage," but now the process may be more "collaborative" in scope—across the boundaries of functional responsibilities or even inside and external to the enterprise. National initiatives using learning as the rubric for change are focused on building a better standard of living through knowledge sharing and innovation.

1. *Education to learning.* Although differences in knowledge are portrayed as separating people, the similarities in innate attributes such as intelligence are seen as "the great equalizer" through education and knowledge sharing. Story telling is recommended as more "compelling" than academic theory in the process of learning, as is direct contact with nature.

2. *Academic to practical.* Participants from developing countries mainly espouse a tension between an "academic" approach, based on studying history, theory, and cases, and the more "pragmatic" approach advocated by a UK participant.

3. *National institutions to innovative networks.* Education is seen to be the key to national success in a global knowledge economy. National success is portrayed in terms of a "better society and quality of life" obtained by people "building on their competencies" through knowledge sharing and innovation.

4. Focus on Distributed Networks

There has been a dramatic shift from hierarchical management to networked learning systems in which all stakeholders—both inside and outside the enterprise—become a source of knowledge. Networked management requires different leadership skills based on inspiration and innovation (i.e., acting upon one's learnings). Motivation comes within the individual, and much success may depend on an understanding of the whole system, involving new views of the management landscape that are holistic in scope. Gone—well, for the most part —are the value chains of activity that have yielded to more robust networked systems in which learning is a two-way street at every point of interaction. The questions of course are how people are receptive to the ideas of others and how they will capitalize on their complementary competencies rather than re-inventing the wheel—a characteristic of an inventive, but not innovative community.

1. *Questioning to initiating.* The main challenge is seen as questioning tradition—"escaping from tacit models"—with the objective of creating wider, more holistic views. One participant warns, "When we do not recognize our own ideas as models of reality, we tend to think of them as the 'truth.'"

2. *Believing to understanding.* Understanding is seen to be the primary means that people have for acting more intelligntly. However, understanding is being severley impaired by the difficulty of assimilating huge amounts of information, the lack of knowledge about intellectual tools, as well as widespread ignorance when it comes to a basic theory of knowledge.

3. *Persuading to inspiring.* Certain individuals are cited multiple times by participants as inspiring re-thinking. The most valuable assets in this new way of looking at things are seen as residing in people's minds and therefore being "as yet" impossible to represent on a balance sheet. The inability to persuade the wider management community of the significance of knowledge innovation is still regretted and is blamed on the continued inability to measure the yield of these kinds of assets.

4. *Instinctual to systems approach.* Despite continuing doubts about how to apply rules and methods to tacit and "experience" knowledge, the value of systematization is recognized, as are the processes of knowledge acquisition and assimilation. Having an open mind to other cultures is seen to be an important source of innovation. Early success is reported in the "complex new metrics" used to measure the value of intellectual capital, while the first standards are said to be "emerging."

5. Focus on Competitive Intelligence

Where it used to be a function of competitive business/market/nation positioning, the rules of the game may have changed. Being competitive used to be a function of understanding the product development capability and business strategy. Today, one must innovate—create ideas and put them into products and services—in advance of the competition. To do so requires a more fundamental understanding of their capacity to innovate and how they collaborate (i.e., their alliance/partner strategy) to get to market. Business intelligence, then, is far more a function of knowing where and how a competitor is going and, then, innovating faster. Success in the new economy is a function of creating new markets; so studying best practices has only limited value.

1. *Size of the enterprise to the innovation capacity.* The development and exploitation of knowledge assets is seen to be the main determining factor in competitive success, whether between people, companies, or countries. The importance of knowledge assets is made even greater by the trend toward globalization. According to one participant, "in [the] Global Economy, it is not size, but innovation that leads to success."

2. *Competition to collaboration.* The opportunities afforded by a dynamic knowledge economy require a flexibility of strategy from competitive to collaborative. Customers can be alliance partners and/or competitors. A highly flexible, adaptive response to a given situation is the only path to success.

3. *Product development to alliance strategy.* It used to be enough to monitor the technology/product development or market strategy of an enterprise to be competitive, but today's market requires an understanding of who is partnering with whom to what end.

4. *Business strategy to innovation strategy.* Monitoring a competitor used to be a function of understanding its business strategy. In today's economy, it is required to have a sense of the competi-

tor's capacity to innovate and how integral that might be to its competitive advantage.

6. Focus on New Products And Services

As the innovation cycle has accelerated and the potential for new markets has increased with the global economy, the opportunity to create knowledge-intensive products, markets, and services has grown exponentially. Subthemes might include smart cards, nanotechnology, robotics, and intelligent learning agents. No longer is the services sector considered the knowledge sector; manufacturing environments rely equally on the leveraging of knowledge in new products and services. Simultaneously, the world has become more cognizant of environmental factors and is looking toward ecological systems as a foundation for new product development. Focus has shifted from analysis of materials and technologies toward how new product ideas—coming throughout the enterprise—can be incubated successfully and expeditiously.

1. *Manufacturing to the services sector.* The Industrial Age relied on scarce resources—land, labor, and capital. The knowledge economy relies upon the bountiful resource of knowledge that operates as a multiplier—the more it is shared, the more it grows. The services industry is well equipped to capitalize on the rapid growth in potential of knowledge-intensive businesses.

2. *Product development cycle to incubation.* Traditional value-chain methodologies—although highly effective—may not be enough in a market that requites continuous innovation of new products and services. There is a need to identify breakthrough technologies and methodologies and provide the necessary incubation capability to enable good ideas to be developed for the market and/or to create new markets.

3. *Economy to ecology.* Global consciousness based on a critical mass of individuals sharing both knowledge and meaning is seen as the way to ecological and economic sustainability. Knowledge professionals are expected to become increasingly "key players" in the world of trade in a "dematerialized" economy. Product life cycles are predicted to be short with waves of new, more complex generations of products spawned by intensive innovation.

4. *Products from materials/technology to intelligent products.* There has been a shift from a focus on technology and materials to the value of knowledge applied to technology. This provides one foundation for smart products and "intelligent series" that will become the backbone of the new knowledge economy.

7. Focus on Strategic Alliances

With heightened global competition and acceleration of product and service life cycles, it is increasingly evident that organizations are unlikely to meet market demands in and of themselves. Essentially, no enterprise is an island. In today's economy, partnering—and successfully managing strategic alliances—is becoming the norm, not the exception. Many of the well-tested competitive management tactics of the industrial era are not suitable for the collaboration strategies of the knowledge era. If it is true that enterprises will rely more on knowledge external to the organization for their own future success, then the art of managing strategic alliances will become ever more critical in the coming decade. Managing such complex relationships requires both foresight and skill to leverage the competencies from which both or all parties might benefit.

1. *Self-interest to group interest.* Alliances are seen as being necessary not just between companies but also between learning institutions and governments, with the goal of replacing "temporary cooperation" with "lasting partnerships" facilitated by

methods for matching offers and wants. The boundaries between nonprofit and for-profit activity are reported as becoming increasingly blurred.

2. *Internal knowledge to external knowledge.* With increased erosion of boundaries—functional, sectoral, and national—the enterprise is being defined as "extended" to include stakeholders (e.g., suppliers, distributors, investors, alliance partners, customers, and even competitors) whose knowledge may be germane to a successful business strategy.

8. Focus on market/customer interaction

Communication—both internal and external—is not often considered an integral part of the innovation process. As global competition has intensified and relationships with customers (and other stakeholders for that matter) become increasingly more important (and more difficult), enterprises are realizing that communication of important information—and knowledge—is critical. Market perception, regardless of accuracy, can make or break the competitive positioning of an organization. Further, the relationship with external sources. especially customers, may be the key to future products and services. "Learning from" and "innovating with" the customer may become a survival tactic for organizations—profit and not-for-profit. Multimedia technologies afford communications to be more multifaceted than ever.

1. *Proactive marketing to interactive partnerships.* The relationship with the customer is seen as changing from proactive marketing to interactive partnerships, as external opportunities replace internal efficiency as the focus of management strategy. Successful marketing in the knowledge economy is reported to be coming from "swarms" of start-up enterprises achieving "hyper-growth" by selling the most advanced products.

2. *Print media to multimedia.* Internet-enabled technologies provide a broader reach for even the smallest enterprise. What may

have once been considered marketing propaganda, becomes essential in many ways to making the case for a given product or service.

9.   Focus on Leadership/leverage

The knowledge economy demands a very different form of leadership—one that is visible internally as well as to the outside world. Leaders are visionary and see the broader picture. They are holistic in their analysis and systematic in their implementation. They have the capability to inspire others to action with effective communications skills. They know how to operate in teams and create a culture of openness, curiosity, innovation, and learning. Further, they can articulate their insights and aspirations externally by being visible in public forums, authoring articles and books, and being respected for their candor and passion. In short, the leaders are learners and espouse a similar ethic with everyone with whom they come in contact.

1.   *Direction to purpose.* Personal drivers making people take on the knowledge challenge are described as a "passion." a "mission," or a desire to "make a difference." Leaders intend to be at "leading edge" where the people are, rather than the "bleeding edge" of development. For others, the purpose is to learn how to change peoples' mental models and to discover why people won't act until it is too late. Many believe that the purpose should be to let go of the simplistic notions of the industrial era, which are so deeply embedded in the woodwork of our intellectual and emotional thinking.

2.   *Toleration to honor.* Honoring other people's culture, intellectual property rights, and motivation by listening, learning, and trust are seen as increasingly important attributes of leadership. In this kind of "authentic partnership" focusing on the process, rather than an us versus them, win or lose result is said to ensure that what needs to be done is done "effortlessly."

3. *Managing to helping.* The nature of leadership is seen as assisting expert workers to achieve (both) their personal and common purposes, rather than setting goals and strategies. One of the common purposes of the kind of knowledge organizations is the benefit of workers and their families.

10. Focus on Computer/communications Technology

The explosion of acceptance of intranets, the Internet, multimedia and collaboration technologies, wireless devices—not to mention e-business, e-learning, e-commerce, etc.—has accelerated the potential foundation for the innovation superhighway. Technology has become a learning tool on the desktop and in the home. Electronic systems, however, are not only mechanisms to serve as a repository of knowledge; they are vehicles to facilitate innovation conversations across borders that increase the global reach of enterprises and the individual entrepreneur.

1. *Internet viewed as promotion to viewed as a learning tool.* Rather than being perceived as another illustration of product brochures or dissemination of annual reports and white papers, progressive companies are realizing the value of learning from those who visit the website in interactive ways.

2. *Passive to interactive.* Technology has previously been perceived as vehicles for diffusion. Recipients are just that—receivers of timely information. We are seeing a shift toward the technology serving more as a vehicle for interaction—an exchange rather than a delivery of information.

3. *Artificial assistant to alien intelligence.* Although the belief is still strong that knowledge creation and thinking can be automated, the implications for the human population of the world are widely seen as cause for concern. Really useful automated knowledge tools are perceived as scarce.

4. *Productivity tools to collaborative technologies.* Knowledge strategy began as an instrument of cost savings and efficiency. It evolved into a tool for decision making. Progressive managers are seeing the value of using the technology infrastructure for learning—person-to-person, team-to-team, function-to-function, and nation-to-nation.

11.3   CASE STUDY: CONSORTIUM FOR ADVANCED MANUFACTURING INTERNATIONAL (CAM-I)[5]

How do these dimensions get put into operation? How does an enterprise—or a collection of enterprises—complete an assessment and build a strategy to leverage its intellectual capital and competencies to ensure its own profitability or prosperity—whichever the case may be. What follows is just one example how the methodology might be used:

The Consortium for Advanced Manufacturing (CAM-I) was founded by a group of manufacturers from the aerospace and defense industries in 1972. Its ongoing role has been to create "communities of interest" in which experts from around the world can collaborate to solve problems that are common to their organizations. CAM-I's original efforts involved research into factory automation issues such as advanced robotics and numerical control of machine tools. It produced a number of ANSI standards through the face-to-face interaction of experts from member manufacturing companies. Today, membership includes over sixty companies in North America, Europe, and Asia working to create solutions to critical business problems through a unique and evolving process for intercompany and international collaboration. The knowledge innovation assessment tool was used by the CAM-I to evaluate the innovation capacity of its cost management system (CMS) program.

In 1998, a group of CMS members and staff completed the ten-part innovation assessment. The goal of the exercise was to better understand the KI assessment tool and to create a tacit awareness of the strengths, weaknesses, and opportunities inherent in the CMS program's collaborative processes. The value of the instrument is twofold: (1) it creates an opportunity for key participants in the innovation process to perform an objective assessment of their competencies and structures; and (2) perhaps more important, it creates a vehicle for dialog about the key dimensions of innovation. The radar chart that resulted from the assessment of the cost management systems program is represented in Figure 11.2.

Using the assessment tool, they concluded that the CMS program is more competent and well balanced with regard to external capabilities than internal capabilities. The nature of the CAM-I organization, consisting of professional staff directing and supporting an international network of industry practitioners and subject-matter experts, seems to discourage the development of formal structures, perform-

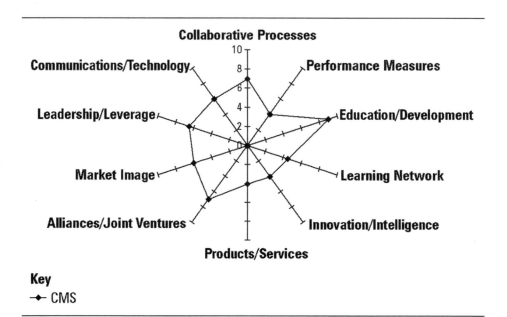

FIGURE 11.2 *CMS innovation assessment.*

ance measures, and documented procedures. Completing the assessment highlighted a few areas in which better documentation and more formal measurement systems could potentially lead to growth and increased flexibility and adaptability within the organization. It also highlighted a unique opportunity for CAM-I to use the unique skill sets of its member engineers, technologists. and accountants with extensive experience in creating activity-based metrics. They can make a critical contribution to the advancement of innovation within any organization. The following paragraphs will highlight some of the learning about strengths and opportunities that resulted from our assessment.

11.3.1   Internal Capabilities

Collaborative process

This is an area in which the CMS program is generally most effective. The nature of the interactions between our industry participants is the main vehicle for value creation. Most of the opportunities in this area result from the lack of structure and documentation around the innovation process. Most of the knowledge of the process is tacit and is transferred informally by seasoned participants to newcomers. Further, explicit recognition of the innovation process could lead to new products or intellectual assets that would create value for members. CAM-I has a very productive collaboration process. The ability of members to replicate that process to create communities of practice within their organizations could be of substantial value.

Performance measures

There is a limited formal measurement system to assess the effectiveness of the members and the staff in creating new innovations. Formal performance measures for staff are tied to level and quality of participation. The lack of formal performance metrics is largely due to the perceived difficulty in quantifying the ongoing effectiveness of the collaboration process. Given the learning that was generated from the assessment and the unique competence of CAM-I members in this area, there is an opportunity to create formal performance measures and objectives around selected dimensions of the innovation assessment. Some of the possible measures will be developmental (creating appropriate structures). while others will be ongoing (sustaining the innovation process). The development of appropriate objectives and measures is one of the key opportunities that the assessment exposed.

Education and development

Given that the CMS program is a forum for continuing education and learning, this was an area of particular strength. In fact, almost every question in the assessment generated a favorable response. The biggest opportunity in this area is to develop structures and approaches to more effectively capture the tacit or fugitive knowledge of the group that emerges during the face-to-face meetings and share that knowledge with the participants at large as well as with other members of their organizations. Audio and videotaping and collecting and sharing notes from structured breakouts and Internet message forums are all being explored to capture this knowledge.

Distributed learning network

While CAM-I does have programs that operate very effectively on an international basis, the CMS program activities are largely centered in North America. The barriers to face-to-face interactions that are created by international time and travel constraints have not been effectively overcome. One of the developmental opportunities that are currently being addressed is the increased use of Internet tools to connect geographic regions and diverse centers of excellence. However, we are still learning how to effectively use this medium to support international collaboration.

Innovation intelligence

While CMS is the acknowledged world leader in management research using the consortium model, increasing connectivity and ease of knowledge transfer are breaking down the barriers to collaboration. As a result, the barriers to informal and ad hoc collaboration are eroding. An important opportunity for the program will be to continually canvass for new collaboration processes and incorporate the emerging practices into the consortium model, thus reducing the effectiveness of the organization and increasing the speed and lowering the cost of collaboration.

Addressing the challenges outlined in the internal categories will ensure that the CMS program continues to be recognized as the foremost organization worldwide for the advancement of cost and performance management research. Meeting the improvement opportunities highlighted by the assessment and formalizing the innovation and knowledge transfer process should continually improve the effectiveness of the organization in creating and transferring knowledge. In this respect, use of the tool has brought the organization into awareness of growth opportunities similar to those that would be identified using the continuous improvement processes of the quality movement.

11.3.2   External Capabilities

Products and services

This dimension is the weakest area for the CMS program with regard to external capabilities. To a large degree, the collaboration process is the value-added activity for members. Members "own" the intellectual capital that results from their investment and in-kind participation. For several years we have held this research as proprietary to our members and offered only limited printed distribution of the work. However. we discovered that the change agents who participate in CAM-I need a broader set of tools to transfer the knowledge within their own companies. As a result, we have expanded our product and service offerings during the past three years to include books and other publications, best practice studies, conferences, workshops, and training. However, there are still additional opportunities to "unbundle" our products and to create more diverse opportunities for participation and knowledge transfer. This is perhaps the area where the organization can create the most immediate growth opportunities.

Alliances and joint ventures

This is an area of particular strength for CAM-I and particularly the CMS program. Partnerships with other organizations for activities as diverse as joint research, conferences and workshops, best practice studies, and joint publications is common. This is an area that the program will continue to pursue very aggressively in order to create the maximum leverage from its investments.

Market image campaign

Aggressive marketing is a relatively new area of competence for the CMS program. The new strategy includes promotions that include conferences to highlight ongoing research, frequent publications in respected industry periodicals, and exhibitions at relevant trade shows and conferences. The challenge of developing promotional messages that fully capture the relevance of the organization's products and services is an ongoing challenge as well as an improvement opportunity that was highlighted by the assessment.

Leadership and leverage

The Program Director and the chairpersons for the research projects play a key role in establishing and maintaining a leadership position for the CMS program in industry. Speaking opportunities, frequent publications, and service on committees and panels are activities frequently undertaken. While this is an area of strength for the program, the assessment highlights the importance of maintaining on ongoing focus on leading thinking.

Communications and technology

Aggressive development of communications technology has led to a world-class tool set for international collaboration via the private member's areas on the CAM-I Web site. An opportunity still exists for improving the state of practice for virtual collaboration. A good deal of training and conditioning is still needed to reinforce consistency in the use of information technology to support collaborative research.

11.4   Key Findings

The assessment is a useful tool for helping organizations evaluate their innovation structures and capabilities. The dialog that occurs between the participants during the assessment is a valuable outcome. It may be useful as organizations record the assessment on audio tape or video-tape the conversations so that the findings can be captured for further evaluation. There may be an opportunity to add scoring or weighting criteria to the assessment to allow organizations to fine-tune their critical success factors and to cause participants in the evaluation to be more precise with their observations and to build greater consensus through dialog and debate.

For the CMS program, the assessment was useful for creating an explicit recognition of the strengths and weaknesses of the organization. By acknowledging these dimensions of performance, the participants are forced to engage in a dialog about improvement opportunities. "How can we better leverage the strengths of the organization and its processes?" "How can we develop structures and processes to support our competencies and improve on our weaknesses?" Further, involving members and staff in the assessment helped us to move toward consensus about what the critical value-creating processes of the organization are and how to measure and improve their performance.

The use of the assessment tool to qualify and quantify the performance of the CMS program and its innovation processes supports one of the fundamental management axioms developed by the program:

- You can't manage what you don't communicate
- You can't communicate what you don't measure
- You can't measure what you don't define
- You can't define what you don't understand

11.5 Summary:

Too little attentions is given to vision activities—the strategies that sustain an organization over time. Too little attention is given to how best to utilize the intellectual capital of an enterprise, public or private. Too much time is given to the short-term fragmented initiatives at the expense of launching holistic and systematic strategies. This need not be the case.

Of course, there is no sure way to predict the future. Indicators are fuzzy at best. This "innovation frontier" leads us into uncharted waters not familiar to managers unfamiliar with—or worse, resistant to—modern management technologies. But, it is succeeding in the difficult tasks that challenge an enterprise and its leadership to distinguish themselves.

Thanks to some of the progressive methodologies and the managerial leadership willing to take "responsible risks," we are discovering that trend analysis based on concept mapping may have some value. If you can define, however sketchily, plausible trends (and the speed of acceleration), an organization may be able to capitalize upon what some might suggest is (almost) inevitable.

In the case of the E100, we are able to discern some of the meta-views providing a foundation for our future. Further, the trends can and must be analyzed according to the process of innovation in order to make strategies operational and effective. The case studies will emerge more rapidly than we think when enterprise leaders realize that they have more to gain from sharing their "story" with others than practicing outdated competitive tactics.

Chapter Endnotes

[1] The detailed report of the ALPBACH 2000 conference can be found at http://www.entovation.com/gkp/alpach.htm.

[2] Many other knowledge experts would consider this a very modest figure.

[3] For more information on the process and other recent trend reports, visit http://www.trendmonitor.com/.

[4] These dimensions are outlined—complete with an assessment—in Chapters 7 and 8 of *Innovation Strategy for the Knowledge Economy* and can be found at http://www.entovation.com/services/tensteps.htm.

[5] Copyright © Consortium for Advanced Manufacturing International (CAM-I). Article originally appeared in *The Journal of Knowledge Management*, vol. 3, no. 1, 1999, pp. 61–65. Reprinted with permission. For further information contact: www.cam-i.org.

PART IV

~

Innovation Leadership in Practice

TWELVE

Modern Knowledge Leadership: the 7Cs

Many mornings I wake up
with a cold gray stone of fear in my solar plexus—
fear that I really do matter…
fear that being afraid won't stop me any more.
If the discovery has frightened me,
it has awakened me
It explains me to myself in a way that says
I have integrity and dignity.
It says that not only can I make a difference, but
I am the difference.

Remarks recorded in
The Aquarian Conspiracy[1]

A new economic world order is emerging—one based on the flow of intellectual, not financial, capital. It is based on emerging concepts of knowledge information and collaboration. Every function, every industry and every region of the world, developing and industrialized nations alike, is experiencing profound changes in the way we manage our most precious resource—human talent. Modern management concepts are evolving from practitioners, not the theoretical academic research base. Leading (and being led) is more a function of navigation and networking than of the traditional command-and-control systems with which we are familiar.

Most astute executive managers have seen beyond the limitations of an information society, technology-enamoured strategies, and the dot.com phenomenon. Modern leaders do not fear the speed of change; they embrace an agenda of learning. They know that effective management is not a matter of having the most knowledge; it is more a matter of knowing how to use it. It is not enough to know modern management concepts and how they get implemented (i.e., put into action). Leadership is more an art than a science, but that doesn't excuse us for searching for appropriate metrics for return-on-leadership (ROL). This or the "new" ROI (i.e., return-on-innovation) might represent possible new performance metrics. In short, enterprises—public and private—must learn to innovate faster than their competitors. We must develop an innovation leadership competence and find out how to measure the performance thereof.

At the heart of the current transformation is the human being within whom knowledge resides. And the path to a sustainable future is an ability to innovate—to create knowledge, convert it into viable products and services, and apply it for the profitable growth of an enterprise, the vitality of a nation's economy, and the advancement of society. It is that simple and that complex.

There is certainly nothing new about the link of knowledge and progress. Since man began to interact with his environment, what he knew was essential for survival. What is different about the knowledge economy is our ability to focus on and manage knowledge—individual and collective—more explicitly. Because of the multiplier effect of knowledge—the more it is shared, the more it grows—we are now evolving a view of executive development demanding a new style of leadership behavior.

The agricultural, industrial, and short-lived information ages utilized linear, competitive, market-share oriented management models. The new economy is far more a function of a system dynamic based on intangible variables—intellectual capital, alliances and partnering, and global communications, both human and technical. Strategic plans, although essential, are not enough to command sustained market positioning. Progress is more a function of strategy; and strategy is the art of effective leadership.

12.1   How Does Leadership Differ In A Knowledge Economy?[2]

Gone are the days when one could measure the effectiveness of employee training and professional development based on the number of days or hours spent on courses. Most business resources are considered in a cost-valuation framework. Leadership must have an impact on the individual and the organization. Real value is created when connections are made between seemingly isolated elements. Margaret J. Wheatley (1992) suggests,

> *The literature on organizational innovation is rich in lessons…[it] describes processes that are also prevalent in the natural universe. Innovation is fostered by information gathered from new connections; from insights gained from journeys into other disciplines or places; from active, collegial networks and fluid, open boundaries. Innovation arises from circles of exchange, where information is not just accumulated or stored, but created. Knowledge is generated anew from connections that weren't there before.*

Twenty-first century leadership demands more vision and visibility. It is not only a function of learned behaviors, but also of how those behaviors demonstrate impact. With global communications, there will be a perceived leveling of competence. Knowledge obsolesce will accelerate. The "digital divide" could exacerbate the gap between the haves and have-nots; but the human (as opposed to the information or technology) agenda will place the emphasis on all people and all cultures—where it belongs! Real-time learning will become the critical success factor for prosperity in both the public and private sectors. Leaders used to focus on "leading" the organization. Tomorrow's leaders will be perceived more as local, national, regional, and international statesmen (and women) who are able to effectively balance economics, education, and the environment.

12.2 REDEFINING THE MANAGEMENT AGENDA

We live in a world of kaleidoscopic change. It is not the speed of change of a variable, or the speed of change of multiple variables. It is the compounding effect of the speed of change of multiple variables creating a landscape for innovation that challenges even the most adept manager. As detailed in Chapter 2, there is a new knowledge value proposition. Cost, quality, and time are no longer the differentiators for market positioning. It is a far more complex relationship between economics, technology, and behavior—sociological, psychological, and managerial—that constitutes the "social capital" of an organization.

In the following subsections we identify seven domains where we might (re)consider the implications for knowledge leadership.

12.2.1 Knowledge Leadership Is a Matter of Context

In the new knowledge/human capital orientation (see Table 12.1), performance metrics are dynamic and based on measuring the intangibles. Organizational structures are networked with self-managing knowledge workers. The processes transcend organization boundaries, linking all stakeholders (e.g., suppliers, alliance partners, distributors, customers, and even competitors) to a strategic innovation system. Information technology is used for knowledge processing—monitoring the flow of knowledge (i.e., how ideas are generated and commercialized).

Most important, it is not one orientation—financial or human—at the expense of another. Both are necessary to ensure optimal flexibility, adaptability, and agility.

Effective knowledge leadership is also a function of vision—and will increasingly be more so. Yet, according to Albert Hochleitner, Director General, Siemens Österrich, "Less than 2 percent of our time is spent on the future perspective. Some companies are even lower than 1 percent! Although the urgent business of everyday life is important, it is not as important as the future."[3] The reality is that executives know that visioning is important; but they haven't a clue as to how to effectively implement given such accelerating uncertainty.

It may not be that the "knowledge leader" is the one to create the vision—far from it. He or she must, however, create the frame within which the vision can be created by a critical mass of organization stakeholders. The leader manages the innovation infrastructure within which ideas are generated and applied. It is a function of listening, guiding thought, and cross-leveraging insights. Once created, the vision can and must be articulated broadly, both inside and outside the firm.

Today's leaders must inspire passion for the work. They need to ensure that teams are stable enough to meet the high-frequency burst of information and complex demands on decision making. They must have an ability to help others maintain focus and balance as they establish priorities. They lead by example, they walk the talk, and they fundamentally understand the "whole." They are able to convey context and meaning in ways that enable others to leverage their own talents.

12.2.2   Knowledge Leadership Is a Matter of Competence

Although Peter F. Drucker (1995) does suggest that innovation is the one competence needed to manage into the future, we know there are several subcompetencies that come into play. For the past seven years, The Banff Centre for Management (now continued through Banff Executive Leadership, Inc.) has been researching and developing a competency-profiling system to assist managers in measuring the impact of their investment in the residential, experiential executive programs. So far, it has been tested with 5,000 executives from over 500 organizations. The results show that 70 percent of organization competencies are generic and 30 percent are specific to the organization, its industry, and regional presence. Through customization, an organization can tailor and monitor its desired proficiency.

A competency map is an assessment tool that outlines the skills and behaviors required to successfully undertake a position or role. There are thirty-five identified competencies organized according to the following categories: direction setting; change leadership; critical thinking; organizational development and diversity; personal/organization balance; and quality, knowledge, and innovation. Each includes four levels of aptitude, an example of which is shown in Table 12.1.

TABLE 12.1   *Sample Competency Map*

Underpinning	Frame A	Frame B	Frame C	Frame D
I Sales/marketing customer service	"pushes product" provides information in format they use	listens for needs provides solution options	builds relationships proactive idea/solution generation	builds partnerships focuses on customer's customer or strategic goals
II Personal/team leadership	personally competent	able to get immediate team functioning competently	works effectively inter-depart-mentally can successfully lead an inter-depart-mental team	works effectively inter-organiza-tionally, cross-boundry often seen as an "industry leader"
III Adult development	focused on "what's in it for me"	works well in defined parameters employs cause and effect thinking/ analysis traditional approaches	"systems" thinker self-directed initiates new ideas, and projects takes responsibility for own career and activities	"network" oriented multisystems thinker/ analyzer systematizes external/ internal input and creative processes

Through the profiles and learning contract, the process provides for (1) evaluation of a leader's competencies against researched standards; (2) agreement between the participants, their supervisor, and the instructor (i.e., the learning triad); and (3) measurement of successful changes in behavior.

It is almost impossible to be taught leadership. You have to learn it, experience it, and be supported in the process. Too often people expect to become better leaders by signing up for courses. The truth is that the process can hardly be left to serendipity. Banff Executive Leadership designed a five-step learning process (Macnamara 2000) as shown in Table 12.2.

TABLE 12.2   *Steps in the Learning Process*

Step One—The Competency Profile

Assess the learners' competence in several aspects related to their role. Peers and colleagues can offer observation and feedback. Some organizations, such as Royal Bank, Stentor, Canadian Occidental Petroleum, CP Rail, and Alberta Agriculture Food and Rural Development have created such maps as a basis for performance management. The more specific and discrete you can be, the more relevance you can create with a prospective learner.

Step Two—The Learning Contract

Identify what is of most importance for the learner and focus. Capable individuals can generally work only on four or five major attributes at a time. By bringing together the learner, supervisor, and instructor, priorities can be established—identifying strengths, particular areas of focus, and strategies for testing learned competencies.

Step Three—The Learning Process

Whether pre-course, on-course or post-course, the profile and learning contract provide focus. However, if the learning environment is simply academic or knowledge-transfer in design, results will be suboptimal. Learning must be hands-on. It must provide participants with opportunities to experiment with new behaviors, receive feedback, and (re)focus their learning. The learning environment must support creativity, critical inquiry, and practical application—the same criteria necessary for successful implementation of new concepts.

TABLE 12.2 (continued)
_____

Step Four—Re-entry Planning

Careful consideration of the return to the workplace is essential. Individuals who have experienced intense remote learning environments cannot be expected to return to their organizations and "teach" others. Re-entry is far more of a listening exercise—identifying language, motivation, and talent in others ready to be nurtured.

Step Five—Measurement of Impact

Successful demonstration of desired skills and learning competencies is essential. You cannot learn about management and leadership by "talking" about it. These knowledge concepts seem new at first. The good news is that they are intuitively obvious and clarify many "fuzzy, soft" management concepts by illustrating how they contribute to the bottom line when put into practice.

Of course, there are new competencies emerging as we write. Research into thirty-three case study examples of knowledge leadership in practice identified new roles and skills for the knowledge age. There are now such position titles as knowledge architect, knowledge engineer, knowledge editor, knowledge analyst, knowledge navigator, knowledge gatekeeper, and knowledge brokers. There is considerable debate among knowledge professionals as to the relative merit of having a chief knowledge officer (CKO). Regardless of your adoption of the knowledge nomenclature, it is essential that someone be designated to oversee the innovation process—how knowledge is created, exchanged, and applied in your organization for future sustainability.

12.2.3 Knowledge Leadership Is a Matter of Culture

Leadership training may be vested in the individual; but impactful leadership must start at the top and become an integral part of the organizational culture. Oftentimes, we see organizations investing in leadership development at the individual level while the corporation values and culture remain unchanged.

Although in a survey administered in 1997, innovation was defined as the number-one advantage of a knowledge program (see

Figure 12.1), developing a culture of knowledge sharing is unquestionably the greatest obstacle.

Over the long term, culture does more to influence the impact of corporate leadership than any other factor. It determines how individuals react and perform on a daily basis. Culture includes years of history—including successes and failures, good and bad decisions, and individual and collective stories. All of these create a set of values—explicit and implicit—that constitute the underpinnings of the enterprise culture. The culture is what determines how leadership is or isn't manifested in an organization.

The two greatest obstacles to successful knowledge leadership are a lack of trust and inadequate communications—specifically regarding values, mission, and critical success factors. These two elements, combined with a lack of vision, appear to be at the root of leadership duress.

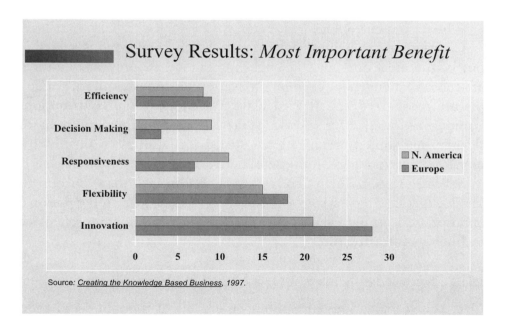

FIGURE 12.1   *Benefits of knowledge programs.*[4]

Trust is a multifaceted and elusive concept that pervades everything we do. It includes other attributes, such as accountability, integrity, honesty, and ethics. Nothing erodes or destroys corporate leadership than mistrust. Untrustworthy leaders may achieve mediocre improvements, but they will never effectively harness the passion for outstanding business results.

Poor communication—both human and technical—may be the greatest leadership weakness. It leads to ineffective performance, poor morale, and internal confusion. With continuous downsizing, constructive knowledge sharing ceases. Worse, organizations became paralyzed with a lack of responsible risk-taking—an essential criterion for innovation.

Without vision, the organization and its constituency are at a loss for a sense of direction. Usually visions are actually only missions. They do not provide an articulation of organization uniqueness or its aspirations. They do not articulate stretch goals that fire the imagination of employees and customers.

Creating and sustaining a culture in which knowledge is valued is one of the most difficult challenges in practice. Appropriate cultures are those that engender change, innovation, openness, and trust. People are recognized and rewarded for their knowledge contribution. Conditions for effective knowledge creation and sharing require more flexible, networked organizational structures; multiple teams; and a climate of intensive and purposeful networking.

Several factors help create the conditions that encourage knowledge-sharing—systems for moving people (e.g., job rotation), appropriate learning events, effective teaming, and a comprehensive technology infrastructure.

12.2.4   Knowledge Leadership Is a Matter of Communities

Over the years, various disciplines or schools of thought—and even functions—have begun to converge in the scope of responsibility and practice. Each area has been broadening its theories and integrating core principles from the domains of others. There is a convergence of functional perspectives, and a common agenda is emerging.

For instance, human resource professionals seek to develop more relevant performance measures as well as new ways to use information technology. Chief information officers, in order to justify investments in technology, have to understand the organization structure, the motivations of people, and cross-boundary processes. Quality experts are building training infrastructures for the transfer of knowledge and best practices. R&D managers are taking on new responsibilities for business development and reducing cycle time with increased customer interaction. Finance professionals are exploring ways to expand their audit capabilities to influence the business strategy of their clients. All are relying upon emerging computer and communications technology advancements to do so.

There is a realization of—and respect for—alternative paradigms that did not exist a decade ago. Value is being created in the organization interfaces—the white space—the connections *between* individuals, organizations, and companies in the same industries and nations within regions of the world.

The notion of communities of practice originated with Etienne Wenger of the Institute for Research on Learning and was actualized and popularized by John Seely Brown, Vice President of Xerox PARC (Palo Alto, California). Likely an outgrowth of quality circles and networked organizations, this is a concept that, when made explicit, helps harness creativity and promotes the cross-fertilization of ideas necessary for prosperous innovation.

> *At the simplest level, they are a small group of people who've worked together over a period of time...not a team, not a task force, not necessarily an authorized or identified group...perform the same tasks...or collaborate on a shared task...or work together on a product. They are peers in the execution of real work. What holds them together is a common sense of purpose and a real need to know what each other knows.[5]*

Even the best strategic planning process often does not provide for an understanding of such natural connections. However, modern managers must take notice of these streams of activity to optimize the innovation process. This is where knowledge leadership resides —where ideas originate, are exchanged, and eventually result in marketable products and services. Observing this convergence of competencies provides insights into how the entire operation may be effectively led.

Innovation becomes the glue that bonds together diverse constituencies. Knowledge and intellectual capital become the mechanisms to build synergy. Such a redefined focus on knowledge and innovation is not the latest consulting fad. It is the essence of sustainable organizations and economies of the future. Instead of operating from the pure perspective of competition, leaders will learn to collaborate and contribute to the success of one another. We are no longer managing a zero-sum game!

12.2.5   Knowledge Leadership Is a Matter of Conversations and Common Language

Of primary importance is the innovation language—a language that transcends the paradigm and biases of one particular function. Ideally, such a language would also encompass industries, sectors, and regions of the world and would, therefore, be universal in scope.

There are several attempts to define the knowledge language with a glossary of terms. One such effort, initiated by Skandia and Ericsson in Sweden, includes an online capability to add to the existing 400 terms. Of course, whatever terminology or language is adopted must apply to the heritage, purpose, mission, and strategy of the enterprise. Such language must pervade all operations and planning efforts.

Once connections are made among internal and external constituencies—with an explicit understanding of potential spheres of influence—attention should be given to purposeful conversations. Mastering the art of structured conversation and dialogue has been the focus of many academic consultants (e.g., Peter Senge, Fernando Flores, and Dan Kim).

Furthermore, there are many successful CEOs beginning to manage according to the quality and level of conversations.[6] One case in point is Ray Stata, Chairman of Analog Devices (Norwood, Massachusetts). In his quest for improvement, Stata began a search for a common language and shared vision. In the process, he discovered that learning and improvement are really two sides of the same coin. Through a weeklong course for his senior executive team, he realized the value of conversations—the flow of meaning, if you will—among and between his senior management. The common bond was the quest for highly effective learning.

Stata's style is to encourage his employees to become a community of inquirers, not advocates. With such a mindset, managers are encouraged to understand and leverage the diversity of knowledge, skills, and experiences. His organization is described as a "network of conversations"—a theme he elaborates both internally and externally.

12.2.6 Knowledge Leadership Is a Matter of Communications

Given the dramatic increases in the functionality of computer and communications technology—including the explosion of the World Wide Web and e-commerce—companies must develop a strategy of how best to leverage the technology. There must take full advantage of both internal and external mechanisms (e.g., groupware, multimedia, and cyberspace) to optimize results. Further, communications is not always technical. Keeping the organization and stakeholders apprised of priorities, changes in direction, success stories, and more is not only difficult; it is essential.

As they say, "You do not get a second chance to make a first impression." These days, with companies being managed by chaos theory and the degree of complexity, simple but not simplistic communications should be the order of the day. A communication strategy must be fully integrated with any plans to leverage the human capital—more specifically knowledge—of all stakeholders in the innovation process.

External messages must be consistent with internal culture, values, and vision. How companies are perceived in the marketplace—branding, ethics, direction, success stories, etc.—must be conveyed skillfully and on a regular basis. More and more companies around the world are using the platform of knowledge-related advertising campaigns, as in the following examples:

- "Knowledge is powerful medicine."—Eli Lilly (Fortune, July 1995)
- "Understanding comes with Time."—Time Magazine (Fortune, July 1995)
- "Prepare to have that idea shattered."—Hewlett-Packard (Fortune, July 1995)
- "A brilliant deduction."—Gifts in Kind America (Fortune, June 1995)
- "Knowledge of the world on-line."—Oracle (CNN ad, November 28, 1995)
- "Old tradition, new thinking."—Harvard Funds (Fortune, June 1995)
- "Your dog is smart"—Purina Dog Chow (CNN ad, February 26, 1996)
- "Travel provides the power of knowledge."—American Express (CNN ad, February 1996)

In the knowledge economy, taglines have taken on a deeper significance. Not only are they designed for marketing products and services, they serve as a concise vehicle to present a timely image to external stakeholders and a motivational tool for employees. Consider all that Federal Express communicated with "The World on Time." It was close to a stretched vision to which all could relate. It was simple, memorable, substantive, and visceral. Sometimes, we forget how important might be the right words in the right context.

Communication strategy may be as much of a learning process as a dissemination tool, perhaps even more so. We need to envision the innovation activity as a value system, not a value chain of events. For example, we may have more to gain from tapping into customer knowledge (i.e., what customers know) than approaching them as the end of a delivery chain. Communications may be more a function of operating a distributed learning network of expertise. It can be the score of an intelligence service as well as a business development function. Leadership is a function of listening and acting upon insights, not merely a receptacle for stakeholder contact.

12.2.7 Knowledge Leadership Is a Matter of Coaching

Coaching is a guided relationship process established between two parties. Both are responsible. The process is forward looking, change oriented, and developmental. It is a tool to enable client success, productivity, revenue growth, and stakeholder value. Coaching is more about "being" than "doing." Effective coaches engage in a process that involves trust, support, and shared values.

The coach's main role deals with expanding the ability to see contexts rather than supplying content. The coaching process affirms the person, seeks to clarify choices, and acts as a catalyst for achieving both individual and organizational purposes. The coaching task connects the inner person (e.g., confidence, values, purpose) with the external manifestation of leadership (e.g., articulating vision, reaching targets, and achieving goals).

Coaching is the opposite of judging and the need for control. This is why its essence is congruent with the fundamental precepts of the knowledge economy. The coaching relationship enables people to work out issues and find answers through their own effective discovery process.

Effective leaders know they do not have the answers. However, they do generally have a healthy curiosity, a sense of direction, standards of excellence, and a track record of success. They genuinely value others and have a need to "know what the others know." They are constantly learning, not afraid to experiment with new ideas nor afraid to make mistakes. They know that facilitating a process is almost always preferable to claiming answers and dictating action. Knowledge leaders will coach as well as be coached. They will navigate through uncharted territory with full confidence in the value of mutual talent.

With the shift to on-the-job learning, it is important to have others—not necessarily managers—guide these leaders through their own innovation process. British Petroleum discovered that personal coaching was an important success factor when it introduced video-conferencing for virtual learning.

12.3　Leadership Starts With You

In the *Knowledge Innovation® Assessment*, one of the ten dimensions of innovation strategy is leadership. Check your own capability, using the test laid out in Table 12.3.

TABLE 12.3　*A Knowledge Leadership Litmus Test*

Can you define a map of your sphere of influence within your industry, across sectors, and around the world?

Do you have an effective strategy to disseminate your knowledge and competencies to the marketplace?

Name the multiple methods of positioning your own intellectual leadership (e.g., articles, books, videos, professional visibility, and participation on committees or commissions)?

How are the learnings from your participation fed back into the organization and used to develop new business strategies?

Is there an internal mechanism to capture, codify, and feed forward expertise in ways that might enhance the business performance of the organization as a whole?

Does your organization perceive external leadership activities as integral to the business? How are they leveraged?

Are there any formal mechanisms to legitimize, encourage, and reward people who impart knowledge and expertise to others?

Use this sample diagnostic as a way to explore with others in your organization how effectively you are developing and leveraging your own leadership talent. Remember that leadership—in all of its facets—is a learning process. True leaders are learners first.

Knowledge leaders are those who inspire the insights of others. They operate on intuition and act with an innovation mindset, knowing that their contributions will make a difference. They know that imagination may be more important than the knowledge per se. They are eager to learn and are not afraid of sharing with others. They take responsible risks, even if it means sharing electronically whereby good ideas can be elevated or killed with a few keystrokes.

- Leaders will understand the nature of complex context —how to make sense of it and how to convey it (with magnetic vision) to others.
- Leaders will know that competencies are based on experience and are more dynamic than static attributes.
- Leaders will know the relationship between the motivation (psychology) of an individual and the culture (sociology) of an organization. They will value heritage (anthropology) and know that more than 2 percent of manager time need be dedicated to visioning—the lifeblood of a future generation of business.
- Leaders will understand the value of the collective—the teams and communities within which work gets done and visions are realized.
- Leaders will know how to evolve a common language and will realize that there is more power in the dialog than what gets documented in a particular planning process.
- Leaders will value the communications process—both technical and human—but not as much for what gets conveyed as for what might be learned.

- Leaders will coach and be coached by people of similar values and vision. Trust will be placed in those able to care more about leveraging the competencies of one another.

A few decades ago, leading was considered different from managing. Today's new economy, full of intensified global competition as well as opportunity, may require managing leaders—an oxymoron?

12.4 SUMMARY

We are at the dawn of a new millennium. The leadership required to carry us forward may not resemble what was necessary in the past. Oh yes, we will always admire those who are now considered to have innovation genius, but this is hindsight. What may be required for future leadership includes a novel set of skills. Considering The Superhighway as a place to test, learn, and leverage new knowledge may be a beginning.

In the industrial era, competition was the path to survival. Leaders understood their own capabilities within the content of others. This has not changed in the knowledge economy. Instead, however, it is not only a matter of where the competition is but where competitors are headed. One doesn't learn where (and how) others are going by studying "best practices." New and successful practices are being innovated every day and from cultures once considered economic observers at best. New rules have been established, but they are not yet very clear. Now, it may be that inherent in the cultural and managerial heritage of others (i.e., different functions, sectors, industries and nations) may lie some answers. Collaboration becomes essential to understanding the innovation of others.

The playing field has been leveled; and only the leaders will survive.

Chapter Endnotes

[1] Taken from *The Aquarian Conspiracy: Personal and Social Transformation in Our Time*, by Marilyn Ferguson (1987 ed.), p. 110.

[2] Material adapted from an article co-authored with Doug Macnamara, then Vice President for the Banff Centre of Management; it was published in the *2001 Handbook for Business Strategy*.

[3] Observations presented at the ALPACH Conference, Austria. July 1999.

[4] From the Skyrme and Amidon Report, "Creating the Knowledge-Based Business" (London, England: Business Intelligence (1997)). p. 55.

[5] Defined by John Seely Brown and Estee Solomon Gray (1995), pp. 78–82.

[6] From Chapter 5, "Innovation as a 'Value-System," *Innovation Strategy for the Knowledge Economy: The Ken Awakening* (1997), pp. 68–72.

[7] Knowledge Innovation® is a registered trademark of Entovation International Ltd.

THIRTEEN
Exemplar Ken Practitioners

Few of the inventors responsible for
the astonishing wave of innovation.
between 1750 and 1860 were scientists;
most were artisans or engineers
with little or no scientific training.
They were men of common sense, curiosity,
energy and a vast ingenuity,
standing on the shoulders not of scholars
but of similar practical types.

Special Millennium Edition of *The Economist*[1]

When I watched the CNN broadcast the dawn of the millennium, as it rippled across the world, I could not help but be encouraged. Whether you believe the year began on January 1, 2000 or 2001 or is yet to come; there is one thing on which we might agree. People underestimate the power of the positive flow of energy we all experience. Y2K aside, individuals and organizations alike appear to have renewed their commitment to change, or as we prefer to call it, innovation (i.e., the capacity to preserve the best of the old and realign the rest to take advantage of future opportunity).

Reflect for a moment on insights provided by the Special Millennium Edition of *The Economist* (December 1999): *Reporting on a Thousand Years*. The discussion on "wealth" was a comment on the last years of innovation. "Mathematics and mechanics had come together.

By the end of the 17th century, understanding and application had converged. Knowledge had expanded, you might say, up to and beyond the point of critical mass. The intellectual foundations for the technological revolution were in place."

I wonder, now, how the story of the evolution of a knowledge economy will be written in the next thousand years. The focus is no longer the technology, nor is it information. In fact, as they write, "Technology is driven by knowledge, and especially scientific knowledge. Knowledge is cumulative; once it exists, it does not cease to exist." This is the multiplier effect of knowledge as the asset to be managed; and we are all actors in this new innovation theater.

If we were to look at the real leaders of the knowledge economy, we'd find they are practitioners. Contrary to popular opinion, the roots of the movement are not in academia; nor has this movement been the brainchild of consulting firms. Instead, the roots are grounded in practice, not theory. In truth, today practitioners sound more like theorists than do the academicians. Modern management theory is being innovated "real-time" and in the executive suite.

The term "ken" was used in my previous book[2] to describe the awakening we are experiencing as participants in the evolving global economy. It is defined in my dictionary as both a noun and a verb:

> **ken** (ken)   v. 1. To know (a person or thing). 2. To recognize. 3. To descry (i.e., discern something difficult to catch sight of; discover through careful observation or investigation); to have an understanding of something.
>
> n. 1. Perception; understanding. 2.a. Range of vision. b. View; sight; to make known.

It is a term that translates into numerous languages—Chinese, German, Celtic, Dutch, Japanese, and even Afrikaans. In short, "ken" is a term that represents having knowledge and a range of vision to know where that knowledge might best be applied. And knowledge applied to action is the process of innovation. These ken practitioners—practicing the art of leadership in this global knowledge economy—come from all corners of the globe.

There are numerous examples of ken practice throughout this book, especially in Chapters 9–11, that provide examples of vision statements and network testimony. And several of the initiatives referenced in Chapter 14 have been directly influenced by the leadership actions of several Entovation colleagues.

We have already featured those Fellows within the Network who are experts in one or more of the domains of innovation strategy. To illustrate how the focus on knowledge and innovation is exemplified in the work of individuals, we have profiled a representative sample of some others.

13.1 Dr. Marcus Speh Birkenkrahe (New Zealand/United Kingdom)

It is becoming clear that we are not in an "old" versus "new" situation—the old economy won't go away because we make space for the new economy. In fact, they are not as different as they pretend to be—the clue here is, integration across boundaries.

Originally trained as a physicist, Marcus Speh Birkenkrahe is serving as a visiting professor at University of Auckland Business School, while on sabbatical from his job in London where he headed knowledge management for the Royal Dutch/Shell Group of Companies until the end of 2001. In this role, his primary task was to develop and implement strategic knowledge management capabilities for Shell, in particular in response to the challenges Shell is facing in the knowledge economy.

Dr. Birkenkrahe is the author of both Shell's Global Knowledge Management Framework and of Shell's Information Security Guidelines, which he created between 1997 and 1998 as a senior adviser to the board of managing directors of the Shell Group. He joined Shell in April 1997 from Andersen Consulting, where he was Director of Knowledge Management for the Maritime Region from 1995. In this position, he was responsible for the central information research and competitor intelligence service in the UK, Ireland, Scandinavia, and South Africa.

Before 1995 Dr. Birkenkrahe worked as a research scientist. Between 1989 and 1994 he worked extensively in the design of online information systems and virtual classrooms. He has received a number of awards for his work as one of the first developers of the World Wide Web on the Internet.

A frequent keynote speaker on the knowledge circles, he is an advisor to the European KnowledgeBoard KM portal and on the editorial boards of the journals *Knowledge Management* and *Scenario & Strategy Planning* (ARK Group Publishing). He is a Fellow of the Royal Society of Arts & Commerce (RSA), London and the author of several thought-provoking articles, one of which is "Turtles All the Way Down and All the Way Up,"[3] which contains the published insights from his keynote speech on the future of knowledge management in the new economy. In addition to describing to others the relationship of knowledge management to business strategy and competitive intelligence, he is lucid about modern management concepts (e.g., adaptive systems and the hierarchy of holons linking tacit and explicit knowledge).

In another article. "Seven Spiritual Laws of Successful Knowledge Management." he explains why KM continues to command greater understanding, in terms of technology, process and strategy. The seven laws are (1) The law of Unity; (2) The law of Giving; (3) The law of Cause and Effect; (4) The law of Least Effort; (5) The law of Intention and Desire; (6) The law of Detachment; and (7) the law of Purpose in Life.

13.2   YVONNE BUMA (THE NETHERLANDS)

Develop a systems communications model that is better suited for the knowledge economy than the traditional linear models.

Think about what we can learn from different cultures…Look for and respect the differences and develop your methods accordingly. Keep our eyes wide open and do not fall for the trap of copying from one dominant culture.

Yvonne Buma is CEO and founder of Gideya. Since 1993 Gideya has provided customized consulting services for local governments and non-governmental organizations, helping them to effectively develop and implement innovative strategies and to effectively communicate these strategies and their implications with all stakeholders, balancing politics and effective communication.

Ms Buma is a behavioral technician, has a background in journalism (e.g., editor-in-chief of a magazine), is experienced in the political decision-making process, holds several degrees in communications, and has a Masters degree in knowledge management from the University of Tilburg (The Netherlands). She is the author of *Knowledge management and communication—towards a new communications model more suited for the knowledge economy.* In this thesis she lays the foundations for a communication model that is better suited for the knowledge economy than the traditional linear communications model that is used by the majority of communications officers at the moment. This view is based on the experience that sharing knowledge, learning, and implementing innovations is definitely not a linear process.

Early in her career Ms Buma was active in international youth work. As secretary general of the Dutch National Youth Council she was responsible for representing the Dutch youth with not only the European Communities, the Council of Europe, and the United Nations but also in bilateral missions and activities where youth (representatives) from all of Europe or the whole world participated. In this period (the early 1980s) the foundation for her development as communications expert and her involvement in knowledge and innovation in organizations was laid. Knowledge management, effective communications and learning from and with different cultures were crucial. Innovative policies and activities stemmed from sharing knowledge (tacit and explicit) through effective communications and respect for different cultures and willingness to learn from them.

In later years. as a government official she was further confronted with the fact that the employee (and his or her knowledge and the ability to use and share it) is the most important asset of an organization. But she saw that this is also the most often neglected asset, and that this and poor communications are usually at the heart of ineffective strategies. Accordingly, she now specializes in creating and maintaining the link of effective (human) communications to organizational strategies.

13.3   DR. JAVIER CARRILLO (MEXICO)

The emergence of a global value system—a critical mass of individuals realizing the potential of knowledge to leverage a universal process of sustainable development. The knowledge management movement has a potential for leveraging a global transformation based on a value balance for mankind as a whole.

Dr. Carillo is a scientist and consultant who has been devoted to knowledge systems and knowledge management since 1980. He is professor of KM at the Monterrey Institute of Technology, where he founded the Center for Knowledge Systems[4] (CKS) in 1992—notably the first such institute in the world. His main interests are knowledge-based business creation and development, knowledge systems audit, and the contribution of knowledge systems to the emergence of a global consciousness. He has developed a KM Model (Knowledge-based Value Systems), which has been applied in more than sixty consultancy projects in several countries. Based on this experience and related R&D, he and his colleagues at CKS developed in 1998 the ITESM graduate KM curriculum program, one of the most comprehensive KM educational offerings available. He holds a Ph.D. in Psychology of Science and Technology from King's College, London, an M.Sc. in Logic and Scientific Method from the London School of Economics, and an M.Sc. in Experimental Analysis of Behavior from UNAM, Mexico.

He serves on the advisory/editorial boards of several international KM organizations and publications such as The Knowledge Management Consortium International (USA), *The Journal of Knowledge Management* (UK*), Knowledge and Innovation: The KMCI Journal* (US), and The Research Center on Knowledge Societies (Madrid) and is a member of several KM networks such as The Entovation 100 (USA), The Sociedades del Conocimiento Community (Basque region), the EVOLVE Project (European Community), the CORGA Network (Venezuela), and the MIK-KM Program (Spain). He is currently vice-president of the KMCI Institute.

Based on the CKS, he has built a KM network throughout the Americas, whose influence has been acknowledged by KM directories, networks, and studies. He is a regular presenter at international conferences. He is the founder and editor of The KMetaSite,[5] a free Web-based reference service that includes four domains: (1) an introductory section with definitions, a glossary, related magazines ,and on-line articles/references; (2) an R&D section with a meta model, philosophic and scientific foundations, organizational KM processes, and related R&D issues; (3) a business section for specialized periodicals, standards, commercial yellow pages, and a KM toolkit; and (4) a reference section for white papers, a directory of who's who in KM, electronic bulletins, and KM forums.

Dr. Carrillo can be credited with building the foundation under KM as a field of study and evolving a community of practice therefor. In his

articles such as "Managing Knowledge-Based Value Systems,"[6] he outlines the origins of value dynamics in knowledge-based economies.
Through his work with the CKS he has expanded the network of alliances building a "community of value." He has even expanded his
curriculum—complete with a video series of knowledge leaders—
through Monterrey Tech's on-site broadcasting studio delivering to
some 200 sites throughout Latin America in addition to digital on-line
Internet delivery worldwide.

13.4   JOACHIM DOERING (GERMANY)

*Very soon the world will be driven by (the
innovations out of) knowing communities.
Self-regulated global communities of practice will
cover every essential topic of our life and transform
this world bottom up. Now we do discover the power
of knowledge and the fission to "unleash" our global
potential.*

Currently vice-president for Siemens Information and Communication Networks (ICN) and president of Group
Strategy, Siemens AG, Joachin Doering began his studies in engineering with business administration at the Technical University of Berlin
and continued in international business at the Haas Business School,
University of California, Berkeley. He has held a variety of line
and consulting functions within Siemens Semiconductor/Fiber Optics
Group (Germany and USA), Business Process Reengineering at
Siemens Components (Malaysia), and Global Supply-Chain Management at Siemens Microelectronics (USA, Japan, and Europe).

Various position responsibilities have included restructuring
Siemens, resulting in a reduction of over 50 percent of headcount and
costs and, within three months; developing customer-centric leadership with six pilot customer integration teams; launching an
Excellence in Partnership program with the annual strategic planning
process; implementing a "bonus on top" program of two new incentive

systems to support international collaboration and strategic alignment of local companies; creating nCubator, an internal incubator/venture capitalist function for entrepreneurial employees with marketable ideas and business plans; and implementing ShareNet, a knowledge-sharing network that connects 15,000 sales and marketing people at Siemens and generating additional revenues in eighty countries.

Joachim Doering managed the marketing activities within the global student network and is co-founder of the Center for Change- and Knowledge Management at the Technical University of Berlin. Joachim lectures on business transformation at the chair for Allgemeine und Industrielle Betriebswirtschaftlehre, Prof. Dr. Reichwald, TU München. He is invited speaker at international congresses and at the Universitätsseminar der Wirtschaft (USW) Schloß Gracht.

His presentations and articles explore the future of work in distributed e-company networks. For instance, the key elements of professional global knowledge sharing are valuable content that enables decision making, a structured global community of knowledgeable people with well-defined knowledge targets, technical systems that allow people to bridge geographical and time distances (enterprise systems, corporate portals, middleware, artificial intelligence, access technology, mobile systems, palms), and a managerial system that encourages and supports the flow of knowledge and must be based on suitable knowledge business models and processes.

Currently, in every industry new growth opportunities for knowledge businesses arise. These opportunities cannot be seen through old-economy eyes and are not to be seized by old-economy hands. The core of these future organizations or, to call them by a more apt name. networks, will be e-lancers, knowledge workers who can be seen as investors and harvesters of their own intellectual capital. The challenge is managing the transformation toward international knowledge business, toward service and people business, managed in networked organizations.

13.5   LEIF EDVINSSON (SWEDEN)

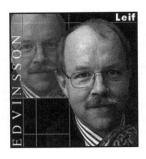

Ideas are, perhaps, the most ethereal resources at an organization's disposal. They fall through the cracks of intellectual property law with worrying ease. They defy classification. No one knows this better than those who work in the great ideas sectors of our age: business schools and consulting firms. Where better to look for clues of where the knowledge economy is headed?

Leif Edvinsson is best known as the first chief knowledge officer in the world because he served as corporate director for intellectual capital at Skandia AFS and was architect of the Skandia Future Centre. He currently serves as Professor of Intellectual Capital, University of Lund and is the founder and CEO of Universal Networking Intellectual Capital AB (UNIC).

Originating his studies at Enköping, Uppsala and the University of Lund, he received his Master of Business Administration degree at the University of Berkeley, California. He is currently a member of the boards of two stock-listed, knowledge-intensive companies as well as of various other IT and IC companies. He serves as a member of the board of trustees for Brain Trust, which in 1998 gave him the "Brain of the Year" award. Most recently, he was listed as being among the top twenty of the most admired knowledge leaders in the world.

Mr. Edvinsson is a well-recognized keynote speaker in the most influential global seminars and conferences at Harvard Business School, Stanford University, the London School of Economics, INSEAD, HHS, HHG, the University of Stockholm, the University of Lund, the American Marketing Association, the Conference Board USA, *Business Intelligence*, and *The Economist*, among others

He is the author of several articles and books, most notably *Intellectual Capital: Realizing Your Company's True Value by Finding Its Hidden Brainpower* (1997) and his new release, *Corporate Longitude: Navigating the Knowledge Economy* (2002). He is well known and cited in the knowledge literature for his ground-breaking series of intellectual capital supplements to the annual reports with titles such as "Human Capital in Transformation," "Intelligent Enterprising," "Customer Value," "Power of Innovation," "Value-Creating Processes," "Renewal & Development Intellectual Capital, " and "Visualizing Intellectual Capital." He has produced CDs on Visualizing IC and Futurizing.

Taking the knowledge and innovation agenda to the national level, he initiated a Coalition of Service Industries in Sweden. He has served as special advisor to the Swedish cabinet on service trade, as well as on the impact of digital economy. He produced the first national intellectual capital (IC) report for Sweden and has helped advise similar projects in other countries (e.g., Israel and Denmark).

Often cited in or participating in seminal reports on IC published in such periodicals as *Fortune*, *The Economist*, *Fast Company*, *The Wall Street Journal*, *Forbes ASAP*, *Financial Times*, *CIO*, and *Computer World*, Edvinsson is now engaged as advisor on intellectual capital at the Brookings Institute (USA) and for the European Commission.

Edvinsson sets the style and then refuses to conform. Always pushing the limits of the application of new concepts, he is the most adept practitioner of knowledge visualization—one of the core competencies of future management. For all practical purposes, Leif represents the future of IC and the accounting thereof.

13.6   ALEJANDRO FERNANDEZ (VENEZUELA)

In Venezuela, 80% of the people have severe formal education deficiencies, threatening the viability of the country as a nation. Learning in action and network technologies enable a new model of unlimited learning opportunities through NGOs. The challenge is to maximize the value of the nation through it underutilized Human Capital in order to construct a more just society and a better quality of life.

Alejandro Fernandez—a pioneer in virtual education in Venezuela—is general manager of human resources for Brenntag Latin America, a world leader in chemical products distribution. Previously he was responsible for managerial development training for Petroleos de Venezuela (PDVSA). His focus was on the rapid development of managers and leaders to deal with the demanding challenges of the oil industry. He played a leadership role in establishing and implementing training and development programs in finance, human resources, leadership, negotiation, corporate culture, planning, quality, language, and service management for clients as well as internally for PDVSA at both the corporate and business-unit level. The areas covered in such activities typically include curriculum development, market and client training needs assessment, technology innovation, and service direction.

During his career of more than twenty years in the Venezuelan oil industry he has held different positions in the areas of human resources, corporate planning and information systems. His achievements in the area of human resources include a corporate incentive program linked with corporate results, a model for reinforcing the corporate culture and values, a development system that includes the individual performance process, competencies, individual, and organizational development models. In January 1996 he was elected president of the National Association of Industrial Relations of Venezuela, where he was responsible for the organization of the HR world Congress held at Caracas, Venezuela in 1998.

With degrees from Universidad Catolica Andres Bello, Cornell, and MIT, he is professor of human resource planning at the graduate school of the "Universidad Metropolitana," author of the book *New Paradigms In the Management of Human Resources*, and co-author of the book *Globalization , Risk and Realities, Knowledge and Competencies for the Organizations for the 21st Century*. Since 1990 he has been director and founder of Pro-Quality of Life, an institution devoted to improving the quality of life in poverty areas, anti-corruption efforts, and improvement of education. He is a pioneer in virtual education in

Venezuela. He is a member of the Administration Board of the Catholic Education Institute for kids with scarce resources and a member of the board of the Virtual Institute of AVEPANE, the Venezuelan Association of Parents and Friends of Exceptional Children.

13.7   Dr. Piero Formica (Italy)

How to fill the gap between individual and organizational knowledge? There has been a shift toward a more advanced culture of co-opetition among all parties in the supply chain...The invisible hand of the market must be accompanied by an invisible handshake (i.e., connectivity and trust-led businesses).

Prof. Piero Formica is Dean of the "International University of Entrepreneurship" in Ijmuiden Amsterdam; professor of economics of innovation at the Master School of Business Law, University of Bologna (where he was a member of the board of directors between 1988 and 1992); and visiting professor at the Institute of Technology, Tartu University, Estonia.

Prof. Formica has over thirty years of experience in the fields of international economics and economics of innovation, working with OECD Economic Prospects Division in Paris, large corporations and small companies, various governmental bodies, and the European Union. In the business world he is involved as director of internationalization to the Zernike Group in the Netherlands, an international company that runs seed capital funds and promotes the commercialization of innovation and know how.

Prof. Formica is member of the Scientific Committee of the International Association of Science Parks (IASP), a member of the board of directors of Transinnova (Rouen, France), and member of the Knowledge Management Entovation Network and of SPICE, an international network of experts on science parks and incubators.

Educated in Italy and the UK, Dr. Formica is a member of the editorial board of the *New Academic Review* (London), editor of the *China High Technology Enterprises Journal*, and coeditor of the *e-Journal of the Business of Experience and Innovation*.

During the past decade Prof. Formica's research has been focused on industrial clusters, business strategies for innovation, new company formation and spin-offs, science parks and incubators, knowledge management, organizational innovation in higher education, the digital economy, and entrepreneurship. He has written widely on these subjects. Among his works are *Tecnopoli—Luoghi e sentieri dell'innovazione*, ISEDI,Torino; *Innovation and Economic Development—University-Enterprise Partnerships in Action*; *Delivering Innovation—Key Lessons from the World-Wide Networks of Science and Technology Parks Spin-offs from Innovative Learning Environment; Doing Business in the Knowledge Economy; Essay Topics in Technology Transfer*; and *Frontiers of Entrepreneurship and Innovation*.

13.8   BOB FRANCO (USA)

My challenge, though, is that in most organizations, appreciation of true value, real knowledge, genuine innovation is a "fringe" activity. I want to see these as core capabilities. I believe these are what we must stand for and must translate across everything we do — our culture, the work we do, our discipline, our intentionality.

Educated at Stevens Institute of Technology and Rutgers College, Bob Franco is a seasoned human resources professional with a strong interest in knowledge and innovation and specific career emphasis in providing consultative services. He is a strong thought leader who has outstanding leadership, collaboration, influence, project and analytical skills.

Currently vice-president for global talent with American Express, his responsibilities include (1) defining talent agenda, strategies, and performance-improvement opportunities for the company's businesses; (2) leading the formulation and application of strategy and methods for realizing opportunities related to performance; (3) assessing strategies for building strategic corporate capabilities and acquiring and developing talent and knowledge management; and (4) developing and integrating strategies related to staffing, human resource development, executive resources, and diversity and meeting regional and business needs while moving toward a long-term enterprise strategy.

Mr. Franco previously led an organization of learning and development professionals, working in strong partnership with business unit general managers to integrate business goals into prioritized performance plans, including product and leadership initiatives. He established necessary capabilities and competencies while reducing costs and introducing new approaches to training service delivery. He also created prioritization and planning tools for various training, HR and quality organization to ensure a properly sequenced approach to solving business problems. His most impressive achievement was improved employee satisfaction with the training organization, showing double-digit improvement in all possible categories of the Employee Values Survey in 1995, 1996, 1997 and 1998 (97 percent) and maintaining performance levels in 1999, 2000, and 2001.

Franco provided HR generalist support in evaluating office climate and management efficiency, analyzing trends, handling conflicts, and developing action plans to address human resources and business issues. He has consulted on compensation, risk management. and staffing plans and strategies. He designed an approach for creating culture change through an employee values survey, employee input and senior management sponsorship; developed a targeted approach to enable clients to implement performance management process; orchestrated a region-wide effort to develop expectations and built consistent standards into the performance appraisal process; played a major role during the company's acquisitions of Thomas Cook and Lifeco Travel.

13.9   CINDY GORDON (CANADA)

We need to understand the tremendous change implications of electronic commerce and the impact of the business models rapidly emerging. As these new solutions are rapidly deployed, organizational boundaries, relationships all shift, the implications of ethics, security, become more imperative to ensure that the knowledge we are creating and distributing in our pursuit of profit reflects the new order we want to create for future generations.

Cindy M. Gordon has more than fifteen years of senior executive experience in the communications and high tech industry. Cindy is currently the CEO of Helix Commerce International, Inc., a company specializing in collaboration commerce services helping companies use e-commerce and c-commerce to accelerate growth.

Prior to joining Helix, Ms. Gordon was a partner with XDL Intervest, a tier-one venture capital firm. She has held senior executive positions with Andersen Consulting, where she was a global practice leader in Andersen's e-commerce and knowledge management strategies and also the national practice partner for their change and strategy practice for communications and high-tech.

During her eight years with Xerox, Cindy was involved in all the large-scale business transformation and new start-up business operations, including professional services, outsourcing services, oversight responsibility for consolidating all call-center operations, and formulating sales and service business effectiveness strategies. She was recognized for the coveted President's Club Award for her global leadership contributions at Xerox.

Cindy has had entrepreneurial experience with Trigon Systems Group and was a founding partner of InfoTech Consultants, a company that specialized in business and technology strategies.

Ms. Gordon is a frequently published author of numerous publications on the new economy, knowledge management, and e-commerce.

She has collaborated recently on three books: *"Chief Knowledge Officers in the New eEconomy"*; *"Knowledge: The Great Business Challenge,"* Negócio Editora; and *"Knowledge Management: Classic and Contemporary Works."* A fourth book, *Realizing the Promise of Corporate Portals*, will be released in summer, 2002.

Currently enrolled in a doctoral program at the University of Toronto, she has degrees from the University of Alberta. She is a board director/advisor to a number of high-technology companies and some nonprofit organizations. Most recently, the University of Western Canada Business School profiled her for her business, community, and board leadership in its new book, *300 Women in the Lead*.

13.10   ADMIRAL BOBBY RAY INMAN (USA)

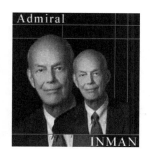

It is a matter of global competitiveness, the relationship between economic and national security and the role of the news media in public policy

Admiral Inman graduated from the University of Texas at Austin in 1950 with a degree in history, and from the National War College in 1972. He then served as assistant and chief aide to the to the Vice Chief of Naval Operations. He became an adjunct professor at the University of Texas at Austin in 1987. He was appointed as a tenured professor holding the Lyndon B. Johnson Centennial Chair in National Policy in August 2001.

Admiral Inman served in the U.S. Navy from November 1951 to July 1982 in a variety of administrative, operational, and intelligence posts and rose through the ranks from ensign to four-star admiral—the first intelligence specialist to do so. While on active duty he served as Director of the National Security Agency and Deputy Director of Central Intelligence.

After retiring from the Navy, he was selected as the first chairman and chief executive officer of the Microelectronics and Computer

Technology Corporation (MCC) in Austin, Texas where he served for four years. As its first leader, he brought several qualities: a national identity, insider know-how and know-who regarding the Washington scene, and a reputation for integrity and intelligence. Inman can be credited with architecting the facility selection in Austin and the recruitment of a significant number of large-scale companies that were, in many cases, arch competitors.

Motivated by President Reagan's Innovation Task Force, lawyers were sending signals to U.S. industry that cooperative research programs were not necessarily illegal, paving the way for the consortium's activities in pre-competitive research. The approval of MCC activity prepared the landscape for many national R&D consortia to follow suit (e.g., SEMATECH and the National Center for Manufacturing Sciences).

MCC used a technopolis framework promoting new kinds of relationships/alliances between public and private sectors—especially government, business, and academia. Technology transfer mechanisms were given a high priority to enhance the transfer of knowledge with MCC and consortium members; the design of the research program was to promote technological commercialization and economic development.

Admiral Inman served as president and chief executive officer of Westmark Systems, Inc., a privately owned electronics industry holding company, for three years and as chairman of the Federal Reserve Bank of Dallas from 1987 through 1990.

Admiral Inman's primary activity since 1990 has been investing in start-up technology companies. He is also a member of the board of directors of Fluor, Massy Energy Company, Science Applications International Corporation, SBC Communications, and Temple Inland. He serves as trustee of the American Assembly, the Center for Excellence in Education, and the California Institute of Technology. He is a director of the Public Agenda Foundation and a member of the National Academy of Public Administration.

13.11   KEITH JONES (CANADA)

Effective leadership is becoming increasingly defined as identifying ways to accelerate knowledge sharing in a way that delivers knowledge "just in time," at the lowest possible transaction cost, to the greatest industrial and societal benefit. Innovation and creativity in knowledge sharing has potential to drive both economic and social gains for the global community.

Keith Jones is the president and CEO of AVAC, Ltd., a not-for-profit private company dedicated to accelerating the growth of value-added agriculture in Alberta, Canada. He has significant experience as a business consultant, international executive coach, and technology entrepreneur. Keith received "Best of the Best" recognition for business excellence, and he is former vice-president of the Agricultural Institute of Management. In addition to his role with AVAC Ltd., Keith contributes to the Alberta Technology Commercialization Network and the Steering Committee of BioProducts Canada, as well as the Agriculture Sub-committee of BioAlberta.

With his business experience in oil and gas, manufacturing, forest products, and agricultural industries both in Canada and overseas, Keith brings a unique perspective to the challenges of growing added value in Alberta's agriculture industry. His work in best practice development and knowledge sharing in RLG International contributed to that firm's growth from 42 professionals to over 150 professionals specializing in performance management, continuous improvement, and executive coaching. He has worked in three Canadian provinces, Hong Kong, and Australia; his "Best of the Best" award recognized his contribution to an Australian corporation's realization of $92 million in profitability enhancement resulting from a two-year strategy implementation project.

Under Jones's leadership, AVAC has launched a series of significant initiatives: (1) a pre-commercial entrepreneurial program for investments of $25K to $2.4 million or more for developing a new product or service, including establishing prototype or pilot plant capabilities for Agrivalue™ technologies; (2) research and strategic initiatives to stimulate Agrivalue™ toward a $20 billion goal; and (3) an idea builder program with streamlined access to seed capital for smaller projects that add value to agricultural commodities. AVAC Ltd. has trademarked the term "Agrivalue® "to focus science and industry on pursuing value-added from a 'consumer's' perspective, rather than from a producer perspective."

AVAC's challenge of facilitating increased "knowledge transfer" across a very traditional and very competitive value chain and industry has required substantial innovation and creativity. AVAC is constructing knowledge networks in support of its focus areas of new and enhanced food products, functional foods and nutraceuticals, and industrial and nonfood applications of agricultural products. AVAC's position as a well-endowed not-for-profit requires a focus on collaboration and recruiting the active participation of others to the challenge of growing an entire industry. AVAC acts from a position of influence, rather than a position of authority, to encourage entrepreneurship and new venture development, linking entrepreneurs to the knowledge they need to grow.

Keith holds a Bachelor of Science degree in agriculture from the University of Alberta and an MBA in international business from the University of British Columbia; he joined AVAC Ltd. in February 2000. He has also been an executive training at The Banff Centre for Management in the knowledge and innovation management program.

13.12   Dr. George Kozmetsky (USA)

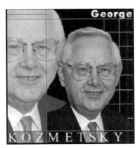

It takes courage as well as wise and lucky leadership to balance short-term, medium-term, and long-term sustainability of a firm. The digital/knowledge industries are ones where walls are coming down between nations, industries, sectors of the economy and between functions of an organization.

George Kozmetsky is a pioneer in the relationship between technology and society. Considered Austin's high-tech father, he co-founded Teledyne, Inc., a major corporation, and the IC² Institute, an important think tank at the University of Texas. He was dean of the business school at the University of Texas at Austin for fifteen years, served as president of The Institute for Management Science, and assisted in the development of more than seventy technology companies, including Dell Computer and Tivoli Systems.

Dr. Kozmetsky currently serves as the E.D. Walker Centennial Fellow and Executive Associate for Economic Affairs in the University of Texas System. Dr. Kozmetsky served from 1966 to 1982 as Dean of the College of Business Administration and at the Graduate School of Business at the University of Texas at Austin. In 1989, he founded both the Austin Technology Incubator (ATI) and its Capital Network (TCN) and still chairs their parent organization (IC² Institute) at the University of Texas.

He has served on numerous boards, including those of Dell, Scientific & Engineering Software, Inc., the Houston Advanced Research Center (HARC), and various KMS ventures. He has also served both state and federal governments as an advisor, commissioner, and panel member of various task forces, commissions, and policy boards, including the National Center for Manufacturing Sciences (NCMA), the Santa Fe Institute, the Claremont University Board of Fellows, the American Friends of Cambridge, the U.S. Air Force Scientific Advisory Board, the AEA Task Force on International Competitiveness, the Advisory Panel to the U.S. Office of Technology Assessment, the Sandia President's Advisory Council, and the board of directors of the Wharton School's SEI Center for Advanced Strategic Management.

To say Dr. Kozmetsky has written extensively is an understatement. He has authored over 20 books and monographs, many of which are considered mandatory reading for university courses. He has published seventy-five articles and supervised dozens of Ph.D. and Masters dissertations—many of students from various corners of the world (e.g., China, Russia, Japan).

An avid learner, his own current research is in leading-edge technologies, technology venturing, systems analysis, organization theory, information technology, quantitative methods applied to economic development, and national and international competitiveness.

Dr. Kozmetsky has been honored and recognized by various professional organizations, was inducted into the Texas Business Hall of Fame for his contributions to the state of Texas, and is a recipient of the 1993 National Medal of Technology as well as the Entrepreneurial Leadership Award from the MIT Enterprise Forum of Cambridge.

13.13   CHIN HOON LAU (MALAYSIA)

The knowledge economy as one that tends to be mediated by knowledge professionals, who will be an increasingly important key players in trade. With knowledge being a more universal language, this is a form of economy that will promote collaboration rather than competition and conflicts, and one that promotes a business environment that reduces wastage of earth resources and human years due to replication and re-inventing wheels, insecurity and isolation.

Chin Hon Lau, founding President of Lagenda Knowledge Systems, a company "where Internet strategy, knowledge innovation and indigenous wisdoms meet." Based in Malaysia and carrying out action research and prototype development at the international innovation front, the company is playing the adaptor function of translating and diffusing global best thinking and practices into Asian community. This includes bridging the gap between knowledge, models, and success stories developed in and for multinational conglomerates and their adoption by local nonprofits and small and medium industries, an effort which they see filling a "glocalization niche."

Lau specializes in Internet-based channels and core competencies for knowledge networking. Having the vision that cross-organizational learning can give rise to hybrid vigor, he works on various types and models of organizations covering local, international, and virtual (Net-based) entities. Lau is a practitioner who strives to incubate the development of micro-knowledge society in the organizations he works with. He is an active member of various local clans and business groups and serves as a community service director of the Rotary Club of Kulai (District 3310). These services enable him to observe issues in the diffusion of technology and knowledge thinking for developing effective solutions serving as the foundation and ground effecter of the society—the grass roots, which the success of any national IT or knowledge agenda depends on.

Lau founded Internet Biologists, a voluntary, purely virtual international organization administered by experts from fourteen countries, with the objective of developing models and mechanisms for online collaboration and learning in molecular life science and bioinformatics. This pioneering organization is in its sixth year, and its virtual collaborative capability has been evidenced by the steady increase in selected, quality membership; successful leadership renewal; development and delivery of numerous virtual collaborative learning programs with an international audience of doctoral and postdoctoral researchers (from over twenty-five countries); and multiple-authored publications.

Lau was trained as molecular biologist with a major in DNA sequencing and genome analysis in New Zealand, Malaysia, Singapore, and various other countries. He was a participant in the first advanced genome sequence analysis course at the Cold Spring Harbor

Laboratory, and also a Fellow of the Salzburg Seminar, Session 358, on the "social and political implications of the Internet". He was involved with some pioneering initiatives in global e-learning (e.g., Global-Network Academy, Learning Corps, and Virtual School of Natural Sciences Biocomputing Division). His past work includes executive directorship and business development in e-learning start-up.

A certified Internet Business Strategist, Mr. Lau is the Webmaster for a few Web sites. He initiated and now moderates the Malaysian Life Scientists list. Through a project applying knowledge management to debate activities, he seeks to illustrate the concept of societal knowledge management and strategic thinking of k-economy to Malaysian community His motto expresses the essence of knowledge economy: "we shall learn, collaborate and shine as a community—be widely propagated, understood, and accepted."

13.14   DOUG MACNAMARA (CANADA)

Competency-based and experiential leadership development really is the epitome of "tacit knowledge" codification, development, transfer and measurement. Individuals, organizations, and nations alike, must continuously re-establish their "Value Quotient" based on knowledge-driven innovation and ingenuity.

Doug has more than twenty-five years of experience in leadership, governance and executive development, strategic facilitation, and overall organizational development. His specialties include strategy formulation and implementation, wilderness/high risk environments, organizational leadership, branding, and sales/marketing/service development. He invented unique competency profiling and active learning processes.

Currently president and CEO of Banff Executive Leadership Inc., he previously served as vice-president of The Banff Centre and general manager of The Banff Centre for Management for over seven years.

During this time he built up annual programming from approximately 35 to over 130 individual programs and increased annual participant numbers from 800 to 4,000. He led the development of dedicated programming areas for aboriginal leadership and management, as well as community and not-for-profit leadership in addition to enhancing both core leadership and management, and governance and executive leadership programming.

His prior background includes time spent as a high school science teacher, an editor in educational publishing, and several years at Royal Trust responsible for leading strategic planning, management development, and technical training (including credit, money market, pensions, benefits, and corporate finance). At Royal Trust, he was founder and managing partner of BRG Associates. This sub-unit of Royal Trust became a national HR, benefits design, communications, and strategic planning consulting team, working with many Top 500 companies, government departments, and nonprofit organizations. As vice-president for sales at Anixter Canada, the leading distributor of wiring systems for telecommunications, data, electrical and electronic infrastructure, he turned around their sales force and financial condition.

In an executive capacity, Doug has successfully led new business unit start-ups, downsizings and turnarounds, and restructurings and transformations. These have included strategic/marketing repositioning and re-branding of image. As a consultant, he has assisted over fifty organizations through these processes in Canada and internationally.

Doug is an active speaker and executive retreat facilitator, with recent sessions/articles including "Leading in a Networked World," "Leadership @ internet.speed," and "High Performance Board Governance."

An active participant in the community, Doug has served United Way Campaigns as a member of the campaign cabinet in Metro Toronto. In addition, he has served Oolagen, The Duke of Edinburgh's Award in Canada and Australia, The Royal Life Saving Society of Canada, the Canadian Red Cross Society, and The Canadian Diabetes Association. He has worked with Indigenous communities, and environmental issues. Currently, Doug serves as chair of the board of The Banff Mineral Springs Hospital and is a member of the Board of the National Geographic Television Channel.

13.15   DR. TOM MALONE (USA)

I believe we are at a historical choice point in determining the kind of world our children's children will inherit. If we make these choices based only on the models of our industrial-age past, we will almost certainly miss the true opportunities before us.

"An environmentally sustainable, economically equitable, and socially stable and secure society in which all of the basic needs and an equitable share human "wants" can be met by successive generations while maintaining a healthy, physically attractive and biologically productive environment."

Dr. Tom Malone is University Distinguished Scholar Emeritus at North Carolina State. A member of the National Academy of Sciences, he was elected Foreign Secretary in 1978. He also chaired the Academy's Geophysics Research Board and its Board on Atmospheric Physics and Climate.

He left a tenured faculty appointment at MIT in 1955 to join The Travelers Insurance Companies where he went on to become Senior Vice President and Director of Research. While on leave from MIT between 1949 and 1951, Malone edited the 1300 page *Compendium of Meteorology* that set the stage for meteorological research in the second half of the 20th century. He returned to academia in 1970 as Professor of Physics and Dean of the Graduate School at the University of Connecticut. A past national president of Sigma Xi, The Scientific

Research Society, he was named Founding Director of the Sigma Xi Center in North Carolina's Research Triangle Park in 1992. He has also served As national president of the American Meteorological Society and the American Geophysical Union

Tom was Secretary General of the Committee on Atmospheric Sciences of the International Council of Scientific Unions (ICSU) that, in a series of reports from 1965 to 1967, proposed the Global Atmospheric Research Program (GARP). He was a co-convener of ICSU's 1984 conference in Ottawa that led to the International Geosphere Biosphere Program (IGBP). Founding Secretary General of ICSU's Scientific Committee on Problems of the Environment, he has been a Vice President of ICSU and was its Treasurer from 1978 to 1984. He chaired the U. S. National Commission for UNECO from 1965 to 1967. He was awarded the International Meteorological Organization Prize in 1984 for "scientific eminence and a record of work done in the field of international meteorological organizations." His international work has also been recognized by an international award from the AAAS in 1994 and by an international jury of twelve scientists from eight countries that selected him for the 1991 St. Francis of Assisi Prize for the Environment.

Among his publications are: "Towards a *Knowledge Society* in the Americas." *INTERCIENCIA*, Vol. 25, No. 2 (2000); "A New Agenda for Science and Technology for the Twenty-First Century." *Proceedings of KOSEF'S 20TH Anniversary Symposium on Issues of Science and Technology in the 21st Century*, June 2-6. Seoul: The Korea Science and Engineering Foundation.; "Reflections on the Human Prospect" in Socolow RH. (ed.) (1994); *Annual Review of Energy and the Environment*. Palo Alto: Annual Reviews;. "Global change, science and the human prospect" in *Science and Public Affairs*, Vol. 6, Part 2. (1991); London: The Royal Society. Malone TF and Yohe GW. 2002 "Knowledge Partnership for a Sustainable, Equitable, and Stable Society." *Journal of Knowledge Management* (2002).

13.16   DR. EUNIKA MERCIER-LAURENT (FRANCE)

Knowledge takes multiple forms—savoir, savoir-faire, savoir-être. Switch from specific problem solving to global knowledge flow through organizing—people + computers + documents— need a common language.

KM is complex and difficult but it is worth an effort. Sometimes…people do not believe, or afraid necessary changes. It's a planetary problem to motivate people to do collaborative work.

Originally an electronic engineer from Politechnika Warszawska, Eunika arrived in Paris in 1975. She obtained her Ph.D. at Paris 7 University, working in INRIA on a microprocessor for intelligent information retrieval from databases. She continued her research on a workstation for collaborative (1981) work and enterprise activities modeling.

In 1982 she joined Groupe Bull and worked in the engineering department, and the scientific unit and artificial intelligence department. During her work on DPS7000 computer design, she built her first decision-support system for diagnosis using an AI "home" tool. To learn more about AI she returned to the University, working at the same time.

In 1989 she created a user's club for Bull clients using artificial intelligence tools, the first initiative of community of practice and innovation with a client. These tools are Le_Lisp, Prolog, knowledge [representation] object-oriented language (KOOL) and Charme (constraint programming), open KADS (knowledge modeling); they are used to solve complex industrial problems. She shared experiences in solving problems, and at the same time tools evolved and were improved with several common research programs. For her last two years with Groupe Bull, she had the responsibility of managing innovative applications worldwide.

In 1993 she contributed to the definition and architecture of the first enterprise memory application (MNEMOS). Lessons learned from all these experiences taught that the optimal way to solve complex industrial problems is to consider them in a global enterprise context, including client interactions. In 1991 the concept of knowledge-based enterprise was born.

She left Groupe Bull in 1994 to found EML Conseil—Knowledge Management Institute and Consulting to help enterprises to organize and manage a "knowledge flow." She works mainly on projects using reasoning by analogy applied to diagnosis, knowledge discovery and fuzzy matching of offer and demand, organizing and exploring past experience. Since 1996 and participating electronically in the KM Forum, she has been an Entovation Fellow, responsible for initiatives throughout France.

Eunika has published over twenty papers on her research and experience and is responsible for the French translation of *Innovation Strategy for the Knowledge Economy*. She contributed to knowledge management Delphi study at KIKM. She is a member of Institut F.R. Bull, a multidisciplinary discussion group on the influence of technology on different domains, the board of the French Association for Artificial Intelligence, and the Transinnova regional and international competency network. She teaches a knowledge approach at the University's engineering and management schools.

13.17   DR. EDNA PASHER (ISRAEL)

Introducing a new topic to a market is not easy. Those of us who have been intensively involved in the global knowledge movement sometimes forget that there are people who are still suspicious, who think we have just invented a new fashion. We are now realizing how even the use of the Internet for virtual conferencing which has become part of our work is still very new too.

Edna Pasher founded an international strategic management consulting firm in 1978. The firm provides customized consulting services to organizations both in the private and the public sectors. Edna Pasher Ph.D & Associates specializes in assisting client organizations to speed up strategic renewal in a fast-changing environment.

Dr. Pasher is a frequent speaker in national and international conferences. She earned her Ph.D at New York University in communication arts and sciences and has served as faculty member at Adelphi University, the City University of New York, the Hebrew University in Jerusalem, and the Tel-Aviv University. She developed the first training program for knowledge managers in collaboration with the Open University in Israel.

In 1994 Edna Pasher Ph.D & Associates identified knowledge management as the critical success factor for organizational renewal, and the firm has become the leader of the knowledge-management movement in Israel and an active participant in the international community of the Intellectual Capital Pioneers. They established the Knowledge-in-Action series of international face-to-face and electronic conferences on knowledge management and intellectual capital, and the Knowledge Cafe' Forum which has met on a regular basis for about thirty times since 1995. In 2001, in collaboration with the Israeli Management Association, Edna Pusher Ph.D & Associates established the Forum for Knowledge Management and Innovation. In 2002 Dr. Pasher started an interest group on innovation and metrics, a community of practice active on-line on Knowledge Board, the portal for the European KM community.

Edna Pasher Ph.D & Associates is one of the partners in a major European Union–funded project—NIMCube, designed to develop a holistic reference method for the re-use and innovation process of knowledge in the field of new product development. This approach —complete with a ToolKit and software application—tries to create new knowledge by transferring existing knowledge into a new context.

Realizing the implications of knowledge strategy at the national level, Dr. Pasher also created the Intellectual Capital Report of the

State of Israel—"Hidden Values of the Desert"—in which indicators provide a benchmark of the progress of Israel against other industrialized nations of the world..

Edna Pasher Ph.D & Associates founded *Status*—the leading Israeli monthly magazine for management in 1991 and Rom Knowledgeware, a firm that provides IT solutions for knowledge management.

13.18   DR. ANTE PULIC AND KARMEN JELCIC (CROATIA)

Each company has unique knowledge, skills, values and solutions that can be transformed into value at the market. If managing the intangible resources (IC) can help to achieve competitive advantage, increase efficiency and market value then it is not a choice, but a necessity. Therefore the key question is: Do we create or destroy value?

Ante Pulic is economics professor at two faculties—Zagreb, Croatia and Graz, Austria— where he has been leading research projects on the measurement of IC performance. His major contribution to the IC field is the development of the value creation efficiency analysis (VAIC™), a new output measure for the new economy. VAIC™ provides information on the performance of key resources, "physical and financial" and "intellectual" capital, based on regular financial data. It has been applied at more than 2,000 companies and banks at various levels of business activity. As business success has traditionally been expressed through accounting and managers are used to react primarily to numerical objectives and feedbacks, he has put all his efforts into finding a way to bridge the gap between new economic reality and traditional accounting standards. It is obvious that the traditional financial metrics do not reflect reality any more; therefore, new output measures for knowledge work have to be introduced. As the key objective of any business is value creation, the ability of employees to transform their knowledge and skills into value-creating actions is of vital importance. The more effective is knowledge utilization, individual and collective, the more successful value creation will be.

As the co-founder of the Austrian IC- Research Center, Ante Pulic has initiated international collaboration on the project "new accounting systems for the new economy." One of the major issues is the inadequate treatment of human capital (represented by all the employees of a company). On the one hand, HC is considered to be the key value-creating factor' on the other hand, salaries and fringe benefits are still considered to be costs rather than investments. It is also important to include additional IC reporting in order to make visible whether and how intangibles are managed and when ROI can be expected. That way investors and shareholders will receive valuable information.

In Croatia Ante Pulic and Karmen Jelcic are currently involved in a major IC project initiated by the Croatian Chamber of Commerce. The objective is to create awareness of the importance of intellectual capital as the key production factor of the new economy through the activities of a newly founded IC association within the Chamber. The activities include publishing and free distribution of an informative IC booklet, lectures and workshops in all twenty Counties of Croatia as well as measurement of the "value creation efficiency" of all the counties (during the past six years) in order to establish a base for future improvement and to create a "national value creation efficiency index."

Ante, Karmen, and their colleagues have been closely affiliated with the sponsorship of the McMaster conference on intellectual capital (Hamilton, Ontario) and the most recent International Conference on Intellectual Capital (Portoroz, Slovenia).

13.19   DR. JOERG STAEHELI (SWITZERLAND)

We consider KM as a product that can be used internally, and you have to advertise, you have to promote like you would to sell a product on the market…We learned you have to continuously feed oil into the furnace, challenging people to come back.

Dr. Joerg Staeheli is global technology officer at Novartis Pharma AG in Basel. His background is in chemical engineering and management sciences.

He joined Sandoz in 1965 and held several positions in chemical development and corporate engineering. From 1990 until the merger of Ciba-Geigy and Sandoz to create Novartis in 1996 he headed Sandoz's department for technology planning and transfer. For facilitating the full use of Novartis' group knowledge and know-how across organizational boundaries he was appointed leader of knowledge networking at Novartis International AG after the merger. From 1990 to 2000 he was also executive secretary of the technology advisory board of Novartis. As of April 1, 2002 Dr. Joerg Staeheli took the position of a global technology officer in pharmaceutical development.

In an issue of *CIO Magazine*, Dr. Staeheli was featured in an article[7] about how Novartis ventures a new strategy for sharing ideas and innovation across the global enterprise. "After the merger of two venerable Basel-based companies, Novartis was the newest and richest beneficiary of Basel's confluence of scientific learning, industry and culture." How does a company that depends on innovation find ways to increase its knowledge? The response was three-pronged: using Web-based technology to foster collaboration within its worldwide workforce; creating a system of development grants for projects that make different business units work together; and hosting periodic knowledge fairs to spark ideas. This form of "knowledge networking" shows that making the most of an organization's intellectual assets is more of a cultural than a technological challenge.

Dr. Steheli has delivered presentations on "the human side of knowledge management," in which he outlines the business case based on company performance; illustrates the impact of knowledge networking; identifies the drivers for knowledge and intellectual capital; and describes cross-organization platforms, including e-communities.

Using socio-technical diagrams, he features the organization network analysis (ONA) that illustrates the flow of knowledge with quantitative metrics. He defines a role for knowledge stewards in the process to increase potential performance.

13.20   XENIA STANFORD (CANADA)

The knowledge economy must integrate customer, competitor, collaborator and corporate capital to unleash the energy necessary to move undaunted into the unknown territory (the future) and slay the dragons of ignorance but to do so let go of the known shore (the past).

Xenia Stanford is currently the president and chief executive officer of Stanford Solutions, Inc., devoted to empowering others to manage knowledge by using practical tools. Stanford's first training and use of knowledge-mapping techniques was at the universities where she was employed as a research officer in the field of education. After many years as a library and records manager, she became a change leader involved in reorganizational design and process restructuring. Throughout her career in business and now as president of her own company, she has helped corporations save millions of dollars.

Born and raised in Alberta with the exception of two years of her childhood in British Columbia, Stanford has studied at several universities and conducted research into learning effectiveness at the University of Calgary in Alberta, Canada and Macquarie University in

North Ryde, Australia. She taught students from nearly every grade including pre-school and university. The teaching locations included the Canadian provinces of Alberta and British Columbia as well as Australia and Fiji. Work and personal travels have taken her to several other provinces in Canada, various states in Australia and the United States (including Hawaii), and several countries in mainland Europe.

Stanford has a Bachelor of Education degree and has completed course work for Master's degrees in several disciplines, including literature and linguistics, library science, and management. She has published many articles and conducted many workshops on the subject of knowledge management and the techniques of mapping and auditing. She wrote a Web column on leadership and won an international writing contest for her article "Delighting the Customer." Her research into the areas of knowledge mapping and auditing is ongoing, and her constantly improving courses reflect the benefit of her continuous learning. She now brings that learning to her latest venture—Know-Map—an electronic publication that reaches thousands of knowledge professionals in more than sixty countries.

An expert in social network analysis, she delivers business development and knowledge mapping workshops for academic, governmental, and industrial firms. She was a leader during the most recent global learn day—a 24-hour around-the-world tour of innovation in education and distance learning.

13.21   HUBERT ST. ONGE (CANADA)

Comprehensive knowledge strategy encompasses— in parallel—the explicit and tacit dimensions of knowledge which can only be generated in highly collaborative relationships. How do we foster values-based leadership?

Hubert Saint-Onge is the former Vice President for Strategic Capabilities at Clarica, where he was responsible for putting in place the strategies, plans, and processes needed to ensure that the firm has the organizational and individual capabilities required to realize its business goals.

Hubert joined Clarica five years ago and before then held various positions in government, the energy sector, and banking. Hubert was the vice-president of learning organization and leadership development for the Canadian Imperial Bank of Commerce in Toronto. Before that, he lived in Calgary, where he worked within the business unit, at the corporate level, of Shell Canada.

Hubert defines success by helping to create a successful organization where its members feel constantly challenged to make a contribution that makes a difference in the realization of worthwhile aspirations.

His business philosophy was cultivated at the earliest stage in his career upon leaving graduate school when he performed community development work in rural Mexico. During that time, Hubert learned that the answer to economic development centered on the self-initiation and empowerment of the individual. It was this experience that led him to focus his career on people and their place within organizations, and how they can assume control over their destinies.

His background includes a political science degree from York University, a masters in economics. Hubert, who calls strategic business planning not only his job, but his passion, says his main hobby is networking with other people around the world who do similar work.

Hubert has traveled the globe giving presentations on organization learning, leadership development, and knowledge value creation in various countries, including South Africa, France, Korea, Australia, and England. He has also published a number of articles on these subjects. In addition, Hubert was a board member of the Canadian Centre for Management Development from 1995 to 1999.

Hubert is the recipient of the prestigious award of the Life Insurance Institute of Canada (LIIC) for Lifetime achievement in people and organizational development. He has also received an honorary fellowship from the Canadian School of Management. He is one of three recipients of the president's awards from the Ontario Society of Training and Development for his contribution to the domain of organization learning.

13.21   SUMMARY

As Tom Peters suggests in his most recent treatise[8] on leadership, "Leadership is confusing....Leaders love a mess....Leaders create their own destinies....Leaders multi-task....Leaders don't create followers, they create more leaders."

These "ken" practitioners represent a diagonal slice of the network. They have worked in the governmental, academic, and industrial environments—and many more than one. They are men and women of vision; but, more important, they are examples of knowledge in action. Through their positions of leadership that often extend beyond the boundaries of their particular enterprise or nation, they are role models of knowledge practice.

According to our research[9] of thirty-three case study examples, the leaders are visionary, holistic, and systematic and encourage an environment of teamwork, learning, and innovation. Truth be known, many of these practitioners sound more like theorists in their presentations and actions than do the faculty researchers.

What that may bode for our future is an unprecedented explosion of economic rewards of innovation based on the flow of knowledge rather than the flow of technology (i.e., materials into products and services). We have yet to witness the benefits of such a self-sustaining, naturally accelerating circle of innovation based on collaborative advantage—not competition any more.

Ultimately, our future depends on individuals—what they are able to imagine and put into practice.

CHAPTER ENDNOTES

[1] Special Millennium Edition, *The Economist* (December 1999).

[2] See *Innovation for the Knowledge Economy*, p. xxii.

[3] Published in a two-part series for *Knowledge Management* (Dec.–Jan., 2001 and Feb. 2001).

[4] For further information, visit http://www.knowledgesystems.org/.

[5] For further information, visit http://www.kmetasite.org/.

[6] Published in the *Journal of Knowledge Management*, vol. 1. no. 4 (June 1998).

[7] The article, "Wiring the Corporate Brain" by Gary Abramson, appeared in *CIO Enterprise Magazine*, March 15, 1999.

[8] Visit FAST Company online at http://www.fastcompany.com/online/44/rules.html.

[9] See *Creating the Knowledge Based Business* (Skyrme and Amidon, 1997), pp. 468–470.

FOURTEEN
Evolving Innovation Infrastructures

We live in an age of interdependence
As well as independence;
an age of internationalism as well as nationalization.
We are partners for peace…
A system of cooperation, interdependence and harmony,
Whose peoples can jointly meet their burdens and opportunities
Throughout the world.
Some say this is only a dream,
but I do not agree.

John F. Kennedy[1]

They came to Malaysia from over 90 countries—some 1,200 participants—to explore avenues of collaboration. Thousands more had been involved in the electronic dialogs that were managed two months in advance, all in preparation for the Global Knowledge Forum and two-day Action Summit. This provided the opportunity to convert concepts and dreams into plans, policies, and programs to build the foundation for a future that does not exist today.

I stood in their midst, reveling in the diversity of talent, the levels of leadership, and the energy in the presentations and conversations. At that moment, I felt a part of "the global innovation village;" and I knew it was only a matter of time.

After I delivered my own remarks, an aboriginal delegate took the microphone and spoke first in his native tongue. Then he offered his thanks for positioning the "person" into the system. I had said that this ICT agenda was to be human and humane—not one only of the wonders of technology and the "information revolution."

We have a great deal to learn from this young man and from others building bridges across cultures as a way of strengthening their own.

14.1   GLOBAL KNOWLEDGE PARTNERSHIP

"The Internet began to impinge on a global consciousness sometime about 1994/95," states one of the background documents for the international forum. In 1996, the G7, meeting in Brussels, decided it was a major issue that required global attention. The Canadian government and The World Bank offered to host the first Global Knowledge Conference, which was held in Toronto in 1997. The Global Knowledge Partnership (GKP)[2]—now numbering more than sixty organizations—was formed in the wake of that meeting. Three years later in March 2000, members of the GKP and other interested parties continued the dialog for a week in Kuala Lumpur, Malaysia,[3] where the current Secretariat is hosted by the Malaysian government and represented by the National Information Technology Council (NITC). For 2001–2003, the chair for the committee is the government of Switzerland, represented by the Swiss Agency for Development and Cooperation (SDC).

The GKP is described as a "network of networks" with a diverse membership base comprising public, private, and not-for profit organizations from both developed and developing countries. This is just one facet of the thousands of cross-border initiatives that emerged during the last decade that constitute the innovation superhighway in which knowledge that is created can move from the point of origin to the point of need or opportunity.

Simply stated, the GKP has a vision of a world of equal opportunities in which all people are able to have access to and use knowledge and information to improve their lives. The mission is three-fold:

- The Global Knowledge Partnership is an evolving network of public, private, and not for profit organizations.
- We aim to promote broad access to—and effective use of—knowledge and information as tools of equitable sustainable development.
- We share information, experiences, and resources to realize the potential of information and communication technologies to improve lives, reduce poverty, and empower people.

Readers may be familiar with their World Development Report (1998–1999) entitled "Knowledge for Development," which set the stage for a new orientation of how The World Bank would assist nations to take advantage of the knowledge economy. The GKP has continued the story-telling method to disseminate the real lessons of leadership, and examples have been published from Africa, Chile, Ghana, Indonesia, Finland, and other countries.

Several major events preceded the Forum and Summit in Malaysia. They focused on the three major content themes of the agenda: access, empowerment and governance. There was a Global Knowledge Development (GKD) discussion[4] in which more than 1,800 participants shared their knowledge on the use of information and communications technologies (ICTs). Building the information community in Africa (BICA) led to an event in Pretoria, South Africa in February 1999. ORBICOM in collaboration with UNESCO, the Canadian International Development Agency (CIDA) and the GKP in Montreal organized "Connecting Knowledge in Communications" in April. The African forum was held in October followed by another regional event in South Asia—the Toward a South Asia Knowledge Network (TASKNET) Conference that was held in New Delhi in November. Over 200 organizations from public, private, and NGO sectors participated—all active in developing the knowledge society of the region. The ASEAN Regional Workshop was held in February to identify the generic issues to be addressed if the vision was to be realized, such as fostering the requisite mindset, allocating and mobilizing resources, bridging the "digital divide," and addressing issues of gender. Priorities were identified in six theme areas: education, politics, technology, culture, economy, and environment.

There was consensus at the GKP that equitable access to information and knowledge on a global scale is crucial to bring about true empowerment and good governance at the local, national, regional, and global levels. GKP's strategic initiatives are important to migrate toward knowledge societies, but this is not enough. The GKP needs to provide the essential platform to build meaningful partnerships in advancing the dimensions of global knowledge. As such, the GKP Action Plan focused on using knowledge to address the following issues:

1. *Poverty alleviation.* Narrowing the income gap between the developed and developing world is on the global governance agenda.

2. *Digital divide.* Providing access and empowering info-poor communities in both Northern and Southern countries is a desired outcome.

3. *Global governance.* Examining the relevance of present arrangements is a step toward providing for an equitable playing field, given the developments in globalization, Internet governance, e-commerce, and intellectual property rights

4. *Human resource development.* Building the capabilities of individuals, groups, and communities based on the principle of inclusion is key to meaningful participation in emerging knowledge economy.

The GKP action plan has translated issues into "action-items" that focus on concrete policies, programs, and projects to address global issues. National, regional, or international institutions are implementing the GKP action plan, using bilateral or multilateral modalities, within a given time frame. The title of the new World Development

Report 2003[5]—"*Sustainable Development in a Dynamic Economy*" —indicates that the agenda has only just begun!

14.2 Development Gateway[6]

There was also considerable progress in building something called the Development Gateway Project—"Where the Worlds of Knowledge Meet"—designed to provide the "value added" to audiences in developing countries and to other stakeholders. There are opportunities to exchange ideas and knowledge, find development projects, explore business opportunities, and access country gateways.

More than twenty countries were initially awarded information development (InfoDev) grants for the planning and establishment of country gateways (CGs). Proposals were considered for regional gateways, which could serve a geographically large and populous region within a country (e.g., the island of Java or the Northeast of Brazil) or a region with many very small countries (e.g., the small island nations of the Caribbean). Many different partnership-building consultations were held in Armenia, Azerbaijan, Georgia, Indonesia, Kazakhstan, Moldova, Pakistan, and Russia. The meetings focused on attracting partners and identifying ways to ensure project sustainability. Key issues discussed included content development, financial sustainability, and technology use.

The Gateway Team presented the Gateway at the UN in New York. Represented were the UNDP, UNICEF, UNIFEM, UNCDF, and UNFPA. The meeting was also well attended by UN permanent missions and non-profit organizations. Discussions are also underway with UNCTAD in the area of foreign direct investment for developing countries; with WHO on the development of health-related content; with UNDP and USAID on the Gateway's aid effectiveness pages; and with ECLAC as a provider of regional economic and social development content and data.

The Development Gateway portal (the Gateway) offers users access to development information, resources, and tools, providing a space to contribute knowledge and share experiences. The Gateway helps users navigate the growing amount of information available online and empowers virtual communities of learning to address key development issues. The gateway is now governed by the Development Gateway Foundation—a not-for-profit organization based in Washington, D.C. and representing major donors and partners from international organizations, the public and private sectors, and civil society, as well as representatives of developing countries.

14.3   KALiF[7]—The European Perspective

A small monograph—"KALiF—To share is to multiply"—was produced as a joint project between Kenniscentrum CIBIT and the European Consortium for the Learning Organization (ECLO) and sponsored by the ESPRIT Project 29255. KALiF is a methodology for creating mutual gain through knowledge sharing.

There is a portal for IT for learning and training in industry (LTI), aiming to promote the European LTI program and to act as a single point of entry to the domain of IT for learning and training in industry. In the LTI program, sixteen European-funded projects are developing innovative tools and techniques, such as virtual-reality environments, knowledge-sharing environments, and simulators to improve knowledge management and learning, not only in various sectors of industrial organizations (e.g., the maritime, aircraft, nuclear energy and transport sector) but also in the designer world and financial services.

In their vision, the key to a realization of objectives is to connect LTI people. They have created a pan-European network of professionals in the field of IT for learning and training in industry intended to survive beyond the life of any particular thematic program. This network exists in both physical and virtual reality so that professionals have opportunities to exchange ideas face to face as well as by electronic means.

Their role is to be the catalyst for making connections, to facilitate conversations, and to serve as ambassadors for the projects to the rest of the world with two types of activities: those aimed at the creation of a "physical network" and those aimed at the creation of a "virtual network." Their Web site includes information on each of the projects: intellectual property rights, venture capital, discussion facilities, and electronic newsletters.

The success of KALiF and the results of many other initiatives funded by the European Union have evolved into another portal called KnowledgeBoard.[8] Originally intended as the portal for the European knowledge management (KM) industry, it has quickly become a worldwide state-of-the-art Internet site for KM discussions, monthly online workshops, and a description of who's who—albeit in the European KM community. Their fortnightly Knowledge-Board newswire, a mix of news, articles, and upcoming events provides the timeliest access to both the concepts and the practice on a global basis.

14.4   THE KNOWLEDGE WAVE—NEW ZEALAND

The Knowledge Wave Trust[9] is an independent body established to build on the ideas and momentum generated by the Catching the Knowledge Wave Conference held in August 2001. The aim is to act as a catalyst to promote existing and new initiatives, stimulate public discussion, and benchmark New Zealand's progress on economic, social, and environmental fronts as we make the transition to a knowledge society.

The Catching the Knowledge Wave Conference convened in August 2001, generated over 100 recommendations on how New Zealand can lift its economic and social performance and create a knowledge society. It was co-chaired by the Prime Minister, Helen Clark, and Dr. John Hood, Vice Chancellor of the University of Auckland.

Thirty-seven national and international speakers and expatriate New Zealanders addressed the conference. It was charged with identifying elements of a national strategy to enable New Zealand's transition to a competitive knowledge society. The proceedings were telecast live, with viewers invited to contribute to the discussion via e-mail.

The conference and its working groups focused on the broad, inclusive view through five themes: innovation and creativity, entrepreneurship, people and capability, sustainable economic strategies, and social dynamism and knowledge opportunities. See the quotes from students in Chapter 15—true examples of the knowledge millennium generation.

Recommendations were consolidated under the following theme headings. Several projects are now underway that support the recommendations made at the conference. Some of the projects listed below have no Knowledge Wave Trust involvement but clearly have the potential to deliver the Trust's objectives:

- Creating a strong vision and brand for New Zealand, promoting our lifestyle and values while building national confidence and pride
- Changing attitudes through celebrating our innovation, creativity, and excellence
- Developing a superlative educational system
- Developing our research and development capability, in both private and public sectors
- Developing specialist industry clusters around areas of competitive advantage, using New Zealand's distinctiveness to win high-value global business
- Developing, retaining, and attracting talented individuals, while engaging and utilizing the Kiwi Diaspora (expatriate network)
- Streamlining and redefining central and local government
- Creating fiscal incentives, regulations, and business support structures consistent with our economic growth aspirations
- Creating innovative societal incentive structures

The "wave" has generated considerable activity. "Innovate" is an initiative to leverage New Zealand's nation of innovators—full of great ideas and inventions—into successful businesses. It focuses on the tools of business development with a variety of seminars, toolkit workshops, multimedia presentations, and keynote speakers from innovative and successful New Zealand businesses. There is a description of the NZ Edge—heroes who are examples of innovators to the world—turning great ideas into great ventures. A new "Innovation Framework for New Zealand" has been drafted and distributed via the KnowledgeWave portal.

There are fiscal incentives, regulations, and business support structures consistent with their economic growth aspirations—namely through the NZ Venture Capital Association—and maybe more telling, innovative societal incentive structures with a Social Capital Venture Capital Fund—a new funding approach that applies venture capital investment disciplines to the funding of nonprofit organizations.

And lest you think that the technology infrastructure involves only computers and Internet communications, The KnowledgeWave celebrates successful Kiwi innovation on prime time television. The producers sensed a need for an attitudinal change to a new confidence and pride in NZ abilities. The "Innovation Wave" is a Knowledge Wave Trust project that showcases New Zealand researchers, business people, teachers, and other innovators through one-minute vignettes on prime time television. There are a total of forty vignettes and one is be played to 700,000 viewers every week night immediately prior to the weather on One Network News. In addition to the television broadcast, the vignettes are archived on one of the highest rated Web sites in New Zealand to serve as a resource for schools.

The efforts of the Trust have enabled what could have been fragmented initiatives to be coalesced under the rubric of the Knowledge Wave—a compelling and graphic image of progress that inspires individuals and enterprises to action.

14.5   SINGAPORE—"THE INNOVATION NATION"

It was the International Productivity Conference (IPO)—the combined fortieth celebration of the Asian Productivity Organization (APO) and the twentieth anniversary of the Productivity Standards Board in Singapore. Delegations from 18 member nations (representing one-third of the world's population) throughout the Middle East and the Pacific participated in several days of thoughtful dialog and exploration of how these nations can create a sustainable future.

Perhaps the most extraordinary realization of this momentous conference coalescing the aspirations of more than 400 participants cold be summed up as follows: What has provided a leadership focus for a generation of quality management has evolved to one of economic prosperity rather than (only) enterprise productivity. For four decades, the quality agenda has maintained a foundation of building competitive advantage. What happened in Singapore in November 2001 does not eliminate competition; it builds on the standard with a spirit of collaboration—across functions, industries, and nations.

Keynotes and panelists alike, one after another, referenced the more fundamental and systematic implications of local initiatives to build effective strategies to ensure social, economic, and environmental sustainability. In an opening video, productivity was represented as the cornerstone of a prosperous future. To quote Peter Drucker, "One cannot manage change; one must stay ahead of change."

New initiatives for the organization focus upon knowledge, technology, innovation and value creation. Strategic business alliances were defined as essential, human capital is more relevant, and people are the "DNA" of an organization. Indeed, a nation's standard of living is defined by how people perform "productively." The theme song referenced the imperative to "make a better life for everyone... hand-in-hand...leading into the future...not afraid to learn...to be the best that people are."

An announcement was made, which could have been unprecedented at the time, of plans of the Prime Minister to create an

Innovation Council—both private and public—to position Singapore as "the innovation nation" with specific plans to stimulate and nurture an enterprising spirit to all Singaporeans.

Prime Minister Goh Chok Tong provided the vision of an Innovative Society as referenced in Chapter 1. Indeed, by the leadership taken at this recent IPC conference, Singapore—with the help of the APO—will lead not only the nation but could set the standards for creating the innovation region of the world.

The administration has put resources behind its words, with such events as a national meeting that attracted 8,000 participating guests at the Singapore indoor stadium. Using a mass-audience technique, more than 400,000 ideas were generated in one hour for the improvement of a wide range of issues (e.g., health care, the transportation system, and education). The exercise carried the message that everyone is creative and everyone has something to contribute. An accompanying effort reaches into the homes and offices nationwide through a Web site. Now, managers are reviewing, prioritizing, and implementing the best suggestions that were placed in the National Ideas Bank—putting the knowledge into practice.

With the new millennium has come a renewed urgency for Singapore to make innovation a way of life. In both promotional materials and programs, leaders of the country have sought to create "an innovation mindset" to sustain the next phase of the productivity—and now the innovation—movement.

14.6 ShareNet: The Enterprise Model

Commensurate with the explosion of activity on the Internet has come an equivalent electronic traffic within enterprises in the form of intranets. Their real value, however, lies in how effective these mechanisms are in driving a common language and shared purpose among an international web of employees—and in some cases stakeholders—in the process.

In the article[10] "Knowledge Communities Going Beyond Repositories and Databases," executives at Siemens AG, Munich, Germany,
have described the evolution and functionality of their global networking system—ShareNet—the company's global knowledge-sharing
system, which, by the way, is both technical and human.

Every company, particularly in fast-changing markets such as
telecommunications, needs to find ways to acquire the requisite know-
how, expertise, and insight to continuously stay at the "leading edge"
with its offerings. Identifying the really business-critical knowledge
and organizing to exploit it consistently, however, goes beyond mere
knowledge management. It requires a strategic approach that leads far
beyond databases and repositories, online directories, and document-
management systems.

Siemens's information and communication networks (ICN) division is a global provider of telecommunication solutions, active in more
than 100 countries. The company's traditional business used to be
quite simple and straightforward; it dominated its home market by
means of a close relationship to a regulated national telecom monopoly. Siemens used this position to sell integrated products to other
national communications providers around the world.

The pace of innovation was accelerated by changes in the market
environment, such as new competitors and advanced technology.
There was a shift from a product to a service focus and solutions
approach, which increases the complexity and knowledge intensity of
the business.

ShareNet is a community of about 7000 sales, marketing, and business development managers of Siemens ICN. The goal is to detect
local innovations and leverage them on a global scale. ShareNet covers
both explicit and tacit knowledge of the sales value creation process
including project know-how, technical and functional solution components, and the business environment (e.g., customer, competitor,
market, technology, and partner knowledge). ShareNet has a strong
focus on experience-based knowledge (e.g., field experience; pro's and

con's of a solution) and providing space for less structured dialog such as chats, community news, discussion groups on special issues, and so called urgent requests (URs).

There is no central or single source of wisdom. The value of the community depends on its ability to create a rich body of knowledge ranging from dedicated editors who regularly complete competitor profiles to project teams who capture the knowledge they created during a certain project. Once the knowledge is on the Web site, it can be re-used not only across countries but also within the sales force of a specific local company, which is a major benefit particularly for a large local organization, because it reduces the need for training and education.

In this way, the work with ShareNet has become a natural and integral part of the day-to-day work of its members, unlike many knowledge repositories, which tend to be disconnected from people's daily job, adding just another task on top of all the other things people have to do.

Knowledge sharing does not simply happen unless there are a number of measurable tangible and intangible benefits not just for the organization but for the individual as well. In the case of ShareNet the main advantages Siemens derives from its knowledge network are as follows:

- ShareNet provides real-life experience knowledge through sales projects, tested customer solution modules ready for application in similar circumstances. Thus, it saves precious time in all phases of the sales value-creation process—for example, in the preparation of an offer, in the negotiation phase, and in the implementation of the network. Time savings range from a few days to several weeks depending on the type of project. The time previously needed to "reinvent the wheel" is now spent in a richer relationship with the customers and creating new opportunities.

- In addition to time, ShareNet saves consulting fees for Siemens because the learnings and analyses of external consultants' reports are made available on a global scale whenever possible.
- By making innovative customer solutions visible throughout the organization, they are re-used in other countries or with other customers, thus generating new income streams.
- By networking the sales frontlines in all countries, Siemens is able to detect new trends and developments in both technology and customer requirements earlier for the benefit of the customer.

Success stories from actual sales projects that highlight these benefits are systematically collected and published on the Web site. A business plan with projections of expected savings and additional revenue created through the use of ShareNet is also in place and communicated.

14.7   CBIRD[11]

Perhaps one of the most progressive experiments in crossing geographic territorial boundaries resides on the border of Mexico and the United States. Imagine if the "border" between two countries did not—in actuality—exist? What might that bode for the innovation capability and economic development of the region?

The Cross-Border Institute for Regional Development (CBIRD) is a bi-national development initiative. By bringing together the academic, governmental, and private enterprise sectors on both sides of the border, as well as foundations and non-governmental organizations (NGOs) in the region, principals assist in identifying opportunities to rethink, reshape, and restructure solutions for a prosperous border region. CBIRD's main objective is to empower the grassroots efforts of local communities to shape their own future. It will help create and share wealth with all citizens of the region, bring equitable prosperity, and protect the environment and the quality of life.

CBIRD offers a unique opportunity for all regional stakeholders to participate through dynamic civic and social entrepreneurship. It will also allow them to promote sustainable development of the border region through the creation of a knowledge-based economy driven by leading-edge technology and industries.

As an independent and neutral catalyst and an advocate for the future, CBIRD assists in transforming the border region into a vibrant and prosperous economic development zone in the Americas. Through communication, cooperation, collaboration, and integration of local and regional communities, CBIRD's vision of "one region—one future" will be realized.

The Texas-Mexico border forms a uniquely intertwined, bi-national and multi-cultural community. In order to respond to the challenge of fulfilling the need to create, shape, and build a dynamic and prosperous twenty-first century border region, the initiative will harness the capability of the region to " think" and "do" as a community-based organization. They are driven by a "bottoms-up" approach using a "think globally and act locally and vice versa" proac-tive process.

Shaping the region, one program at a time, the principals plan to create a bi-national region through planning and analysis as well as hard work and determination. CBIRD is committed to working with local communities and their leadership to establish collaborative core programs that help grow and shape the region.

14.8   NEPAD: Africa's Initiative[12]

The New Partnership for Africa's Development (NEPAD) is a pledge by African leaders, based on a common vision and a firm and shared conviction, that they have a pressing duty to eradicate poverty and to place their countries, both individually and collectively, on a path of sustainable growth and development and, at the same time, to participate actively in the world economy and body politic. NEPAD embraces the following initiatives:

- *Peace, security, democracy, and political governance initiative.* This section covers the conditions for sustainable development—namely, peace and security and the democracy and political governance.
- *Economic and corporate governance initiative.* This section covers the conditions for sustainable development—namely, improved state capacity to promote economic growth and development.
- *Bridging the infrastructure gap.* The infrastructure sectoral priority includes all infrastructure sections (on the subregional and continental level)—namely, information and communication technologies, energy, transport, and water and sanitation.
- *Human resource development initiative.* The human resource sectoral priority includes poverty reduction, education, reversing the brain drain, and health.
- *Capital flows initiative.* This section includes topics related to capital flows such as increasing domestic resource mobilization, debt relief, ODA reforms, and private capital flows.
- *Market access initiative.* This section covers market access issues such as diversification of production, agriculture, mining, manufacturing, tourism, services, promoting the private sector, promoting African exports, and removal of non-tariff barriers.
- *Environment initiative.* This section supplies information on the systematic combination of initiatives to develop a coherent environmental program.

14.9   THE UNITED NATIONS

The UN resolution[13] adopted at for the World Summit on the Information Society provides a platform for an innovation superhighway if you substitute the word "innovation" for the word "information."

It recognizes "the urgent need to harness the potential of knowledge and technology for promoting the goals of the United Nations Millennium Declaration, and to find effective and innovative ways to put this potential at the service of development for all." It recognizes "the pivotal role of the UN system in promoting development, particularly with respect to access to and transfer of technology, especially information and communication technologies and services, inter alia, through partnerships with all relevant stakeholders."

It is convinced of "the need, at the highest political level, to marshal the global consensus and commitment required to promote the urgently needed access of all countries to information, knowledge and communication technologies for development so as to reap the full benefits of the information and communication technologies revolution, and to address the whole range of relevant issues related to the information society, through the development of a common vision and understanding of the information society and the adoption of a declaration and plan of action for implementation by Governments, international institutions and all sectors of civil society."

It recognizes "the need to harness synergies and to create cooperation among the various information and communication technologies initiatives, at the regional and global levels, currently being undertaken or planned so as to promote and foster the potential of information and communication technologies for development by other international organizations and civil society."

14.10 Summary

In societal, regional, national, and enterprise initiatives, the objective is universal: to discover useful information (i.e., knowledge) and disseminate it (i.e., creation and diffusion) via the network (i.e., facilities and services). This is the essence of The Innovation Superhighway.

It is a highway not necessarily based in the information per se. It is, rather, an active mechanism to ensure the movement of knowledge from the point of origin to the point of use. It is a highway that is dependent as much—perhaps more so—on the intellectual and social, albeit virtual, connections among people as it is the sophistication of a technology infrastructure. It is a highway of networked knowledge operating in the best interest of our common good, but not at the expense of individual development.

Imagine what might be possible if the "architects" envisioned their portals as vehicles for innovation. stimulating the development of new knowledge and moving it in real time to the point of opportunity or need? Each of the initiatives above can function as a node of this evolving network of innovation. Enabled by the most sophisticated technology and carefully developed by professionals from various industries and regions of the world, this highway of the "best" knowledge of the world is being made accessible to all.

These initiatives, viewed collectively, could be considered as examples of global interdependence operating for the success of an enterprise, the vitality of a nation's economy, and the advancement of society as a whole. At last—a common language and a shared vision.

CHAPTER ENDNOTES

[1] Speech delivered at the Paulskirche Assembly Hall, Frankfurt, Federal Republic of Germany, June 25, 1963. Recorded in Sorensen (1988) p.322.

[2] For further information, visit the Web site at http://www.globalknowledge.org/.

[3] The GKP has since held its annual meeting for 2002 at Addis Ababa, Ethiopia.

[4] This electronic discussion has continued after the Malaysia conference and is still one of the most robust sources of knowledge about the progress of initiatives worldwide.

[5] To review previous and current editions of the WDR, visit http://econ.worldbank.org/wdr/.

[6] For further information, visit http://www.developmentgateway.org/.

[7] For further information and a downloadable version of the study, visit http://www.lti-portal.org/.

[8] For further information, visit http://www.knowledgeboard.com/.

[9] For further information, visit http://www.knowledgewave.org.nz/.

[10] The article references Tom Stewart in *Fortune*, JUNE 7, 1999, p. 220.

[11] For further information visit http://www.cbird.org/.

[12] For further information, visit http://www.africanrecovery.org/.

[13] For the complete resolution, visit
http://www.itu.int/newsroom/press_releases/2002/UNGA_res_56_183.html.

PART V

The Millennium Vision

FIFTEEN
The Knowledge-Millennium Generation

Seeds of so much of our future lie with our young people.
We should spend more time on them.
We should educate far more of them for far longer.
We should set them better examples
And, when they join our corporations,
We should give them every opportunity
To practice what they are learning,
even if they occasionally
get it wrong.

Charles Handy
Beyond Certainty[1]

Our future is in good hands.

I find this to be true in every corner of the world; but in March 1999, I discovered the students at the University of Cologne, Germany, who accomplished something extraordinary. Originating in 1984, the Organisations Forum Wirthchaftskongress (OFW)—now a 34-member (all honorary) student team—works to gain practical experience in addition to the theory the university provides. These bi-annual conventions bridge the gap between generations and nations and provide a common prospect of the opportunities and risks of the future.

In addition to the Congress content and format innovation, OFW reaches all over the world for student essays on the topic of the convention: "Rethinking Knowledge." In an intensive competition complete with review committee, 1,111 papers from students in eighty-three countries—from Albania to Zimbabwe—were received. 400 of the best were selected, and those individuals came from over seventy countries to participate in the dialog.

In short, it was an exceptional pooling of expertise and the closest I have seen to the harnessing of our worldwide collective intelligence. The substance of the dialog was so robust that I cannot do it justice here.

Here are some of the themes that emerged from many of the speakers.

1. It's not the technology, it's the social implications thereof—the human dimension.

2. We can create and incentivize the environment to produce more knowledge and sharing.

3. The focus on knowledge goes well beyond the enterprise in terms of economic policies and practices; it is a matter of establishing modern managerial standards.

4. It is a matter of function of balance and harmony, not either/or or win/lose scenarios.

5. There may be some answers in collaboration.

6. Developing nations are using the knowledge economy as one way to level the playing field.

7. This is only the beginning of a major societal transformation, the implications of which we are just beginning to comprehend.

More relevant to this chapter, thanks to a grant from Joachim Doering, vice-president for information and communications networks (ICM), Siemens AG, we were able to submit the original 1,111 papers to Trend Monitor International[2] for analysis. What follows are the results of the concept mapping of a vision of the future from the youth of the world.

15.1   A VISION OF THE FUTURE

This vision of the future is laid out in the nine subsections that follow.

15.1.1   From sharing knowledge and practice to sharing meaning and goals

Despite the huge investment in time and technology in the cause of promoting knowledge sharing, the results have been disappointing, because people continue to hoard what suits them and make multiple copies of messages that are in their interest to broadcast (thereby creating information overload amongst their colleagues). IT actually makes both hoarding and broadcasting easier. High-performance teams who are aligned and complementary need to share meaning and goals. Only when meaning and goals are shared, does effective knowledge sharing become possible.

15.1.2   From arrogant certainty to humble doubt

As the environment in which people live becomes increasingly destabilized and seemingly complex, the expectation that knowledge provides solutions to problems is diminishing. As knowledge becomes more relative and less certain, humility and flexibility are increasingly being seen as virtues.

15.1.3   From value based on money to value based on wisdom

This trend is still very much in the new-thinking domain. The question is, What do people really exchange during a mutually valuable transaction?

Wisdom implies always taking into consideration the wider context. So a really wise exchange between the buyer and seller of a car, for example, should consider the consequences for the environment of manufacturing the car, running it, and disposing of it. Clearly, there will be occasions when making no exchange will be wiser than making one. Growth would have to be measured by quality of learning rather than the quantity of transactions.

15.1.4   From progress based on novelty to sustainability based on experience

The artificial culture of consumerism is based on creating and exploiting demand for the "new and improved," which always promises to be better than what people are actually experiencing. The process works simply by breeding dissatisfaction. If people were encouraged to be satisfied with the basics of life rather than to want remade, new versions of things all the time, they would make a much smaller impact on the ever-surrounding environment. Sustainability would be a direct consequence of this trend.

15.1.5   From private knowledge sold by experts to public knowledge shared to increase social responsibility

Of course, the last thing that the large majority of experts want is to make their specialist knowledge generally available. The successful presentation and dissemination of expert knowledge is liable to sharply curtail the amount of work needed. The reason, though, that this knowledge will become available in a form non-specialists can use is that fortunes are to be made by experts who succeed in disseminating their expert knowledge far and wide, through the Internet and knowledge-publishing techniques. Ironically, the more intellectual forms of knowledge will be most at risk. Knowledge requiring hands-on experience will be relatively safe.

15.1.6   From organizations based on structures of roles and tasks to organizations based on cultures of relationships

Culture underpins meaning. It engages both emotional and abstract intelligence; it addresses motivation; and it involves caring and trust.

Bureaucratic structures are not without culture, which grows like weeds around paving stones. They also tend to distort cultural relationships by imposing arbitrary structural hierarchies on people, often making what would otherwise be excellent teams dysfunctional. Cultures of relationships are, by their nature, self-selecting and self-managed.

Abstract management techniques, which are designed to manage roles, tasks, and processes, are ill-suited to these kinds of culture-based organizations, which are growing up both inside big corporations and among the exploding networks of micro-businesses.

15.1.7 From individual points of view to group perspectives

High-performance teams create knowledge out of their relationships. All members of the team must widen their perspectives to include an understanding of each other's viewpoints. In this way, understandings can become both wider and richer. Through iterations of relationships and communications, a meta-perspective can be constructed that can provide teams with higher-level group reflection capabilities, making possible a new dimension in consciousness. People have worked together as high-performance teams since hunter, gatherer times. These days, the only time that people really get to work together in this way is during crises as well as in many team sports, voluntary activities, and some project activities within corporations.

15.1.8 From digital technology as a knowledge delivery mechanism to digital technology as a knowledge creation tool

The growing supply of data-mining software and other "knowledge tools" is the latest attempt by artificial intelligence enthusiasts to create "artificial knowledge" that would be of strategic value to organizations. A great deal of money is being spent on creating a market for this new form of knowledge. It is too early to say what its real value is likely to be.

15.1.9   From environmentally destructive knowledge exploitation to environmentally sustaining knowledge contribution

Knowledge has been traditionally used by business as the way to extract the most physical value from the environment at the cheapest cost.

Knowledge could as easily be used to discover ways to extract as little nonrenewable value from the world as possible, while at the same time contributing as much renewable value as possible. Scientific and technical knowledge would, of course, have a great deal to contribute to such a quest. However, the most valuable contribution would come from the values and knowledge by which people actually live their lives.

15.2   TRENDS

In the following subsections the number of arrows—> to >>>—indicates the strength of the trend.

15.2.1   Organizations

1.   Sharing knowledge and practice: > sharing meaning and goals

2.   Private knowledge sold by experts: >> public knowledge shared to increase social responsibility

3.   Organizations based on structures of roles and tasks: >>> organizations based on cultures of relationships

4.   Individual points of view >>> group perspectives

15.2.2   Values

5.   From arrogant certainty > humble doubt

6.   Value based on money >> value based on wisdom

15.2.3 Purposes

7. Progress based on novelty > sustainability based on experience
8. Environmentally destructive knowledge exploitation >> environmentally sustaining knowledge contribution
9. Digital technology as a knowledge delivery mechanism >> digital technology as a knowledge creation tool

This represents a well-researched vision of the future that, if innovated (i.e., knowledge put to action) could provide a foundation for sustainability and more. It could be a platform for world peace, nothing less. And the knowledge-millennium generation, as I call it, could assume the leadership. Now, let's explore a few other examples.

15.3 GLOBAL KNOWLEDGE PARTNERSHIP

There was a unique feature of the GKP Forum reported in Chapter 14. The event that brought together young people from as many as eighty countries also included several weeks of electronic dialog moderated and synthesized by able knowledge experts, including a Youth for a Knowledge Society (YKS) focus that addressed youth perspectives on ICT and development.

The Global Knowledge Partnership is committed to ensuring that young people (ages 15 to 30) are recognized as full partners in bridging the digital divide. To assist in this task, the GKP draws upon the networks and experience of the Youth Advisory Council established in January 2000, which plays a leading role in providing insights into how ICTs can best be used to empower young people around the world.

According to the Global Knowledge Partnership (GKP) Web site, "young people are often the leading innovators in the use and spread of information and communication technologies (ICTs).[3] Increasingly, young people are adapting and using these technologies (including, for example, telephone, fax, radio, television, film, computers and the

Internet) to meet local information and communication needs. But young people can remain an untapped resource if decision-makers do not integrate their knowledge, vision and experience."

Recognizing the expertise of young people, the Global Knowledge Partnership requested the International Institute for Sustainable Development (IISD)[4] to help involve youth from developing countries in policy dialogs seeking to develop strategies for bridging the digital divide. IISD convened a GK Youth Advisory Council in December 1999 to assist the GKP in learning from the expertise of young professionals around the world who are using ICTs to produce, disseminate, and employ knowledge for sustainable development.

From January to March 2000, the advisory committee facilitated a Youth Building Knowledge Societies (YBKS) e-conference to collect information on youth perspectives on bridging the digital divide. The YAC presented its report at the Global Knowledge II Action Summit in March 2000.

From January to May 2000, more than 350 young people from 57 countries came together in an on-line conference[5] to explore how youth are using ICTs to produce, disseminate, and employ knowledge for sustainable development. The e-conference, titled "Youth Building Knowledge Societies (YBKS)," focused on the experiences of young people in Africa, Latin America, Asia, and Central and Eastern Europe. The e-conference was structured around three interrelated themes: access, education, and sustainable livelihoods.

In March 2001 the Youth Advisory Council reconvened to update the YBKS report as an input to the G-8 Digital Opportunities Task-force (DOT Force). The "Youth DOT Force process" highlighted the need for more active involvement of youth organizations and networks in intergovernmental dialogs on information and communication technologies. A directory of digital divide initiatives by and/or for youth was incorporated into the GKP portal.

In September 2001 young people from Taking It Global[6], the Global Youth Action Network, and Nation took up the challenge of GK Youth to continue the youth-led dialog, networking, and advocacy on behalf of digital divide issues. This led to the launch of the Youth, ICTs and Digital Opportunities Network in February 2002.

Young people are now harnessing the power of information and communications technologies (ICTs) to assure opportunity, empowerment, and inclusion for all. The "Youth, ICTs and Digital Opportunities" portal was launched on January 31, 2002 to enable young people from around the world to share their experiences on how ICTs can further development. The site features news, people, events, organizations, and online discussions about closing the digital divide.

According to Terri Willard, project manager, knowledge communications, IISD, these interactive features aim to foster a global network of young social entrepreneurs (ages 16 to 24) on the cutting edge of applying old and new communication technologies to confront the challenges of sustainable development. All GKP members to use the site to

- Promote youth-oriented ICT projects and activities
- Locate possible speakers and participants for ICT conferences and workshops
- Identify upcoming young consultants and entrepreneurs
- Seek collaboration from youth organizations and networks on ICT projects and activities
- Highlight opportunities for young people to become involved in regional, national, and international policy consultations
- Find inspiration and ideas for their work

A strategic framework entitled "Youth Creating Digital Opportunities"[7] has been drafted. It includes the case for: youth as leaders in information and communication; youth as social entrepreneurs technologies; and youth as a large untapped resource for creating digital opportunities.

The UN will be holding a world summit on the information society (December 2003 in Geneva and one in Tunis in 2005). It is a summit that focuses largely on the digital divide and the rules governing cyberspace and information. The summit plans to adopt: a declaration including a set of principles and rules aimed at establishing a more inclusive and equitable information society; and a plan of action outlining specific proposals and concrete measures to be taken so that people the world over will benefit more equitably from the opportunities presented by the information society.

15.4   WORLD CONGRESS OF THE YOUNG ENTREPRENEUR ASSOCIATION

The Young Entrepreneur Association of Zaragoza, Spain celebrated in collaboration with the European Union, The Spanish Kingdom, and the Government of Aragón the first Virtual World Congress of Young Entrepreneurs and SMEs that lasted until the end of March 2002. It provided an opportunity to foment transactions between SMES around the world.

The first Virtual World Congress of Young Entrepreneurs and SMEs simulated a traditional congress, including numerous interactive seminars, exhibitions, workshops, and activities of prime interest to young entrepreneurs. The Virtual Congress made use of the latest technological innovations and communication tools to allow for 24 hours a day/365 days a year participation at the simple click of a mouse. The methodology of this Virtual Congress was based on the creation and running of debate workshops and workgroups centered on topics proposed by the Congress organizer or other collaborating organization and are topical and interesting for today's entrepreneurs and SMEs.

The Congress's objectives included

- Creating a forum for debate and the exchange of ideas and experiences about the problems facing the young entrepreneurs and SMEs
- Maximizing the commercial exchanges among the participants
- Creating an entrepreneurial culture and spirit in Europe and indeed worldwide that is open to the digital culture

- Diffusing new information technologies among young entrepreneurs
- Promoting an entrepreneurial culture
- Divulging good business practices
- Contributing to and transmitting information about the new global economy

The Virtual Congress was open to all young entrepreneurs from all corners of the globe regardless of the sector, activity, nationality or size of the business, as well as to all SMEs and to anybody with an interest in economy and entrepreneurial activity in general. The Congress officially opened with a simultaneous videoconference whose participants included key figures from the business and economical worlds from several locations across the globe: Washington, Buenos Aires, Brussels, Cairo, St. Petersburg, Zaragoza, Madrid, and New Delhi.

There were two types of inscriptions—an individual one for virtual participants and one for organizations related to the business world that wished to participate in an active way in the event, thus acting as collaborators. The following were the initial areas and themes:

- E-business: new business models
- New ways of doing business between businesses—business to business (B2B)
- Electronic commerce—business to customer (B2C)
- Systems of geographical information (SIG) in the implantation of new businesses
- Financial institutions on the Internet
- Logistics in the e-commerce value chain

Communication during these debate forums was bi-directional—in other words, participants could establish direct contact only with the speaker and not among themselves, although all participants could read their questions and messages. At a determined time and date, the expert speaker could launch a chat forum whereby a real-time debate could be initiated with other invited experts from organizations related to the business world.

Of course, this does sound like any conference, albeit one that used advanced computer and communications technology. The uniqueness lies in the connections that made between young entrepreneurs, linking competencies and aspirations in unprecedented ways.

15.5   Junior Alpbach

This annual European Forum Alpbach is financed through—contributions (in the form of subsidies and scholarships) from the Austrian federal government, the provincial government of the Tyrol, and a number of Austrian institutions under public law, such as the Austrian National Bank and the Federal Economic Chamber. Financial support has also been received from the European Commission. Contributions are received from private sponsors, including private individuals, companies, and representative groups such as the Confederation of Austrian Industry.

On of the most novel features of this conference is an activity called Junior Alpbach, which runs parallel with the week-long conference. In this event, selected students are invited to spend a week interfacing with Nobel laureates in a variety of activities ranging from scientific experiments, cultural and performing arts expressions, and one-on-one interface that would be the envy of any child with aspirations.

15.6   The Jade Network

One of the most remarkable examples of knowledge being put into action is teh worldwide movement of Junior enterprises—student-run consulting companies. The idea is simple and powerful—young, entrepreneurial people get together to gain some practical experience during their studies by managing their own company and working on consulting projects. They use what they have learned at the university, and transfer that knowledge with great enthusiasm and professionalism to companies, solving the clients's problems for a remuneration that is a fraction of standard fees in the industry. The results are often unexpected and innovative. The client lists can speak for themselves: all kinds of organizations—from a small bakery to huge multinationals, are using such services in areas ranging from market research to complex process re-engineering, or IT implementation. In a fast moving economy those who are learning fastest win; and the student teams grasp all the new concepts and ideas very quickly, being able to advise on a selected topic just after some weeks of in-depth research.

Although based in Belgium, the model has been adapted in many countries, mostly in europe, where there are now over 300 such initiatives, working together in the JADE network—the European Confederation of Junior Enterprises. JADE was founded in 1992 as an international non-profit organization that connects national Junior Enterprise movements all over Europe. JADE animates the development of Europe's Junior Enterprises by implementing European projects and encouraging cross-border co-operation on multinational studies, organizing international congresses and meetings that facilitate exchange of knowledge and ideas.

Celebrating their 10th anniversary in Berlin, 233 registrants came from many countires. The organization has support from the European Commission, and a great house in Brussels, where 5 students from all over Europe come to work and live together for a one year term on the executive board; and others join them as project managers. There are problems for international exchange of consultants, shared spaces for electronic dialogue and exchanting methodologies, and best practice workshops. The network—with also 300 Junior Enterprises in Brazil—is developing quickly; and as it unites over 20,000 student consultants, it could be considered one of the largest consulting companies in the world.

15.7   New Zealand

The KnowledgeWave[8] initiative described in more detail in Chapter 14 is a typical example of an effective program on the national level. The initiative in and of itself is an illustration of exemplary practice, but what is rather unusual in this national initiative is the integral involvement in students.

The twelve senior secondary students were selected to attend the 2001 Conference "Catching the Knowledge Wave" on the basis of the their submitted essays, which raised thought-provoking points. The following are a selection of comments from the students' essay on the theme of the kind of knowledge society they wanted for New Zealand. The students presented their combined perspectives in a special youth forum at the conference after hearing from national and international speakers.

"These students demonstrated real insight into the issues New Zealand faces in becoming a knowledge society," said Colin Prentice, University of Auckland Schools Director and Coordinator of the essay competition. "The judges were really impressed with the liveliness of the students' thinking, the depth of research, the quality of thinking and the genuine concern they expressed for this county," he added. What follows is a representative sample of submissions, but I recommend that you review them all and, more important, initiate opportunities in your country to do same.

Melissa James, Tokoroa High School, Tokoroa writes, "Stephen R Covey defines a habit as the intersection of knowledge, skill and desire. Knowledge is the theoretical paradigm, the 'what to do and why,' Skill is the 'how to do,' and desire is the motivation—the 'want to do'. But to make excellence a habit rather than an act, we should have all three of these principles operating. A knowledge society is one where dreams become reality, and excellence becomes a habit."

Adrian Ranaweera, St. Paul's College, Auckland, states, "A knowledge society can only come about from a public that is well educated, innovative and creative; from people who live in an environment that holds economic strategies for growth which raise standards of living and encourage national development. Only when New Zealand has set itself a proper vision that is understood and accepted by all, can the first positive steps be taken. Productivity must be kindled and economic reform brought about with a government drive on strategic economic policies. Only when these conditions are satisfied will New Zealand finally take its proper place as one of the world's great knowledge societies."

Kesaia Waigth, Gisborne Girls' High School, Gisborne writes, "In order for vision to become reality we must put in place economic strategies. Firstly we must achieve prosperity to raise the living standards of New Zealanders and improve the quality of life. To do this we must work towards improving the productive and innovative capacity of the economy to increase its operational effectiveness. This means using knowledge led innovation to create higher value commodities and services, and improve the efficiency with which traditional products are produced. This will allow us to compete in the global market."

Rosemary Wilkinson, Kaipara College, Helensville, declares, "It is from new ideas and innovations that new products and services develop. This leads to more jobs and economic growth. A culture of innovation and creativity needs to be nurtured. New Zealand already has a colorful history of ingenuity and a can-do philosophy. We need to build on this to provide an environment that allows creativity and innovation to blossom. We need a system that supports creative thinkers, entrepreneurs and new businesses by providing them with the resources they need and making sure they are aware that these resources are available."

Robert Tilbey, King's College, Auckland writes, "Becoming a knowledge society is a realistic dream, but in order to succeed we must move forward as one nation, corporations and government alike. I would like to see a society that seeks to inspire individuals, while retaining the capabilities to support their ideas. Ultimately I would like to see a knowledge society in New Zealand that attracts the international community. I would like to see New Zealand with international authority, a nation in which I would be happy to create a future."

In the words of Pascal Millaire, King's College, Auckland, "Knowledge, creativity and innovation are the most valuable natural resources in the 21st Century. What is in our heads is increasingly more important than what is in the countryside. New Zealand's potential is only limited by the knowledge, creativity and innovation of its people. As a small country we will always be on an "edge" but whether that is the leading edge or trailing edge will be dictated by the decisions and direction New Zealand is taking now."

15.8   SUMMARY

There is now a critical mass of talent dedicated to innovating the future; and it includes the youth of the world. In various corners of the globe, there are many creative initiatives making progress on such topics as access to technology, the digital divide, the inequities experienced by certain minorities, and other topics relevant to building a sustainable future.

These students have benefited from the best education possible. They have grown up with the technology and the global benefits of the Internet providing access to global sources of information, both technical and human. They've been labeled the 'click-and-go" generation; but the depth of insight is recorded in the trends and quotes that preceded. It is apparent that in addition to being technologically astute, they have a grasp of the diverse variables necessary for a sustainable knowledge economy. They also realize that innovation is the process wherein lies some of the answers to their future positioning in the world—as individuals and as nations.

Clearly, the solutions to modern progress do not lie within the existing leadership, especially those who are glued to the managerial practices that made them successful in the first place. Look instead to the new leaders—those learning form the young entrepreneurs poised to take advantage of the opportunities afforded a knowledge economy. It is only a matter of time before the potential is unleashed.

CHAPTER ENDNOTES

[1] Handy (1996), p. 100.

[2] For further information on Trend Monitor International and the concept-mapping methodology, visit http://www.trendmonitor.com/.

[3] Of course, they refer to the "global information society," and we would encourage the terminology "the global *innovation* society"!

[4] For more information, visit http://www.iisd.org/networks/gkyouth.asp, supported as Knowledge Networks of the International Institute for Sustainable Development (ISSD).

[5] There were several of us from the "older generation" who were also privileged to participate.

[6] For more information on the Taking IT Global initiative, visit http://ict.takingitglobal.org/home.html.

[7] For the document, visit http://users.netcon.net.au/~denise/digitalopportunity62.doc.

[8] For further information, visit http://www.knowledgewave.org.nz.

SIXTEEN

Blueprint for
Twenty-First Century Innovation

Information at the speed of light. Instant communication.
Satellite services can place information on any spot
with the precision of a surgeons knife.
Our planet is ringed with data that practically circles the globe,
binding one continent to another.
We have become a global village,
where a sneeze in the Tundra
can be heard in Antarctica.

The World Development Report 1999[1]

I was visiting a country (which shall go unnamed) and meeting with the Minister of Education who had just launched an initiative called "Knowledge Management in the Information Society." I queried why it was the information—and not the knowledge—society. He asked me "What's the difference?" I responded that there are at least two distinctions.

- First, when the focus is on the information or the technology, we are placing the attention on things and not people. I believe that this is actually increasing the digital divide.
- Second, when the focus is on knowledge, the knowledge of everyone is important. The knowledge agenda is a very human and humane agenda.

These distinctions are not insignificant, and leaders worldwide are acting on the promise of the new management future. Much activity may be launched with only a cursory understanding of the principles and practice. This is not bad—far from it, but it is suboptimal.

Instead, there should be ways to design the frame for the discussion, promote astute awareness, develop the leadership that has a considerable sphere of influence, and collectively evolve a compelling vision that provides a quantum impact rather than relying upon incremental improvement.

16.1   THE CASE FOR INNOVATION

The business intelligence (UK) research project documented in *Creating the Knowledge-Based Business* (Skyrme and Amidon, 1997[2]) contains thirty-three leadership case studies that illustrate the various dimensions of knowledge management. In almost every case, references are made about the need to create a culture of sharing, openness, learning, collaboration, trust, and innovation. As stated earlier, Peter Drucker claims that innovation, along with the ability to measure the performance thereof, is the one competence needed for the future. In the accompanying survey performed by Ernst and Young (see Figure 16.1), innovation is the primary attribute most important to an organization's future in both Europe and the United States.

The graphic in Figure 16.1 portrays the next wave beyond reengineering and quality. In what has become known as Charles Handy's sigmoid curve, enterprises must transform at point *A*. For enterprises reaching point *B*, it is too late.

Overlaid on the graphic are the five business generations defined in an earlier *Research-Technology Management* article (Amidon, 1996). A sixth stage was added representing work done with Leif Edvinsson, then vice president for intellectual capital at Skandia, where managing the future is the real agenda for the twenty-first century. In *Power of Innovation*, the 1996 supplement to the interim report, the image used

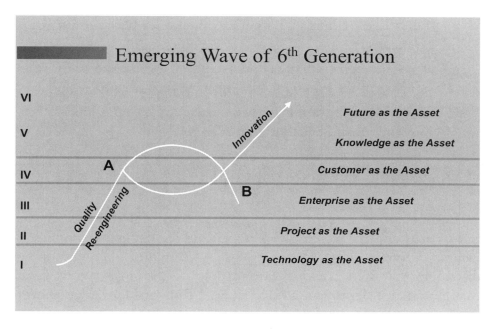

FIGURE 16.1   *Emerging sixth wave of management.*[3]

is that of a powerful wave to depict the complex, but robust innovation system needed to manage the intangible assets of an enterprise.

16.2   A SOLID FOUNDATION[4]

Every architectural effort—especially one that proposes to integrate elements that may not have been heretofore connected—should begin with some planning assumptions. Many of these elements were detailed in Chapters 4–8. There was a combined effort with expertise across the sectors to think through what might constitute sustainability in the knowledge economy; and their collective wisdom identified these five[5]:

1.   Knowledge is the primary of innovation.

2. The value of human potential can/should be linked to economic results.

3. A systems approach (i.e., understanding the whole and the relationship of the parts) enables optimal performance.

4. A prosperous future is based increasingly on interdependence, interaction, and collaboration.

5. The flow of knowledge—not just cash flow—must be visualized, monitored and incentivized.

There is more than enough evidence of activity that we are on the right path, and the voices are being heard in the most prominent forums of our society. There is hardly a functional orientation or discipline that is not taking careful note of the implications from this perspective. Companies have launched major knowledge and/or learning initiatives usually residing in the responsibilities of a C*O. Government agencies have followed suit with swift embrace of e-government initiatives. Academic institutions—realizing now that they are but a "node" on the learning network—have launched assessments of their own programs and the value of distance learning, some on a regional or worldwide basis. All has not been as serendipitous (or naturally evolving) as many might think.

This focus on knowledge was originally shared with the OECD in Paris in 1988[6]. Many readers are aware of the resulting articles and the superb research on the topic, some of which is outlined in *Blueprint of 21st Century Innovation.*[7]

For example, the OECD has produced a series of reports that have provided both leadership and direction on the topics of human capital, learning and society, national systems of innovation, and, most recently, the knowledge-based economy. A bi-monthly *OECD Observer* features the most recent thinking and research results. One issue featured an editorial by Jean-Claude Paye, Secretary-General of OECE, on the rationale for national innovation systems:

*Performance in the knowledge-based economy depends to a large extent
on the functioning of such national innovation systems, particularly the
ability to distribute knowledge and technology to a wide range of
economic actors... Coherent policies for the knowledge-based economy
must therefore create incentives for expanded investment in human
resources, technology, innovation, and information networks. (Paye,
1996)*

In the same issue, three main aspects of industrial innovation
deserve to be mentioned. First, technological change impinges on
codified and tacit knowledge. Second, the sources of innovation may
be either internal or external to the firm. Third, innovations can either
be embodied in capital goods and products or disembodied. These
interdependencies in purpose may be a result of the cross-divisional
activity within the OECD. It may be that the time has come to step
back from the details of current analysis and see the entire picture.

In 1993[8], we took the knowledge agenda into The World Bank, and
you have seen the results in the stellar work of Stephen Denning and
the report *Knowledge for Development*, which has helped convert The
World Bank from financial to intellectual capital. And we know that
industrialized nations do not have a monopoly on knowledge—far
from it! I believe that the knowledge agenda has actually created a level
playing field and inspired developing economies to innovate their
own future.

Years later with the creation of the World Development Report
(1998–1999) and according to Stephen Denning, knowledge became
the major strategic theme—getting organized to create, capture, distill,
and disseminate relevant development knowledge[9]. It is aimed initially
at increasing individual effectiveness, transferring information and
knowledge to the organizational level, and ultimately making it accessible so that all individuals can take effective action. This constitutes
not only a corporate memory of information and best practices' it also
incorporates the best knowledge from outside organizations. The
knowledge management system will interconnect with universities,

foundations. and other world-class sources of knowledge so that the Bank becomes a clearinghouse for development knowledge.

We are "neighbors in a global village." In May 1997, the Dutch Ministry of Education, Culture and Science, together with the European Union, held a three-day invitational conference on knowledge management and learning organizations as a step toward creating the European Knowledge Union. Coordinated by Kenniscentrum CIBIT, the meeting brought together knowledge leaders from all over the world. As background material, a compilation of speeches by the Honorable J.M.M. Ritzen was provided, outlining concepts (e.g., a continuous Europe, neighbors in a global village, co-ownership) that have been part of what is described as the "knowledge debate" (Ritzen, 1997).

In a study by Brown and Herzfeld (1996), the authors find that in the emerging global environment, the nation's capacity to innovate will play a dominant and probably decisive role in achieving that goal. Deborah Wince Smith, former Assistant Secretary for the U.S, Department of Commerce, outlines the incentives for investment in innovation: human resources; technology; intellectual property rights; physical infrastructure; capital formation and allocation systems; regulatory framework; international trading systems; reciprocal access to international investment opportunities; and industrial structure for innovation and business, management, and manufacturing practices. She concludes that a national innovation system is a dynamic, holistic system of mutually reinforcing elements. No one element can exist independently from the impact it exerts on the overall system vitality.

There are many world economic surveys. Perhaps the most succinct and comprehensive overview is contained in a survey produced by *The Economist* (1996). It describes how the future prosperity of rich economies will depend increasingly on their ability to innovate and capacity to adjust to change. The rich economies are coming to depend increasingly on the creation, distribution, and use of information and knowledge, involving both technology and human capital. The most distinctive feature of the knowledge-based economy is not that it churns out information for consumers—it does that too—but that it uses knowledge pervasively as both an input and an output throughout the economy.

Connecting with the movement on organizational learning is a parallel study. The Economist Intelligence Unit produced a research report in cooperation with the IBM Consulting Group, entitled *The Learning Organization: Managing Knowledge for Business Success*. (The Economist Intelligence Unit and IBM Consulting Group 1996.) It involved a questionnaire sent to 3,000 executives in 26 countries and 50 in-depth interview with 37 companies. The study was not a focus on innovation, nor did it examine the role of knowledge in the economy; however, the interview findings do reveal implications germane to this chapter:

- Learning enhances a company's speed, innovativeness, and adaptability.
- Formal business procedures must be balanced with the freedom to create.
- Every company has a different approach.
- Work is personal.
- Culture is key.
- Individuals must commit to personal change.
- Day-to-day operating demands conflict with learning.
- Business performance measures do not value knowledge assets.
- Learning builds shareholder value for the long term.
- Effective information systems meet both business and human needs; and with economies of thinking, bigger and better ideas emerge.

The point is that this transition has been well documented in both the academic and professional circles and the trade press. Something fundamental is changing, and we are all a part of its evolution.

16.3   CREATING AN INNOVATION CULTURE

Creating the culture in which knowledge is valued and shared effectively is one of the most difficult challenges faced in practice. One of the primary influences may actually be the competitive environment that has been developed over time and begins with a child's birth. Competition is healthy when it involves sports, and it was appropriate for an economic climate in which resources were plentiful. Once global competition became a reality, available resources shrank rapidly overnight. However, the knowledge economy promises an abundance of resources if the metrics and measurement systems can be properly defined.

Of primary importance is the innovation language—a language that transcends the paradigm and biases of one function or another. Ideally, such a language would also encompass industries, sectors, and regions of the world and, therefore, would be universal in scope. There are several attempts to define the language with a glossary of terms. Of course, the language must be adapted to the heritage, purpose, mission, and strategy of a particular entity. It is important that the language be established and pervade all operations and planning efforts. The intent of this chapter is to suggest that the language can best be created under the rubric of innovation strategy—redefined, of course, according to the flow of ideas.

Culture extends beyond the enterprise. When the stakeholders in the process are considered (e.g., suppliers, alliance partners, distributors, customers, competitors, and even the customer's customer), the view of the knowledge base from which organizations might learn becomes expansive. The strategic business network (SBN) as model is in direct contrast to Alfred Sloan's multidivisional structure (SBU) for organizations, which was well suited to the Tayloristic industrial paradigm. Dividing the large enterprise into independent strategic business units was considered the optimal way to measure performance.

However, the dynamic economic climate demands a networked, fluid organizational structure that balances accountability with responsible risk taking. It is not the parts themselves that add value, but the synergistic nature of the whole, the value of which is greater than the sum of the parts. This is the nature of fusion and the result of symbiotic learning networks, both human and technical. Demonstrated value resides in the interfaces between the boxes, sometimes described as the white space, which must be the object of our performance-management systems.

Shared purpose is essential for an enterprise to thrive in the dynamic global economy. Amidst the turmoil and chaos of the past decade, throughout downsizing and reengineering processes, many organizations have lost their sense of direction. Initiatives have become fragmented and, worse still, internally competitive. Interestingly enough, it may not be the financial resources that are scarce today as much as the mindset and available commitment time of the enterprise leaders.

Too often, managers operating in the traditional, competitive work climate are managing initiatives with unnecessary duplication of effort and suboptimal allocation of resources. In many instances organizations must find a way to coalesce, rededicate themselves to a common agenda, and respect the complementary competencies that can be brought to bear. Creating the community of innovation practice may be one way to begin the process.

16.4   MULTIPLE ECONOMIC LEVELS

Innovation management must be viewed within a global context. The complexity of managing within a global economic system creates a dissonance between strategy and operations at multiple levels. An adjustment on one level automatically has an effect on, and is affected by, another. During the past decade researchers have documented the challenges of cross-boundary activity. Enterprises have a sense of what it means to convert an organization from a domestic to a national or even transnational business. Systems dynamics tools and collaborative technologies provide a way to visualize scenarios, understand relationships among factors, and experiment with options for action.

What is not so well established in the literature or in practice is how to optimize the allocation of resources across the multiple boundaries. Perhaps the best-known and most practiced model is that of the stage-gate developed by Cooper and Edgett (1999). In general, modern frameworks for analyzing technology strategy, innovation management, and strategic alliances are so complex that it is difficult to capture their meaning.

In 1989, research on the nature of alliances in this transnational economy was reported in *Global Innovation Strategy*[10] By contrasting activities in different parts of the world according to diverse functional perspectives, the researchers were able to uncover the managerial implications on three economic levels: microeconomic (intra-organizational); mesoeconomic (inter-organizational), and macroeconomic (transnational). Following are the three economic levels of analysis that proved useful for contrasting activities. The results of that research suggest that optimization demands a balance among all three levels simultaneously.

16.4.1 The Microeconomic (intra-organizational) Level

Each enterprise consists of separate functions from each of which R&D discoveries need to be transferred into products and services that are created, marketed, sold, and maintained. However, as already discussed, these are no longer linear value models, for ideas indeed come from throughout the enterprise. In fact, it is through the simultaneous development process and sharing of expertise that much of the breakthrough thinking occurs.

16.4.2 The Mesoeconomic (inter-organizational) Level

With intensified global competition and increased consumer sophistication, it has become increasingly important to consider the relationships with external stakeholders (e.g., suppliers, distributors, alliance partners, investors, government, academia, customers, and competitors). This is the economic level least documented in the literature and the one most responsible for competitive threat from the Japanese during the late 1980s because of their keiretsu. It is also the most important level for economic development experts building national infrastructures. These interdependent relationships are dynamic, evolve over time, and are necessary to strengthen organizations.

16.4.3 The Macroeconomic (transnational) Level

Advancements in computers and communications and the explosion of the number of users of the World Wide Web have provided global opportunities unforeseen a decade ago. John Naisbitt claims, "The bigger the world economy, the more powerful its smallest players." With the emergence of electronic commerce and international networks of professionals across every border imaginable, the strength of the entrepreneur in a global context is a reality. Enterprises, both regional and national, need to consider the advantages of linking with global partners for idea sourcing, joint ventures, marketing partners, or contributors to one's distributed learning system, however that might be defined.

Organizations need to determine what connectors might be developed at the interfaces to link these economic levels and what would be the relationship among the levels. After years of research, it has been determined that a focus on knowledge (content) and innovation (process) with learning (method) is the optimal core an enterprise might create. With such a common focus, all initiatives at and across levels can be synchronized. That may be the place where most value is created

When these economic levels are viewed as overlapping circles, such as in a Venn diagram, the boundaries of the interfaces become apparent. This is also the locale in which similarities in intent might be discovered and leveraged (see Figure 3.2 for an example)]. These represent the value-creating opportunities in cross-functional integration in a firm, cross-sectoral integration within a nation, and cross-cultural integration in the global infrastructure. How enterprises effectively manage this dimension of collaboration will determine how they survive and prosper.

16.5   CRAFTING AN ENTERPRISEWIDE INNOVATION VISION

The challenges that confront institutions approaching the third millennium are complex, diverse, and compelling. Such change dynamics are kaleidoscopic in nature, transformative in impact, and international in scope. One could take on the traditional planning role of identifying and overcoming obstacles in attempts to control the environment so as to minimize any negative impact. Such has been the focus of competitive strategy for the past three decades.

A more constructive strategy is collaborative and synergistic. It embraces the inevitability and strength of change in ways that catapult learning forward, stretch imaginations, and define common ground for contributions from diverse paradigms. Such a strategy recognizes the value of the whole and its interrelated parts, operating as an evolving ecological system in which streams and cross-currents of activity are opportunities to harness the value of knowledge.

People from developing nations have often said to me me: "We are an agricultural society just transforming to an industrial society, and you want us to become a knowledge economy? Is it possible?" My response is that not only is it possible, it is necessary. You can gain learnings from industrialized economies—the good and the bad—and chart your own future in full realization that the knowledge of every human being is important and the process to be managed is one of innovation.

Innovation must be in the head, heart, and hands of every participant in the system. It does not mean everyone is an expert technician or marketer. Everyone should have knowledge of the entire innovation system and his or her particular role. There must be a common language and shared purpose, and boundaries must fade between functions, sectors, industries, and cultures. There must evolve a basic trust, mutual respect, and collegial competencies and, above all, a thirst for learning.

A knowledge agenda—whether for an enterprise or for a nation—cuts across the aspects of the new knowledge value proposition (i.e., economics, behavior, and technology) noted in Chapter 2; but it also operates on the three economic levels simultaneously— micro-, meso-, and macroeconomic) (see Figure 16.2).

To do so, we need a frame of the activities—how resources might best be allocated.

Innovation must be in the head, heart, and hands of every participant in the system. It means is that everyone has knowledge of the entire innovation system and his or her particular role in that process. It does mean that there is some common language and shared purpose

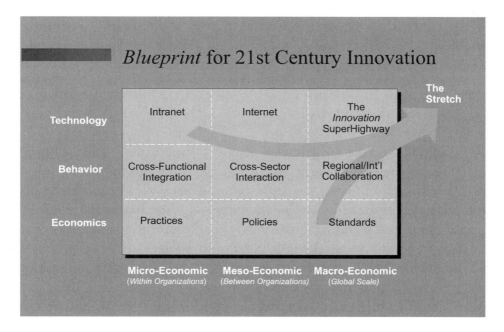

FIGURE 16.2   *Nine-box blueprint for the innovation superhighway.*

and that the boundaries fade between functions, sectors, industries, and cultures of the world. It means that there are basic trust, mutual respect, and collegial competencies. In addition, it is likely that a thirst for learning pervades the culture.

That being the case, players at all enterprise levels (from microeconomic to macroeconomic) can share these modern management philosophies and in so doing overcome the barriers and obstacles to progress. Academics, government officials, industrial executives, and nonprofit practitioners may all participate in this community of innovation practice. With this in mind, a three-dimensional transformation matrix has been formulated and can be applied. It includes the activities that can be mapped according to the different economic levels, as well as the three elements of the knowledge value proposition (See Chapter 2): economic, behavioral, and technological.

Not only are the language and concepts transforming, but also the basic principles of our professions—and what some might suggest is the new knowledge profession. Some will see it as a challenge; others will perceive it as a threat. Progressive managers will see an opportunity to shape the very foundations for the future. What was managed previously will pale in comparison.

16.6   SUMMARY

If we are able to take a worldview of how to best utilize our most precious resources—the insight and imagination of the human mind—and vow to avoid unnecessary duplication of resource, we can envision interaction that expands our assets with—as some have suggested—a multiplier effect. Building The Innovation Superhighway of today that enables free trade for marketable goods and services is more a function of the human capacity to create and apply new ideas—or old ideas in different ways (i.e., the ability to innovate). Too much emphasis has been placed on the technology, which has likely exacerbated the digital divide. Similarly, too much emphasis has been placed on the "information" economy, given that the new economy is not one that is digital as much as it is human.

Increasingly, management responsibilities will be viewed as facilitating the learning process, which includes external stakeholders (e.g., suppliers, distributors, alliance partners, customers, and even competitors). How these relationships are managed is far more a matter of collaborative expertise than the competitive skill with which most are familiar. Values, valuation. and valuing will gain prominence as executives search for what to measure and how and when to evaluate performance. Only when we have a common language across borders —functions, industries and countries alike—can we begin to explore the prospects for collective prosperity.

The core premise of the future is collaboration. This does not mean that organizations do not compete; competition is inevitable. It does mean that the orientation shifts to one of sharing and leveraging one another for mutual success. The common language will emerge as well as the shared vision—one that might be realized in our lifetime. In national and global terms, this is described as creating the common good from which all benefit. Previous eras have experienced reliance upon resources that are depleted. Perhaps the era based upon the bountiful resource of knowledge provides an opportunity for true global symbiosis.

Chapter Endnotes

[1] Opening of the World Development Report, "Knowledge for Development," (1999).

[2] Pp. 67–68.

[3] Originally appeared in Chapter 1 of *Innovation Strategy for the Knowledge Economy* (p. 6) and then adapted for *Power of Innovation*. Supplement to Skandia's 1996 Interim Report: 8.

[5] Published in *Collaborative Innovation and the Knowledge Economy*, p 1.

[6] "Managing the Knowledge Assets into the 21st Century" was brought to Graham Vickery, an OECD principal administrator, in the fall of 1988.

[7] For an electronic version, see http://www.gkii.org/articles/blueprint1.htm.

[8] Materials were passed to Carl Dahlman. the executive responsible for producing the World Development Report.

[9] Author's note: This is precisely the process of innovation.

[10] MIT thesis published by the IC² Institute of the University of Texas at Austin (1989).

SEVENTEEN
Creating the World Trade of Ideas

The kaleidoscope has been shaken.
The pieces are in flux;
soon they will settle again.
Before they do,
let us reorder the world around us.

Prime Minister Tony Blair (2001)[1]

Change was inevitable, and constructive change is innovation.

We knew the current conditions—founded on models of financial capital and even linked with technology in the form of the dot.com—were built on unstable (or perhaps incomplete) economic assumptions. The technology/productivity paradox must be resolved—and once and for all. The behavior implications of the new knowledge value proposition are fundamental to that resolution. And we must plan for the world we want to innovate, not the one that exists today.

Tomorrow will not look like today; yet the future is not unlike the uncharted waters sailed by the explorers during the Middle Ages. Today, there are better navigation devices, but there is little understanding about what might lie over the horizon. Ours is the challenge to innovate our future in ways that leverage the best of every human being, every enterprise, and every nation.

Knowledge has emerged as the strategic focus for business and has been growing in importance over the last decade. Of course, Peter F. Drucker described the knowledge worker as long ago as 1963. Ever since the early descriptions, interest in knowledge as a lever of strategy and the number of organizations with formal knowledge programs has grown inexorably.

- We've learned that in the new domain of knowledge economics, what we count matters. As imprecise as it may seem, what we need to calibrate is the intangible, hidden, intellectual wealth of an enterprise—how it is created and leveraged.
- We've learned that the knowledge structures operate as holonomies—nesting of networks—with both local and global scope. We need to understand how they operate as communities and spheres of influence.
- We've learned that the category of knowledge workers—although originally described as high-technology or white-collar—includes everyone; we all have a role to play. We need to determine what motivates constructive behaviors—new modes of interdependence and collaboration.
- We've learned that all knowledge processes can fit under a rubric of innovation—but innovation redefined according to the flow of knowledge. We need to make the process explicit and discover ways to measure performance—how knowledge is created, shared, and applied.
- We've learned the power of knowledge processing technology—advancing in features and receptivity beyond our wildest dreams. We've learned that technology isn't an end but a means for prosperous innovation. We need to find ways to take advantage of the advancements and use it as an instrument in the new economy.

Understanding of these complex facets and the interdependencies thereof provides a solid foundation for what was originally envisioned in 1982. The prosperity of individuals, enterprises, and nations relies upon knowledge as the resource and innovation as the process.

The United Nations was created to maintain political stability around the world. The World Bank and the IMF were created after World War II to ensure the movement of financial capital. Today, we need a similar infrastructure for the worldwide flow of intellectual capital. If knowledge is the modern asset—the most precious resource —of the twenty-first century, we have a premise behind the need to create The Innovation Superhighway for the world trade of ideas.

17.1   A Vision-In-Progress

The foundation for a new economic order has been laid. This does not mean the answers are known, but there exists a better understanding of the elements of the infrastructure and the right questions to be addressed. This is a very different paradigm from previous agricultural, industrial, or service economies. It is one that truly rests on the value of human potential and how it might be systematically leveraged for the benefit of mankind. The challenge is to determine the integral linkage between human potential and economic performance.

This vision, as articulated in the 1999 interviews of the Entovation 100, suggests that something of unprecedented significance and transnational in scope is emerging.

> *A new economic world order*
> *Based upon the flow of knowledge—not technology,*
> *Innovation value systems—not chains,*
> *Stakeholder success—not satisfaction, and*
> *International collaboration—not competition.*[2]

The changes are far more fundamental than people realize. And all the focus on knowledge has always been in actuality a focus on innovation. But people were locked into the traditional 50-year-old industrial management models of managing things. The transformation is a human one as well as a humane agenda that has touched the hearts and minds of all peoples of the world.

Even some of the best knowledge management professionals—and the related up-springing of the KM press, the KM societies, the KM business press, and even the premature KM standards—were moving in the right direction. The process—the future survival and prosperity of our organizations and the world—should not be left to serendipity.

Enterprises will need to balance the old and the new, competition and collaboration, short- and long term goals. Banerjee and Richter (2001)[3] describe a new generation not unlike the knowledge millennium generation illustrated in Chapter 15, a new economy and a new capitalism that is changing the way business is done in Asia. They describe the "virtual keiretsu" (unlike the traditional keiretsu) created by the Japanese firm Softbank that aims to "accumulate and share knowledge resources and technology to exploit the explosive growth of the Internet—a mix of 'new economy' wisdom and old Asian values."

Most of the focus to build the national and global infrastructures (NII/GII) has been a focus on innovation, not information. The quest for information societies might better be labeled a quest for innovation societies. Even the progress made in ICT development describes knowledge networks, learning systems, innovative practices, and entrepreneurial incentives—all in the name of stimulating both enterprise and national productivity and prosperity. Therefore, perhaps the "I" in ICT should stand for innovation, not information!

There is an abundance of case study examples describing real benefits that organizations are gaining through a systematic approaches to harnessing existing and new knowledge—better products and services, faster time to market, improved customer service, and reduction of cost through avoiding reinventing the wheel. And we've shown that further evidence of the globalization of the knowledge agenda is its acceptance as a pivotal point of policy by both nation states and international agencies alike.

We know from the trends that have been carefully documented in Chapters 11 and 15 that there are prospects for a more sustainable future. For enterprises, this would mean progressive management policies and practices that take advantage of the value of collaborative networks and empowered and inspired individuals. If adequately architected—as much as anything can be "constructed" in this new economy—this could be a realizable vision for The Innovation Superhighway one that may not be far from what the original architects of the NII/GII intended.

17.2 FIVE ENTOVATION PRINCIPLES FOR HOMELAND SECURITY

On 9/11/01, the world changed—forever. We've had a chance to absorb the tragedy, gain some perspective, and begin thinking about what actions we might take as individuals and organizations. We can now appreciate the dynamics of "kaleidoscopic change." It is not the speed of change of a variable, nor the speed of change of multiple variables. It is the compounding effect of the speed of change of multiple variables that has created a management landscape unfamiliar to us all. On 9/11, everything changed.

As I watched the World Trade Center, a concrete representation of a, if not the, financial capital of the world crumble, I now had a better vision of the rising sun. Within days, I knew that the Center would be rebuilt, but how and on what foundation? What meaning would it carry forward, and how would whatever was constructed in its place be not only a memorial to the past, but an inspiration into the future?

For many Americans—and citizens of the world for that matter—these events have given us great pause for reflection. Now it is time to construct a platform for action that provides a foundation for the protection of our future. Indeed, this crisis affords us an opportunity—and a global one at that—to architect a commonality of purpose that transcends any particular culture or spiritual orientation. This is a chance to value the diversity of perspectives and come to a common language and shared vision of what might be possible. Together, we could crystallize a compelling message for leaders of this new world that is "innovating" before our eyes.

17.2.1   Principle 1: The Best Defense Is An Offense

When people are wounded—either physically or emotionally—the tendency is to withdraw. This is essential to deal with immediate injuries and to develop some strategies to prevent further injury. However, depending on the magnitude of the infliction, the results can lead to panic and paralysis. These conditions lead to increased fear, additional downsizing, and protectionist actions that exacerbate the problem. Bad economic conditions produce bad economy, low morale, absence of risk-taking, and bad economic conditions. It is a death spiral without a forward agenda to motivate and inspire action. All the innovation (i.e., responsible risk-taking) gets squeezed out of the system precisely at the time it is needed.

17.2.2   Principle 2: The Battle Is An Economic One, Not Necessarily A Military One

Despite the attacks on the World Trade Center and subsequent apparent biological warfare, we must not forget that the military response is only part of the solution. The damage to human life is evident; the real damage to the quality of life is incalculable. The numbers of the unemployed; the stagnation of investment; the damage to small, medium-sized, and large-scale enterprises across every industry; and the loss of world trade all have implications far beyond the boundaries of the United States.

17.2.3   Principle 3: Knowledge, not Technology, Is the Engine of Economic Prosperity

We now know that knowledge, in the form of "intellectual capital," is the most precious resource to be managed; unlike land, labor, or financial capital, it is an asset that multiplies. It is the one resource, in coordination with environmental conditions, that leads to the prosperity of a company or a country. The knowledge economy, as opposed to a digital or information economy, affords us a human and humane agenda within which the potential of every person is valued. It is the agenda that had leveled the playing field and enabled all nations —developing and industrialized—to envision modern management policies and practices. Knowledge in the form of imagination coupled with action is what enables us to envision a world that doesn't yet exist.

17.2.4 Principle 4: Innovation Is the Process by Which Knowledge Is Created And Harnessed

If knowledge, embedded in the learning capacities of people, is the resource to be managed, then innovation is the process whereby visions are realized. According to Peter F. Drucker, it is the one competence for the future. Therefore, innovation strategy—developing the capability to create, share, and apply knowledge—is a process that should not be left to serendipity. Innovation operates on all three economic levels: the profitability or prosperity of an enterprise (microeconomic), the vitality of a nation's economy (mesoeconomic) and the advancement of society (macroeconomic). It is the one process around which can be created a common language and a shared vision.

17.2.5 Principle 5: Any National Strategy Must Be International And Collaborative In Scope

Although there are definite implementation boundaries, no strategy—not even one for national defense—can be developed as an "island" in this global economy. We have too much to learn from one another as a way of dealing with the inevitable complexities and uncertainties. The days of developing competitive advantage may finally be past. Instead, nations will discover ways to leverage the uniqueness of their heritage and culture with strategies to develop new, better standards of excellence. With 9/11, we have an opportunity to shape the vision: "We are building a new economic world order based upon knowledge, innovation, stakeholder success and international collaboration; and this is the platform for world peace, nothing less."

We know that according to President George W. Bush, up to $20 billion may be allocated in funds for the recovery of New York alone; but how many of those previous resources will be allocated to start-up businesses and to revitalizing those businesses that have suffered severe financial and morale consequences. We know that Donald Trump and other financiers will be instrumental in reconstructing the WTC site, but will they just reconstitute the financial capital of the world, or will they innovate to represent the extraordinary value of international collaboration and the harnessing of intellectual capital worldwide? We know that Homeland Security Director Tom Ridge understands the value of innovation by virtue of the successes within his state of Pennsylvania. Will he realize that Homeland Security is as much about prosperity (based upon growth) as it is about protection?

In some post 9/11 scenario planning, faculty at the Wharton School of Business, in conjunction with Canadian consultants of the New-bizDev.org[4], have identified four alternatives based on internal and external events and the degree of response from industry and government: (1) paralysis/survival, (2) slow growth, (3) thriving on chaos, and (4) the most optimal global growth.

> *Countries and peoples of the world recognize common goals and focus on economic development and peace as the route to permanent stability. The key features of this scenario would be that the recession proves short-lived and the business cycle would return to normal; the global coalition against terrorism would evolve into a coalition for peace and commerce, and the threat of terrorism would fade. Investments in new technologies for energy management would reduce the role of oil in Middle Eastern politics. Consumers would feel confident about the future, increase their spending, and lay the foundations of a sustained economic recovery. Trade barriers would be lowered and the developing economies would grow in tandem with the developed ones.*

These are the goals most consistent with the vision referenced in the preceding text; they may provide the most promise for taking advantage of the events of 9/11 and converting tragedy to triumph.

17.3   A GLOBAL HOLONOMY

With the emerging community of innovation practice, it is understood that various practitioners throughout the value system can contribute. How they are engaged in a common mission determines how they are able to leverage their complementary competencies. Rather than competing for resources and spheres of influence, individuals, groups, organizations, and nations can realize what they have to gain through collaborative versus competitive strategy.

We can expect the complexity of what we are managing to increase and the speed of innovation (i.e., idea to action) to accelerate. We expect that understanding a global context could become increasingly more important even if a business is local. We anticipate that strategic alliances and communities of knowledge practice will become more important for survival. How might we make sense of these multidimensional webs of innovation?

Imagine a transnational community in which the collective learning of all participants—employees, academics, government officials, and other stakeholders—is applied to the problems that plague society. Imagine an environment in which intellectual pursuits, pushed to the leading edge of a given field, provide insight to capitalize on global opportunities that advance the state of the art and the state of the practice simultaneously. Imagine a network of interdependent individuals, departments, and research centers linked across the globe to share and leverage the knowledge of one another through symbiotic partnering. By definition, this community operates as a formal and informal nesting of networks.

The complexity of relationships seems unmanageable. It is absolutely critical to understand and leverage the links among the spheres. Strategies are needed at each level to properly mine each source of interaction. This is precisely the challenge: to create an optimal strategy for sustainable growth in an economy of such dynamic movement.

There are some answers in the writings of Jessica Lipnack and Jeffrey Stamps (1994). Consider yourself as an individual within the context of the whole. Consider your enterprise within the context of a nation. Consider your nation in the context of societal transformation. There are ways with common purpose and alignment of competencies, oftentimes diverse and complementary, to ensure your sustainability.

Figure 17.1 provides a few examples of what might be included in the map of an organization's own spheres of interaction. Each organization is unique in the interfaces it seeks to manage. The first step is making those interfaces explicit. Mapping both individual and organizational time lines and spheres of influence provides excellent analytical insight as to how well the person or organization is placed to succeed in the knowledge age.

The core premise of the future is collaboration. This does not mean that organizations do not compete; competition is inevitable. It does

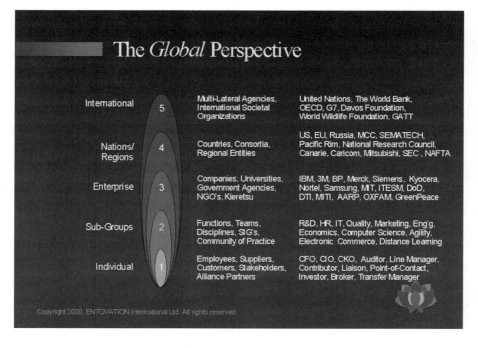

FIGURE 17.1   *The global perspective.*[5]

mean that that their orientation shifts to one of sharing and leveraging one another for mutual success. In national and global terms, this is described as creating the common good from which all benefit. Previous eras have experienced reliance on resources that are depleted. Perhaps the era based on the bountiful resource of knowledge provides an opportunity for true global symbiosis.

We are seeing the emergence of several societal initiatives, such as the Earth Charter,[6] that call for organizing principles that link respect and care for community life, ecological integrity, societal and economic justice, and democracy, non-violence and peace. These initiatives— similar to the initiatives of the Global Knowledge Partnership described in Chapter 14—are increasingly exploring the implications of knowledge and innovation in building the sustainability they envision.

17.4   PROSPECTUS[7]

What if there was a way to link these initiatives in a way that cross-fertilized intent and aspiration? Further, what if there were mechanisms in place to ensure that the concepts and theories being developed and practiced provide a solid foundation for optimal performance and results were not at the whim of marketing fancy or political influence. What if there was a way to chart a direction forward that would resolve the productivity paradox? What if we could define universal innovation metrics to measure the one competence deemed necessary for the future? What if we could use the technology to share learnings in ways that eliminate unnecessary duplication of effort destructive competition and reinventing the wheel?

What follows in Table 17.1 and the following text is one way to structure the international dialog necessary, across disciplines, functions, sectors, industries, and cultures—developing and industrial alike.

TABLE 17.1   *Proposal: The Innovation Superhighway—Networked Competence for Shared Prosperity*

Vision	A new economic world order based on knowledge, innovation, stakeholder success, and international collaboration.
Project Scope	A structured, international dialog—electronic and face-to-face—with a cross-generational network of theorists and practitioners from fifty countries operating as a holonomy of expertise across functions, sectors, industries and geographic regions innovating a world that does not exist today.
Rationale	This is a defining moment in the evolution of the world. In the knowledge economy, our most valuable resource is the knowledge we can create and apply for the benefit of an enterprise, the vitality of a nation's economy, and the advancement of society. Innovation (and the ability to measure its performance) is the one competence needed for the future. It is that simple and that complex. We can resolve the productivity paradox with a new knowledge value proposition. The agenda cuts across three levels of society: micro-, meso-, and macroeconomic. Global sustainability is a function of collaborative—not competitive—advantage. With aligned values and vision, we have an opportunity to innovate our future.

Frame	**Roundtable Roots**	"Managing the Knowledge Assets into the 21st Century" (1987)
	Value Proposition	Economics, behavior and technology
	Constituency	Global knowledge leadership map
	Innovation Architecture	Ten dimensions of innovation

TABLE 17.1 (continued)

	Format	E-collaboration and residential learning—An international center of learning
	Trend Analysis	ENTOVATION 100—Five meta-views
	Proof of Concept	Global Learn Day—Seven vignettes of international dialog

17.4.1 Concept

The future belongs to those able to traverse boundaries (e.g., disciplines, social and civic communities, etc.) Innovation is the hands of those able to make connections that weren't there before. The process can be managed systematically—or can at least be architected—rather than just leaving the future to serendipity. In the 1980s, the management architecture was created. Since 1994, the network of professionals who share some common values and vision has been featured on the global knowledge leadership map. The time is right to put them into a structured dialog.

Based on the interviews, trends have been identified that set a standard for the twenty-first century. The plan is to put these 100 people into communication with a combination of electronic conferencing and face-to-face meetings in which their respective competencies and constituencies will be leveraged. Insights will be published on a periodic basis and distributed to worldwide leadership.

The global map will evolve into a series of national and/or regional maps through which progress can be reported and new initiatives imagined. The collective talent will operate as a global innovation management system, the infrastructure for which will be The Innovation Superhighway. This will be as a demonstration of knowledge innovation (i.e., creation, conversion, and commercialization). As experts from industrialized and developing nations alike work in collaboration, the economy now based on financial capital will adjust to learn how to link human capital to economic results. This common language and shared vision provides, ultimately, a platform for world peace.

17.4.2 Problem and opportunity

In the early 1980s, there were only about a half dozen people worldwide discussing the new economy in terms of intellectual capital, learning organizations, and intangible assets. Today there is a community of knowledge practice that spans the globe—expounding the principles, practice, and potential. Conferences proliferate, college degree programs have been instituted, and knowledge certification programs now abound. Most consulting firms have developed knowledge practices and the business and trade press have featured editorial sections and complete journals on the subject. Enterprises have established chief officer positions (e.g., CKO, CLO) for knowledge learning and innovation. But the downsizing and economic decline continue worldwide because we are transitioning to the new economy and the new economic rules have yet to be discovered. With all the best intentions, unnecessary duplication of effort thwarts progress that might provide an accelerated solution—the innovation infrastructure.

17.4.3 Toward the Innovation Superhighway

The following are the characteristics of the innovation superhighway.

- It builds upon the foundation of the infrastructure of the information superhighway—ready for grass roots enterprise innovation as well as G-8 level discussion and policy making.
- It provides a systematic frame for resolution of the productivity paradox on a worldwide basis.
- It places the focus on the human being, within which true insight and imagination resides, as well creating as an action-

oriented agenda for initiatives that are both human and humane.

- It establishes a common base for learning from each other's progress—our competencies, projects, and aspirations.
- It defines—in collaboration—a new economy based on the flow of intellectual capital.
- It coalesces, rather than duplicates, current leadership initiatives underway, providing optimal results.

Individuals and enterprises of all nations are welcome and encouraged to participate. It will take all of us—developing and industrialized nations alike—to create a sustainable future and an increased standard of living around the globe.

17.5 SUMMARY

It is not insignificant that with the events of 9/11, the World Trade Center collapsed. We now entertain a vision of creating the "World Trade of Ideas" that is as much a human infrastructure as it is technical. It is not insignificant that the financial capital of the world has been fledgling ever since. In fact, many economies of the world are suffering similar consequences. Perhaps now is the time that we reconstruct based on intellectual, not financial, capital?

The knowledge economy affords an unprecedented opportunity for creating the future. This is a climate in which ideas will be valued, but only as they are applied to advance society, however that may be defined. The answers lie in an effective innovation strategy, redefined according to the flow of knowledge: ideas to prosperity. The mandate is quite clear, but the role of the management professional is yet to be fully understood. What legacy will there be in ten, twenty, or fifty years?

Organizations must create the integral connection between the value of human capital and economic prosperity. Technology is the integral enabler, but it is people—their intellect, insights, and imagination—that will fuel innovation prosperity. We all have a responsibility to bring clarity, meaning, and methods to the process. What is equally obvious is that this cannot be done in a vacuum. Creating the knowledge innovation language, culture, and shared vision is by definition a collaborative process. History will document how well this transition toward the innovation superhighway is led.

Chapter Endnotes

[1] Remarks by Tony Blair in a CNN broadcast during the aftermath of the 9/11 events.

[2] Documented in "The Global Momentum of Knowledge Strategy" (Amidon 1999).

[3] *Intangibles in Cooperation and Competition*, p. 30.

[4] For further information, visit http://wwwNewbizDev.org.

[5] Holonomy adapted with permission from *The Age of the Network* by Jessica Lipnack and Jeffrey Stamps (1994), p. 98.

[6] For the full Charter Web site, visit http://www.earthcharter.org/earthcharter/charter.htm.

[7] The research design can be reviewed at the Web site http://www.gkii.org.

APPENDIX A
Knowledge Innovation®

Imagine intellectual assets harnessed to solve collectively the problems that plague society.

Much has been written about technological innovation. Indeed, its strength has been tied to U.S. economic competitiveness. However, those dedicated to the learning profession—whether their classroom is corporate or on campus—know that real value also lies in the benefit to society. There is hardly a function, organization, industry, or nation that is not undergoing massive transformation. These structural changes will set in motion some impacts we may not realize for decades.

In the twenty-first century, knowledge about products and services is likely to become as important as—perhaps even more important than—the discrete products themselves. Given the acceleration of technology development and worldwide global communication systems, enterprises will have to become far more innovative in how they partner with customers to create, transfer, and apply new knowledge within and across industries.

Looking at the future of our research enterprise from a pessimistic perspective, we could envision decreased investment from industry, continued fragmentation of the science and technology community, and an academic research agenda "driven" by the needs of industry. An optimist might see, instead, a collaborative strategy emerging with innovative relationships that benefit all partners. The network of expertise, enhanced by modern communication systems, enables us to advance the standard of living in our country and throughout the world. I believe such a vision is attainable.

In the evolution of technology transfer systems; I see the emergence of a knowledge innovation system in which people recognize the dynamic nature of the innovation process. Networked enterprises would be defined beyond the confines of a particular company, laboratory, or geography. With a multitude of research consortia, joint ventures, and alliances, managers will seek a more systematic understanding of how ideas originate and enter the marketplace.

Imagine a science and technology community interconnected without unnecessary or counterproductive duplication. Imagine the scientific breakthroughs of one entity leveraging the discoveries of another. Competition plays a role, but only as a catalyst for new ideas or to preserve the identity of individual partners. Imagine intellectual assets harnessed to solve collectively the problems that plague society.

The new focus on what I call knowledge innovation—the creation, exchange and application of new ideas into goods and services—could fuse many diverse interests into a shared vision. Rather than allow serendipity to dictate our future, now is the time to take steps together and embrace the opportunities posed by the changes ahead.

Debra Amidon, formerly a global innovation strategist with Digital Equipment Corporation, is head of Entovation International Ltd. in Wilmington, Mass. This article first appeared in *PRISM, the Journal of the American Society for Engineering Education* (June 1993). Knowledge Innovation® is a registered trademark of Entovation International Ltd.

APPENDIX B
Sample Definitions of Innovation

The three stages in the process of innovation: invention, translation and commercialization.

> Bruce D. Merrifield. 1986 in "Forces of Change Affecting High Technology Industries," a speech delivered by the U.S. Assistant Secretary of Commerce.

Invention: the power of inventing or being invented; ingenuity or creativity; something originating in an experiment. Innovation: the act or process of innovating; something newly introduced, new method, custom, device, etc.; change in the way of doing things; renew, alter.

> *Webster's New World Dictionary*, 1982, Second College Edition.

Phases of Growth: entrepreneurial; divergent; inventive; creative; exploratory management; duplication; modification; improvement; commonality/likeness; shared leadership; divergence and innovation; sharing and integrating differentness; partnering/vision. Innovators can hold a situation in chaos for long periods of time without having to reach a resolution...won't give up...have a long-term commitment to their dream...innovators introduce a maximum of tension into the thinking process, unifying concepts that often appear to be opposed, solving problems which appear impossible.

> George Land and Beth Jarman. 1992. *Breakpoint and Beyond: Mastering the Future Today* (New York: Harper/Collins Publishers).

This (innovation) life cycle is an S-shaped logistic curve consisting of three distinct phases: emergence (the development of the product or service, its manufacturing capabilities, and its place in the market), growth (where the product family pervades the market), and maturity (where the market is saturated and growth slows).

William G. Howard, Jr. and Bruce R. Guile, 1992,
Profiting from Innovation (New York: The Free Press) p.12.

Innovation cuts across a broad range of activities, institutions and time spans. If any part of the pipeline is broken or constricted, the flow of benefits is slowed. This is felt ultimately in lower productivity and lowered standards of living. In this sense, the cost of capital is crucial not only at the early stages of research and product development but also at the later stages when high-technology products are installed in production processes, in both manufacturing and service industries, as new tools to improve worker effectiveness.

James Botkin, Dan Dimancescu, and Ray Stata, 1983,
The Innovators: Rediscovering America's Creative Energy
(New York: Harper and Row).

Matrix of the four types of Innovations: I. Architectural Innovation; II. Market Niche Innovation; III. Regular Innovation; and IV. Revolutionary Innovation.

William J. Abernathy, Kim B. Clark, and Alan M. Kantrow, 1983,
Industrial Renaissance (New York: Basic Books).

Continuous innovation occurs largely because a few key executives have a broad vision of what their organizations can accomplish for the world and lead their enterprises toward it. They appreciate the role of innovation in achieving their goals and consciously manage their concerns' value systems and atmospheres to support it.

James Brian Quinn, 1986, "Innovation and Corporate Strategy:
Managed Chaos," in *Technology in the Modern Corporation:
A Strategic Perspective* (New York: Pergamon Press, p.170.

Five Stages of the Innovation Process: 1. Recognition; 2. Invention; 3. Development; 4. Implementation; and 5. Diffusion.

Modesto A. Maidique, 1980, "Entrepreneurs, Champions and Technological Innovation," *Sloan Management Review* (Winter).

The literature on organizational innovation is rich in lessons...describes processes that are also prevalent in the natural universe. Innovation is fostered by information gathered from new connections; from insights gained by journeys into other disciplines or places; from active, collegial networks and fluid, open boundaries. Innovation arises from ongoing circles of exchange, where information is not just accumulated or stored, but created. Knowledge is generated anew from connections that weren't there before.

Margaret J. Wheatley, 1992, *Leadership and the New Science* (San Francisco: Berrett-Koehler Publishers), p.113.

To explain innovation, we need a new theory of organizational knowledge creation....The cornerstone of our epistemology is the distinction between tacit and explicit knowledge...the key to knowledge creation lies in the mobilization and conversion of tacit knowledge.

Ikujiro Nonaka and Hirotaka Takeuchi, 1995,
The Knowledge-Creating Company
(New York: Oxford University Press) p.56.

APPENDIX C
Calibrating the Innovation Strategy

How might one get started? A Knowledge Innovation® litmus test is provided below as a sample of questions to be answered for an organization to assess its capacity for innovation. There are actually over seventy questions in the full assessment available in text or software application form (Amidon 1997a, pp. 62–63). The questions below provide a sample of ten carefully researched dimensions of innovation and may be answered individually or in a group. Using this as a dialog tool, participants may get a better understanding of the complementary competencies that can be brought to bear.

Yes   No

1.   Has one person been charged with the overall responsibility to manage the corporatewide innovation process?

2.   Are there performance measures—both tangible and intangible—to assess the quality of the organization's innovation practices?

3.   Do the training/educational programs have provisions to incubate and spin out new products and businesses?

4.   Does the local, regional, or international presence operate as a distributed network of expertise which learns from as well as distributes to customers?

5.   Is there a formal intelligence-gathering strategy to monitor the positioning of both current and potential competitors?

6.   Does the rate of production of new products and services exceed the industry norms and create new markets in which to excel?

7.   Has a strategic alliance manager been designated to create and manage the network of partnerships and joint ventures to leverage the firm?

8.   Does your marketing image portray an organization with the capacity to create and move ideas into the marketplace to make the firm's customers successful?

9.   Have resources been allocated to articulate a compelling vision internally and share company expertise externally through publications and participation in major forums?

10. Is the computer/communications capability treated as a learning tool for internal conferencing and external business leverage on the World Wide Web?

If seven out of the ten questions were answered in the affirmative, it is likely the organization has a good handle on the innovation process and knows how to create an environment for the optimal flow of ideas contributing to the vitality of the enterprise. Primarily negative responses to these basic innovation questions should drive an organization to examine its processes for bringing ideas to market and leveraging intellectual capability into the future. Even if the score is high, the questions can frame an innovation dialog.

APPENDIX D
The Momentum of Knowledge Management

What began almost ten years ago—Knowledge Innovation®—has now reached the stage of a critical mass of insight. Dedicated experts across all disciplines are exploring and defining new management practices fundamental to capitalizing upon the knowledge-based economy.

Although there has been a plethora of articles and books on the topic, the seminal cookbook (if there ever be such a thing) is only "work-in-process." In the 1920s, when Alfred Sloan divisionalized General Motors, it sent a clear, consistent, concise message of the techniques necessary for large-scale business management. However, today—driven by the acceleration of computer/communications technology and the value of collaborative networks, the real competitive differentiator—human talent—provides the enterprise advantage.

Today, there is an emerging "community of practice," which transcends any function, sector, industry, or geography. Participants include theorists and practitioners from education/learning systems, economics/finance, quality/benchmarking, human resources, information/Internet technology, R&D/innovation strategy, and more. The concurrent engineering, agile manufacturing, and reengineering initiatives are all coming to a common theme: transformation of the enterprise—profit or not-for-profit—through knowledge management.

The first conference in the United States that focused on knowledge—beyond the theories of artificial intelligence—was entitled "Managing the Knowledge Asset into the 21st Century." It was convened by Digital Equipment Corporation and the Technology Transfer Society at Purdue University in 1987. The second on "Knowledge Productivity" was coordinated by Steelcase North America and EDS in April of 1992. The third was hosted by the Industrial Research Institute (IRI) in Vancouver, British Columbia in October 1992. McKinsey and Company initiated its Knowledge Management Practice during the same time. "The Knowledge Advantage Colloquium" was co-sponsored by the Strategic Leadership Forum and the Ernst & Young Center for Business Innovation in 1994. This Fall alone, there have been a half dozen major conferences on the topic, including the three contrasted for this report. Several more planned for the Spring.

D.1 COLLECTIVE FINDINGS ARE EMERGING

D.1.1 The knowledge movement is pervasive

Whether it is defined in terms of learning, intellectual capital, knowledge assets, intelligence, know-how, insight or wisdom, the conclusion is the same: manage it better or perish. Initiatives in industry, education, and government are trying to tackle the same problems, issues, and opportunities.

D.1.2 The unmeasurable must be measured

If it cannot be measured, it isn't considered of value. However, traditional financial accounting mechanisms fail to calculate/calibrate the most important resources of the firm—its intellectual capacity. Instead, current mechanisms treat people as liabilities or expenses instead of assets. The business case must be defined in order to justify necessary investment strategies in the human and social (i.e., interactive) capital of the firm.

D.1.3   A collaborative research base must be established

There is minimal research activity for service functions or the services industry of the economy. There is no equivalent to the Industrial Research Institute for the services industry—the fastest growing sector of the economy. There is minimal government funding and few consortia that are non-industrial in mission. Enterprises are embarking upon individual R&D efforts when a collective degree of research—on a pre-competitive basis—is essential for establishing a solid foundation for the future of the industry.

D.1.4   Initiatives must be designed as "middle-up-down"

Top-down leadership continues to be essential for management because traditional hierarchical structures will not disappear overnight. Grass-roots activities that are networked can have the insight for change validated by those closest to the point of sale. Often, those closest to service delivery are not the people empowered in an organization. Experts describe the strategy as middle-up-down as a way to balance and integrate the best of both methods.

D.1.5   Insight is being gleaned rapidly

For those who embrace change as reality, there is little time to be spent on barriers. The future is far more exciting to create. In each profession, those who were deemed philosophers and futurists are being sought for counsel on business operations. What was theory yesterday is fundamental to business survival tomorrow. There is a cumulative effect between and among disciplines as leaders seek to understand the principles and policies of one another. Indeed, the field has become sufficiently sophisticated to warrant the benchmarking of best practices for even further dissemination and leverage.

D.1.6 Implementation takes many forms

The variety of new titles and program initiatives vary from company to company due to the uniqueness of each corporate culture. New titles range from novel verbiage to relabeling of traditional functions. There are many ways to (re)configure the knowledge puzzle, and leadership can come from any level, function ,or position in the company.

D.1.7 Management architectures are useful but should not be limiting

A frame of reference is essential in order to scrutinize and interconnect the variables. However, exploration of the factors leads to identification of new variables and interconnections that are fundamental to the business. The frame provides a way to organize the discussion and fuse the diverse values within the company culture. The process must be dynamic—not static—in order to capitalize on new business opportunities coming from unserved markets and unarticulated needs.

D.1.8 The nature of "the collective" must be understood and harnessed

Enterprises are now defined as including multiple stakeholders: suppliers, partners, alliances, customers, and—in some cases—competitors. These infrastructures are a combination of evolving, ecological systems and carefully architected schemes for profitable growth. The combination is what is of most value. Attention must now focus upon the definition of the whole and the interconnections of the pieces.

D.1.9 Technology is integral to the successful functioning of the knowledge enterprise—but how?

Similar to the misconceptions of computer-based education, artificial intelligence, and the early renditions of groupware, there is confusion as to the appropriate role for the supporting technology. The "productivity paradox" explains why there has not been a commensurate economic return for the investment on technology investments (i.e., behavioral disconnects), but it does not provide a path forward for the ideal technical solutions. This will take some time and considerable trial and error.

D.1.10 The knowledge phenomenon must be managed and not left to serendipity

As incomplete as the systems might be, some influence and control is better than none at all. Consider the kaleidoscope which when moved in small degrees changes the image; still, there are the inevitable unexpected forces that cause a major shift in orientation. Management must be understood as both a science and an art in order to reap optimal advantage.

D.2 CONCLUSIONS

The interest generated during the past year is significant. Business schools have created interdisciplinary initiatives by necessity. Industrial investments have forged connections that were not likely to occur otherwise. Government agencies are also, by necessity, forced to produce significantly more results to the consumer than can be provided with incremental improvements. Reengineering and quality efforts, along with massive restructuring, have produced what financial results are possible. Considerable alignments are now needed in order to fulfill expectations of stakeholders.

The paradigm must shift; that is inevitable. This new focus on knowledge as the foundation for a successful future has been embraced. Creativity is being reborn in ways to contribute to the bottom line of an enterprise. As impure as this new science may be, it provides insights not easily discerned with traditional management methodologies. Experimentation is rampant, and people seek to learn from their mistakes as well as the successes and failures of others.

The conferences attended have all created some form of evaluation tool(s) as a way to move the dialog forward. All have sought to learn, some in more systematic ways than others, from their participants. There is a realization that this is, indeed, a journey and that no one has the answers. This is a movement born within industry, not the academic corridors or even the consulting firms. In fact, those parties are playing catch-up trying to determine their own role in this emerging economy. One attendee commented "The universities are a decade behind; the consulting firms are half that. Industrialists are creating the future real-time." The knowledge movement is shaking the very foundation of how an organization is created, evolves, matures, dies, or is reformed. These are fundamental shifts in the way we do business, how economies are developed and societies prosper.

APPENDIX E
Knowledge Leaders and Laggards

What are the characteristics that distinguish organizations that are leaders in knowledge management and those that are less successful or even failing in their knowledge initiatives? In research for *Creating the Knowledge-based Business* we found ten recurring characteristics that separated the leaders and the laggards. The report also illustrates these characteristics through case studies of thirty-three knowledge leaders.

E.1   TEN CHARACTERISTICS OF LEADERS

1. They have a clearly articulated vision of what the knowledge agenda and knowledge management is about. Their thinking about their business, their business environment, and their knowledge goals is clear.

2. They have enthusiastic knowledge champions who are supported by senior management.

3. They have a holistic perspective that embraces strategic, technological, and organizational perspectives.

4. They use systematic processes and frameworks (the power of visualization).

5. They "bet on knowledge," even when the cost benefits cannot easily be measured.

6. They use effective communications, using all the tricks of marketing and PR.

7. There is effective interaction at all levels with their customers and external experts. Human networking takes place internally and externally on a broad front.

8. They demonstrate good teamwork, with team members drawn from many disciplines.

9. They have a culture of openness and inquisitiveness that stimulates innovation and learning.

10. They develop incentives, sanctions, and personal development programs to change behaviors.

E.2   TEN CHARACTERISTICS OF LAGGARDS

1. They simplify knowledge to an information or database model, often applying the "knowledge" label without a comprehensive understanding of what knowledge is about.

2. They package and disseminate the knowledge that is most readily available (as opposed to that which is the most useful).

3. They work in isolated pockets without strong senior management support. Thus, they may hand over responsibility for knowledge systems to one department, such as MIS, without engaging the whole organization.

4. They focus on a narrow aspect of knowledge, such as knowledge sharing, rather than all processes including new knowledge creation and innovation.

5. They blindly follow a change process (e.g., BPR) without understanding the associated knowledge dimension.

6. They downsize or outsource without appreciating what vital knowledge might be lost.

7. They think that technology (alone) is the answer—for example, that expert systems by themselves are the way to organize and use knowledge.

8. They have a major cultural blockage, perhaps caused by a climate of "knowledge is power."

9. They "know all the answers" (i.e., they are not open to new ideas).

10. They get impatient. They think knowledge management is simply another short-term project or program. They do not allow time for new systems and behaviors to become embedded.

References

————, *Breaking the Barriers to the National Information Infrastructure*, A Conference Report published by the Council on Competitiveness: Washington, D.C. (December, 1994).

————, Survey of the World's Economy: The hitchhiker's guide to cybernomics," *The Economist* (September 28, 1996).

————, Economist Intelligence Unit and IBM Consulting Group, *The Learning Organization: Managing Knowledge for Business Success*, The Economist Intelligence Unit, New York, 1996.

————, *Vision for a 21st Century Information Infrastructure*, The first in a series of policy reports published by the Council on Competitiveness: Washington, D.C. (May, 1993).

————, "Power of Innovation Capital," Supplement to the Annual Report, Skandia A.F.S. (1995).

————. "Vital Intangibles," *The Economist* (April 4, 1997).

————, *Information in the Technology in the Services Society: A Twenty-First Century Lever*, published by the Computer Science and Telecommunications Board, National Academy Press: Washington, D.C. (1994). p. 190.

————*Knowledge for Development* – the 1998–99 edition of the World Development Report (WDR), The World Bank: Washington, D.C. (1999).

————"Companies have made innovation an organization-wide priority," *Trendsetter Barometer*, PriceWaterhouse Coopers (June 27, 2001).

————*Collaborating for Innovation: 2nd Annual Innovation Report*, The Conference Board of Canada, pp. 303–400 (2001).

————"Country intelligence for the digital age," promotional brochure for the Economist Intelligence Unit, The Economist Group (2001).

————*Stories from the Edge: Managing Knowledge through New Ways of Working within Shell's Exploration and Production Business*, published by Shell International Exploration and Production B.V.: Rijswijk, The Netherlands (November 2001).

————*Investing in Innovation 3ʳᵈ Annual Innovation Report*, The Conference Board of Canada, 336–401 (2002).

————, "Gartner Advises on Managing Innovation: Is it Possible?," *Gartner Insight* (an electronic publication), Gartner Research, vol. 4, issue 3 (March 2002).

———— "The Economic Consequences of terror," *The World in 2002*, The Economist: London, (2002).

————"Collaborative Knowledge Networks: Driving workforce performance through Web-enabled communities," monograph produced by Deloitte Research: New York (2002).

————*Global Information Technology Report 2002-2002: Readiness for the Networked World*, published by the Center for International Development, Harvard University, Cambridge, Massachusetts (2002).

Ackoff, Russell L., *Redesigning the Future: A Systems Approach to Societal Problems*, John Wiley & Sons: New York (1974). p. vii.

Amidon, Debra M., "The Collective Challenge: Optimizing the Technology Alliance," *Managing the Knowledge Assets into the 21ˢᵗ Century: Focus on Research Consortia*, Technology Strategy Group and Digital Equipment Corporation: Cambridge, Massachusetts, April, 1987, pp. 14–27.

————"Technology Challenge to Management," *Entrepreneurial Management: New Technology and New Market Development* (George Kozmetsky et al., eds.), Ballinger Press (1989).

————, *Global Innovation Strategy: Creating Value-Added Alliances*, graduate MIT thesis published by the IC2 Institute of the University of Texas at Austin, Texas (1989).

————, "Knowledge Innovation: The Common Language," *Journal of Technology Studies*, Epsilon Pi Tau (Fall, 1993).

————"Momentum of Knowledge Management", *Research-Technology Management*, Industrial Research Institute: Washington, D.C. (May/June 1996).

————"The Challenge of 5ᵗʰ Generation R&D: Virtual Learning," *Research-Technology Management*, vol. 36 (July–August 1996).

————*Innovation Strategy for the Knowledge Economy: The Ken Awakening*, Butterworth-Heinemann: Boston (1997).

————, "Customer Innovation: A Function of Knowledge," *Journal of Customer Partnerships* (December, 1997).

————, *Collaborative Innovation and the Knowledge Economy*, Society of Management Accountants of Canada: Hamilton, Ontario, Canada (1998).

————. "Blueprint of 21st Century Innovation," *Journal of Knowledge Management*, vol, 2, no. 1 (September 1998).

————, "Global Momentum of Knowledge Strategy" published on the Entovation Web Site and in *I³ Update/ENTOVATION News* (February, 1999).

————"The Virtual CKO: Leading by Strategic Conversations," *Leading Knowledge Management and Learning*, ASTD Action Series, American Society for Training and Development: Alexandria, Virginia, Dede Bonner, ed. (2000) pp. 101–112.

Amidon, Debra M. and David J. Skyrme, "Creating the World Trade of Ideas: A Global Knowledge Innovation Infrastructure," *Knowledge Management Review* (Spring 1999).

Amidon, Debra M. and Darius Mahdjoubi, "The Atlas of Knowledge Innovation: Migration from Strategic Planning," *2000 Handbook of Business Strategy*, Faulkner & Grey: New York (Fall, 1999).

Amidon, Debra M. and Doug Macnamara, "The 7C's of Knowledge Leadership," published in the *2001 Handbook of Business Strategy*, Thompson Financial Media: New York (Fall, 2000).

Amidon, Debra M. and Jan Wyllie, *Voice of the ENTOVATION 100: Innovation Trends of the Knowledge Economy*, produced by Trend Monitor International, Ltd. (2002)

Anielski, Mark, *The Alberta GPI Blueprint: The Genuine Progress Indicator Sustainable Well-being Accounting System*, Pembina Institute for Appropriate Development: Drayton Valley, Alberta (September 2001).

Asacker, Tom, *The Four Sides of Sandbox Wisdom*, Eastside Publishing: Manchester, New Hampshire (December 2001).

Banerjee, Parthasarathi and Frank Jurgen Richter, *Intangibles in Competition and Collaboration: Euro-Asian Perspectives*, Palgrave of Anthony Rowe, Ltd.: Chippenham, Wiltshire, UK (2001).

Bartlett, Chris and Sumantra Ghoshal, "Managing Across Borders: New Strategic Response," *Sloan Management Review* (Fall, 1997).

Beazley, Hamilton; Jeremiah Boenish; and David Harden, *Continuity Management: Preserving Corporate Knowledge and Productivity when Employees Leave*, John Wiley and Sons: New York (2002).

Becker, Gary Stanley, *An Economic Approach to Human Behavior*, University of Chicago Press: Chicago (October 1978).

————, *Human Capital: A Theoretical and Empirical Analysis, With Special Reference to Education*, University of Chicago Press: Chicago (December 1993).

Bonner, Dede (ed), *Leading Knowledge Management and Learning*, ASTD Action Series, American Society for Training and Development: Alexandria, Virginia (2000).

Bontis, Nick, "National Intellectual Capital Index: Intellectual Capital Development in the Arab Region," report produced for the Intellectual Capital Research Inc., McMaster University and the United Nations Office of Project Services (2002).

————, (ed.), *World Congress on Intellectual Capital Readings: Cutting edge thinking on intellectual capital and knowledge management from the world's experts*, Butterworth-Heinemann: Boston (200).

Borgman, Christine L. *From Gutenberg to the Global Information Infrastructure: Access to Information in a Networked World*, MIT Press: Cambridge, Massachusetts (2000).

Botkin, Jim Botkin, *Smart Business: How Knowledge Communities can Revolutionize your Company*, The Free Press: New York (1999).

Brown, John Seely and Estee Solomon Gray. "After Reengineering: The People are the Company." *Fast Company* (premier issue, 1995), pp. 78–82.

Brown, John Seely and Paul Duguid, "Organizational Learning and Communities-of-Practice: Toward a Unified View of Working, Learning, and Innovation," *Strategic Learning in a Knowledge Economy: Individual, Collective and Organizational Learning Process*, Butterworth-Heinemann: Woburn, Massachusetts (2000).

Brown, Harold and Herzfel, Charles (eds.), *Global Innovation/National Competitiveness*, The Center for Strategic and International Studies, Washington, D,C,, 1996.

Bush, Vannevar, *Science—The Endless Frontier*, a report to President Roosevelt, Order No. NSF 90-8, National Science Foundation, Arlington, Virginia (1945).

Carter, Barry, *Infinite Wealth: A New World of Collaboration and Abundance in the Knowledge Era*, Butterworth-Heinemann: Boston (1999).

Cooper, Robert G. and Scott J. Edgett, *Product Development for the Services Sector*, Perseus Publishers (1999).

Cortada, James W., *The Rise of the Knowledge Worker*, Butterworth-Heinemann: Woburn, Massachsuetts (1998).

Cothrel, Joe; Karina Funk; and Crystal Schaffer, "Learning to Innovate," an electronic *Focus E-zine* for Cap Gemini Ernst & Young (2001).

Cross, Rob and Sam Israelit (eds.), *Strategic Learning in a Knowledge Economy: Individual, Collective and Organization Learning Process*, Butterworth-Heinemann: Boston (1999).

Davenport, Thomas H. and Laurence Prusak, *Working Knowledge: How Organizations Manage What They Know*, Harvard Business School Press: Boston (1998).

Dawson, Ross, *Developing Knowledge-Based Client Relationships: The Future of Professional Services*, Butterworth-Heinemann: Boston (2000).

De Kerckhove, Derrick, *Connected Intelligence: The Arrival of the Web Society*, Somerville House Publishing: Toronto, Canada (1997).

De Geus, Arie, "__?___", *Harvard Business Review* (1989).

Denning, Stephan, *The Springboard: How Story-Telling Ignites Action in Knowledge-Era Enterprises*, Butterworth-Heinemann: Boston (2001).

Drucker, Peter F. *The New Realities: In Government and Politics, In Economics and Business, in Society and World View*, Harper & Row: New York, N. Y. (1989).

———, *Post Capitalist Society*, Butterworth-Heinemann: Boston Massachusetts (1993).

———, *Innovation and Entrepreneurship*, Harperbusiness: New York, NY (May 1993)

———, "From Capitalism to Knowledge Society," *The Knowledge Economy* (Dale Neef, ed.) Butterworth-Heinemann: Boston (1998). pp. 15–34.

———, "The Information Executives Truly Need," *Harvard Business Review* (January–February, 1995). pp. 54–62.

Edvinsson, Leif and Michael S. Malone, *Intellectual Capital: Realizing Your Company's True Value by Finding its Hidden Brainpower*, HarperCollins Publishers: New York (1997).

Edvinsson, Leif, "The Knowledge Capital of Nations," *Knowledge Management*, ArkGroup: London (April 2002), pp.27–30.

Ehin, Charles, *Unleashing Intellectual Capital*, Butterworth-Heinemann: Boston (2000).

Fountain, Jane E. "Social Capital: A Key Enabler of Innovation in Science and Technology" in *Investing in Innovation: Toward a Consensus Strategy for Federal Technology Policy*, L.M. Branscomb and J. Keller, eds., MIT Press: Cambridge, Massachusetts. (1997).

Forrester, Jay, *Industrial Dynamics*, MIT Press: Cambridge., Massachusetts (1985).

Galbraith, John Kenneth, *Ambassador's Journal: A Personal Account of the Kennedy Years*, Houghton Mifflin Co.: Boston (1969).

Gibson, David V. and Everett M. Rogers (1994). *R&D Collaboration on Trial*, Harvard Business School Press: Boston, pp. 31–38.

Goldfinger,. Charles, "A Necessary Illness," *WorldLink* (January–February 1997).

Goldman, Steven L.; Roger N. Nagel; and Kenneth Preiss, *Agile Competitors and Virtual Organizations*, Van Nostrand Reinhold: New York (1995).

Granell de Aldaz, Elena, *Managing Culture for Success: Challenges and Opportunities in Venezuela*, Ediciones IESA: Caracas, Venezuela (1998).

Hamel, Gary and C.K. Prahalad, *Competing for the Future*, Harvard Business School Press: Boston (1994).

Handy, Charles, *Beyond Certainty: Changing Worlds of Organizations*, Harvard Business School Press: Boston, (1996). p. 100.

Harris, Douglas H. (ed.) *Organization Linkages: Understanding the Productivity Paradox*, Report of the National Research Council, National Academy Press: Washington, D.C. (1994).

Harris, K.; M. Grey; and C. Rozwell, "Changing the View of ROI to VOI—Value on Investment," *Strategic Planning*—SPA-14-7250, published by The Gartner Research Group (November 14, 2001).

Harris, Trevor and Elmer H. Huh, "Valuing and Measuring Technological Edge: Finding FASSTEST Companies," Report for Global Valuation and Accounting published by Morgan Stanley Dean Witter (October 11, 2000).

Huang, Kuan-Tsae, "Capitalizing on Intellectual Assets," (James W. Cortada and John A. Woods (eds.)), The Knowledge Management Yearbook 1999–2000, Butterworth-Heinemann: Woburn, Massachusetts (1999).

Hughes, Paul, "The Evolution of Price Modeling: From Billing to Dynamic Transaction Management," Yankee Group Report for Billing & Payment Application Strategies, The Yankee Group (2002).

Ishikawa, Akira, *The Global Information Network: Fundamental Revolutions based on the study – research into the corporate use of communications networks in Japan, United States and Europe*, Nikkan Kogyo Shimbum: Tokyo, Japan (1992) Translated by Sachiko Gardner and Hiroko Smith, IC2 Institute: Austin, Texas (1995).

Itami, Hiroyuki, *Mobilizing Invisible Assets*, Harvard University Press: Cambridge, Massachusetts (1987), p. 23.

Judge, W.K.; G.E. Fryxell; and R.S. Dooley, "The New task of R&D Management: Creating Goal—Directed Communities of Innovation," *California Management Review*, vol. 39. no. 3 (1997).

Kanter, Rosabeth Moss, *Evolve!: Succeeding in the Digital Culture of Tomorrow*, Harvard Business School Press: Boston (2001).

Kaplan, Robert S. and David P. Norton, "The Balanced Scorecard: Measures that drive performance," *Harvard Business Review*: Cambridge, Massachusetts (January–February 1992).

Kelleher, Michael et al., *KALiF: To Share is to Multiply*, CIBIT bv: Utrecht, The Netherlands (2001).

Kozmetsky, George and Raymond Smilor, *The Technopolis Phenomenon*, published by the IC2 Institute of the University of Texas: Austin, Texas (1990).

Krebs, Valdis, *Managing Core Competencies of the Corporation*, The Advisory Board Company (1996).

Lampe, David R. (ed), *The Massachusetts Miracle*. The MIT Press: Cambridge. Massachusetts (1988).

Leonard-Barton, Dorothy, *Wellsprings of Knowledge: Building and Sustaining the Sources of Innovation*, Harvard Business School Press: Boston (1995).

Lev, Baruch, *Intangibles: Management, Measurement and Reporting*, Brookings Institute Press (2000).

Levine, Rick et al., *The Cluetrain Manifesto: The end of business as usual*, Perseus Press: Cambridge: Massachsetts (2000).

Lipnack, Jessica and Jeffrey Stamps, *The Age of the Network: Organizing Principles for the 21ˢᵗ Century*, OMNEO, an imprint of Oliver Wight Publications: Essex Junction, Vermont (1994).

Macnamara, Doug, "Competency Profiling and Learning Contracts: Building Partnerships in Leadership Development and Maximizing Impact" *Leadership Compass* (Winter–Spring 2000). pp.19–21.

McNamee, Mike, "New Yardsticks for Investors," *BusinessWeek*, (November 5, 2001).

Mieszkowski, Katherine, "Are You on Craig's List?," *Net Company*, Issue 002. p. 26.

Miller, Riel, *Measuring What People Know: Human Capital Accounting for the Knowledge Economy*, OECD, Paris (1996).

Miller, William L., and Langdon Morris, *Fourth Generation R&D Managing Knowledge, Technology and Innovation*, New York: John Wiley & Sons (1999).

Mintzberg, Henry, *The Rise and Fall of Strategic Planning*, The Free Press: New York (1994).

Molz, R. Kathleen, a presentation—"NII Principles and Actions: A Checklist of the Clinton Administration's Progress" (September 1993–94).

Morville, Peter, "Social Network Analysis," published electronically by Semantic Studios LLC (February 21, 2002).

Naisbitt, John, *Global Paradox*, Avon Books: New York (1994). pp. 5–6.

Neilson, Robert, *Collaborative Technologies & Organizational Learning*, Idea Group Publishing: Hershey, Pennsylvania (1997).

Nonaka, Ikujiru and Hirotaka Takeuchi, "The Knowledge-Creating Company," *Harvard Business Review* (November–December, 1991) p.97.

Nonaka, Ikujiru and Noboru Konno, "The Concept of 'Ba': Building a Foundation for Knowledge Creation, *California Management Review* vol.40, no. 3 (1998).

——— "Drucker on Asia: A Dialogue Between Peter Drucker and Isao Nakauchi," Butterworth-Heinemann: Oxford, UK (1997).

Paye, Jean-Claude, "Policies for a knowledge-based economy," *OECD Observer*, no. 200 (June–July, 1996), p. 5.

Petzinger, Jr. Thomas, *The New Pioneers: The Men and Women who are Transforming the Workplace and Marketplace*, Simon & Schuster: New York (1999).

Pinchot, Gifford and Elizabeth, *The End of Bureaucracy & the Rise of the Intelligent Organization*, Berrett-Koehler Press: San Francisco (1994).

Polanyi, Michael, *Personal Knowledge: Toward a Post-Critical Philosophy*, University of Chicago Press: Chicago (September 1974).

———*Tacit Dimension*, Peter Smith Publishers (June 1983)

Por, George, "Nurturing Systemic Wisdom Through Knowledge Ecology," *The Systems Thinker*, Pegasus: Boston (October 2000).

Porter, Michael F., *Competitive Advantage: Creating and Sustaining Superior Performance*, The Free Press, New York (1985),

Portes, Alejandro, "Social Capital: Its Origins and Applications," Lesser, Eric L., (ed.) *Knowledge and Social Capital: Foundations and Applications*, Butterworth-Heinemann: Boston (2000).

Preiss, Kenneth; Steven L. Goldman; and Roger N. Nagel, *Cooperate to Compete: Building Agile Relationships*, Van Nostrand Reinhold: New York (1996.

Prior, John E. C., *Knowledge Management & the Wealth of Intangibles: An ABC of Terms with Comment & Illumination*, J.P. Consultancy: Toronto, Canada (December 1999).

Quinn, James Brian, *The Intelligent Enterprise: A Knowledge and Service-Based Paradigm for Industry*, The Free Press: New York (1992) p. 310.

Rifkin, Glenn and George Harrar, *The Ultimate Entrepreneur: The Story of Ken Olsen and Digital Equipment Corporation*," Prima Publishing & Communications, Rocklin, California (1990).

Ritzen, J.M.M., *Toward a European Knowledge Union*, Ministry of Education, Culture and Science, The Netherlands, 1997.

Rothschild, Michael, *Bionomics: Economy as Ecosystem*, Henry Holt & Co.: New York (1990).

Saint-Onge, Hubert, "Shaping Human Resource Management Within the Knowledge-Driven Enterprise," *Leading Knowledge Management and Learning* (Dede Bonner, ed.), ASTD Action Series, Alexandria, Virginia (2000).

Scharmer, Claus Otto, "Presencing: Learning From the Future as it Emerges," presentation at the Conference on Knowledge and Innovation, May 25–26, 2000, Helsinki School of Economics.

Senge, Peter, *The Fifth Discipline: The Art and Practice of the Learning Organization*, Bantam Doubleday Dell Publishing: New York (1990).

Skyrme, David J. and Debra M. Amidon. *Creating the Knowledge-Based Business*, London: Business Intelligence (1997) p. 55.

————"Measuring the Value of Knowledge." *Handbook of Business Strategy*, New York: Faulkner & Gray (1999).

Skyrme, David J. *Knowledge Networking: Creating the Collaborative Enterprise*, Butterworth-Heinemann: Oxford, UK (1999).

————, *Capitalizing on Knowledge: From e-business to k-business*, Butterworth-Heinemann: Oxford, UK (2001).

Simpson, John et al., "Scenarios for Future Work in the Knowledge Economy," European KM Forum IST Project No 2000-26393 (2001).

Smilor, Raymond W.; David V. Gibson; and George Kozmetsky, "Creating the Technopolis: High Technology Development in Austin, Texas. *Journal of Business Venturing* (1988), vol. 4, pp. 49–67.

Smith, David E. (ed.), *Knowledge, Groupware and the Internet*, Butterworth-Heinemann: Boston (2001).

Sorensen, Theodore C. *"Let the Word Go Forth": The Speeches, Statements and Writings of John F. Kennedy—1947 to 1963*, Delacorte Press: New York (1988).

Stabulnieks, Janis, *"National Concept on Innovation,"* Accepted by the Cabinet of Ministers of the Republic of Latvia, Protocol No. 9. § 39 (February 27, 2001).

Stata, Ray, "Organizational Learning: The Key to Management Innovation," *Sloan Management Review,* (Spring, 1989) pp. 63–74.

Stewart, Thomas A., *Intellectual Capital: The New Wealth of Organizations*, Nicholas Brealey Publishing Limited, UK (1997).

———, *The Wealth of Knowledge: Intellectual Capital and the 21st Century Organization,"* Currency Doubleday: New York (2002), Ch. 1.

Stanford, Xenia. "Social Capital and Innovation Analysis of the E100—Part I: Foundations & Assessment Overview," *KnowMap* vol. 2. no. 2.,(April 2002).

Sveiby, Karl-Erik and Tom Lloyd, *Managing Know-How: Add Value by Valuing Creativity*, Bloomsbury Publishing: London (1987).

Sveiby, Karl-Erik, *The New Organizational Wealth: Managing & Measuring Knowledge-Based Assets*, Berrett-Koehler: San Francisco (1997).

Tatsuno, Sheridan, *The Technopolis Strategy*. Prentice-Hall Press (1986).

Thurow, Lester, *The Future of Capitalism: How Today's Economic Forces Shape Tomorrow's World*, Penguin: New York (1997).

Ward, Arian, "Lessons Learned on the Knowledge Highways and Byways," *Strategy & Leadership* (March–April 1996).

Wenger, Etienne; Richard McDermott, and William M. Snyder, *Cultivating Communities of Practice: A Guide to Managing Knowledge*, Harvard Business School Press: Cambridge, Massachusetts (March 2002)

Wheatley, Margaret J. *Leadership and the New Science: Learning about Organization from an Orderly Universe*, Berrett-Koehler Publishers: San Francisco (1992) p. 113.

Wiesenfelder, Joe, "The Information SuperHighway (This is not a metaphor)," *Wired* Archive 4.02 (February 1996).

Wiig, Karl M., "Knowledge Management: An Emerging Discipline Rooted in a Long History," *Knowledge Horizons: The Present and the promise of Knowledge Management* (Charles Despres and Daniele Chauvel, eds.), Butterworth-Heinemann: Boston (2000).

About the Author

DEBRA M. AMIDON is Founder and CEO of **ENTOVATION International, Ltd.** (Wilmington, Massachusetts)—a global innovation research and consulting network linking 80 countries throughout the world. She's been featured in notable biographical publications such as *The International Book of Honor* and the *Woman of the Decade*. Recently, she has been announced a finalist for the Competitive Intelligence (CI) Champion of the Year.

Considered an architect of the Knowledge Economy, her own specialties include knowledge management, e-learning networks, customer innovation and enterprise transformation. For the last few years, her presentations have been heard throughout the North and South America, Europe, Asia and South Africa. Her advice has been sought by diverse organizations such as the National Research Council, The

Agility Forum, the Industrial Research Institute, the European Union, PBS, BBC and The World Bank.

Author of many publications including: *Managing the Knowledge Assets into the 21st Century* (1987); *Innovation Strategy for the Knowledge Economy: The Ken Awakening* (1997); *Creating the Knowledge-Based Business* (1997); *Collaborative Innovation and the Knowledge Economy* (1998); *The Architectural Primer for Knowledge Innovation* (2001); *The Global Knowledge Primer* (2001); and *The Innovation SuperHighway* (scheduled for 2002 release).

Known among her peers as a management pioneer, philosopher and visionary, she has captured the imagination of academic, government and industrial leaders around the globe. With her seminal conference in 1987, she set in motion what has evolved to an expansive 'community of knowledge practice'—comprised of theorists and practitioners from diverse functions, sectors, industries and geographies. Her *"Momentum of Knowledge Management"*—and subsequent *"Global Momentum of Knowledge Strategy"*—is available in many languages over the Internet. Her books have also been published French, Chinese, Spanish, Portuguese, and German.

She has served in a variety of executive management positions as Assistant Secretary of Education for the Commonwealth of Massachusetts, Executive Director of a higher education consortium, established the first industrial-strength management systems research office and a variety of leadership or advisory positions, including the National Conference for the Advancement of Research, the Industrial Research Institute, and the National Science Foundation.

Her articles have appeared in *Research-Technology Management, Knowledge Inc., PRISM, Journal of Customer Partnerships, Exec!, 2000 The Handbook of Business Strategy*, and the *International Journal of Innovation Management* to mention a few. Her publications—selected for Business Literacy 2000—have been cited in *The Financial Times, Management Service, Innovacion, The Observer, Management Today, Director, Silicon Valley North, Ottawa Citizen, KM Magazine, Singa-*

pore Business Times, *TRACK*, *AMA Management Review* et al. She was featured as the 'Leading Light' in *Knowledge Inc.*

Married with four children, she holds degrees from Boston University, Columbia University and the Massachusetts Institute of Technology where she was an Alfred P. Sloan Fellow. E-mail: debra@entovation.com; URL: www.entovation.com

Index

3Cs, 29–30

ARPA-net, 6
Arthur Anderson/APQC model, 102
Awareness, creating, 159–60

Bartlett, Chris, 55
Behavior, in knowledge value
　　proposition, 24
*Benchmarking the Netherlands 2000:
　　On the Threshold of the new
　　Millennium*, 60
Best practice guidelines, 65
Biological metaphors, 102
Bionomics, 54
Bontis, Nick, 53
Borgman, Christine L., 7
Brookings Institute, 65–66
Brown, John Seely, 213
Buma, Yvonne, 227–28
　　as author, 227
　　background, 227
　　as government official, 228
　　youth work, 227–28
　　See also Ken practitioners
Business intelligence model, 102

Canada
　　Conference Board of Canada, 79
　　GPI Blueprint, 61
Carrillo, Dr. Javier, 228–30

background, 228–29
Center for Knowledge Systems
　　(CKS), 228–30
KM network, 229–30
　　See also Ken practitioners
Carter, Barry C., 87
CBIRD, 274–75
　　defined, 274
　　functions, 275
　　objectives, 274–75
　　See also Innovation infrastructures
Center for Knowledge Systems
　　(CKS), 228–30
Change
　　effects of, 99
　　kaleidoscopic, 20, 98
　　leadership and, 204
　　learning as rubric for, 184
　　in market environment, 272
Chief knowledge officer (CKO)
　　merits of, 210
　　virtual, 147
Clarica, 105–6
Coaching
　　defined, 217
　　judging vs., 217
　　leadership as, 217–18
　　See also Leadership
Collaboration
　　to cohesion, 181

Collaboration (continued)
   competition to, 186
   as core future premise, 315, 326
   emerging economic conditions and,
      77
   environment, 77
   research base, 343
   structure support of, 80
   technologies, 116
   technology stimulus of, 22
   as underlying theme, 9
   in win/win scenarios, 10
Collaborative advantage, platform for,
      77–79
"Collaborative individualism," 5
*Collaborative Innovation and Knowledge
    Economy*, 33
Collaborative knowledge networks,
    78, 320–21
Collaborative process
   in CAM-I case study, 194
   as innovation strategy dimension,
    180–81
Collaborative Strategies, 116
Communication(s)
   in CAM-I case study, 198
   distributed learning network of
    expertise and, 217
   face-to-face, 145
   as innovation strategy dimension,
    191–92
   internal/external, 189
   knowledge leadership as matter of,
    215–17
   poor, 212
   strategy, 109, 215–16, 217
   technology, 123, 191–92
Communities
   innovation, 146
   knowledge leadership as matter of,
    212–14
   knowledge management, 146

   role of, 72
   transnational, 325
Communities of practice, 75
   concept origination, 213
   emerging, 325, 341
   participants, 341
   to shared meaning, 181
Community networks, 16
Competence
   leadership as matter of, 207–10
   "new" leadership, 90
   role of, 86
   successful, 94
Competency
   map, 208
   profile, 209
   profiling system, 207
Competitive intelligence
   in CAM-I case study, 195–96
   focus on, 186–87
   system, 123
Competitive management tactics, 188
Computer technology, 191–92
*Connected Intelligence: The Arrival of the
    Web Society*, 115
Consortium for Advanced
    Manufacturing (CAM-I)
   alliances and joint ventures, 197
   background, 192
   case study, 192–94
   collaborative process, 194
   communications and technology, 198
   cost management system
    (CMS), 192, 193
   distributed learning network, 195
   education and development, 195
   innovation assessment, 192–93
   innovation intelligence, 195–96
   key findings, 198–99
   leadership and leverage, 197
   market image campaign, 197
   performance measures, 194–95

products and services, 196–97
See also Innovation strategy
Control to humility meta-view, 176–77
comments, 177
defined, 176
questions, 177
See also Meta-views
Corporate Longitude, 56
Cortada, James W., 85
Creating the Knowledge-Based Business, 302
Critical success factors, 64
Cross-Border Institute for Regional Development. See CBIRD
Cross-organizational processes, 102–3, 105
Culture, 143
beyond enterprise, 308
honoring, 190
innovation, 74
innovation, creating, 308–9
knowledge leadership as matter of, 210–12
knowledge-sharing, development of, 80
knowledge structure and, 74–76
Customer Relationship Management (CRM), 31–32, 135
as a movement, 31–32
focus, 86
programs, 32
Customers
interaction process, 31
knowledge gleaned from, 99

de Kerckhove, Derrick, 115
Denmark, 59
Denning, Stephen, 134
Development Gateway, 265–66
country gateways (CGs), 265
defined, 265
portal, 265–66
team, 265

See also Innovation infrastructures
Digital divide, 205, 264
Distributed networks
in CAM-I case study, 195
as innovation strategy dimension, 184–85
Diversity, discovery of, 81
Doering, Joachim, 230–31
background, 230
position responsibilities, 230–31
presentations and articles, 231
See also Ken practitioners
Drucker, Dr. Peter, 29, 50, 83, 85, 97, 207

Earth Charter, 327
Eco-efficiency, in WHKP vision, 15
Ecology
economy to, 188
role of, 72
Economic levels, 309–12
macroeconomic, 311–12
mesoeconomic, 310–11
microeconomic, 310
as overlapping circles, 311–12
Economic(s), 18
dynamic climate, 80
kaleidoscopic, 39
knowledge performance, 49–66
OECD, 63
performance, 23
surveys, 306
Economy
to ecology, 188
to holonomy meta-view, 176
Ecosystems, in WHKP vision, 15
Education, 18
in CAM-I case study, 195
as innovation strategy dimension, 183–84
in WHKP vision, 15
Edvinsson, Leif, 51, 56, 65
as author, 232–33

Edvinsson, Leif (continued)
  background, 232
  as government advisor, 233
  as ken practitioner, 232–33
  as representative of the future of IC, 233
  as speaker, 232
  See also Ken practitioners
E-government, 150
E-learning
  development of, 125
  investments, 108
Energy, in WHKP vision, 15
"Enterprise ideas economy," 117
ENTOVATION 100, 133, 142, 151–54
  accomplishments, 158–59
  analysis, 142
  challenges, 156–58
  influences, 156
  knowledge economy visions, 160–61
  meta-views of, 175–79
  Network affiliation, 166–71
  questions, 153
  responses by question, 155
  sample comments, 161–65
  structure and credibility, 145
  yet to accomplish, 159–60
ENTOVATION Fellows, 132
ENTOVATION Network
  affiliation benefits, 166–71
  case study, 129–48
  as CI Champion of the Year finalist, 166
  credibility, building, 147
  customer success vignette, 135
  defined, 130
  distinctive competencies definition, 130
  engagement process, 132–33
  entrepreneurialism vignette, 137–38
  evolution of, 131, 148
  executive leadership vignette, 140–42

Global Knowledge vignette, 136
  growth stages, 130–32
  homeland security principles, 321–24
  knowledge-sharing vignette, 138–39
  Latin-American learning vignette, 139–40
  lessons learned, 145–46
  leveraging collective competence, 132
  members, 134, 141
  model, 102
  network structuring, 130–31
  Old Mother Europe vignette, 137
  proof of concept, 133–42
  reciprocity and, 147
  sharing the wealth, 131
  size, 132
  as source of insight, 171
  summary, 147–48
  transformation into innovation system, 132
  value of, 165–71
  as virtual organization, 134–35
  what went right?, 146
  what went wrong?, 146–47
Entrepreneurialism role, 85–86
Environment, 18
  collaboration, 77
  market, change in, 272
Ernst & Young model, 102

Fernandez, Alejandro, 233–35
  background, 234
  as Pro-Quality of Life director, 234–35
  in Venezuelan oil industry, 234
  See also Ken practitioners
Financial capital, 58
Financial focus, 56
Formica, Dr. Piero, 235–36
  background, 235
  research, 236
  See also Ken practitioners
Franco, Bob, 236–37

background, 236
current endeavors, 236–37
HR generalist support, 237
See also Ken practitioners
"From e-Learning to Enterprise
    Learning: Becoming a Strategic
    Learning Organization," 108
*From Gutenberg to the Global Information
    Infrastructure: Access to
    Information in a Networked
    World,* 7

Galbraith, John Kenneth, 49–50
Gartner Research Group, 107
Genuine Progress Indicator (GPI), 61
Ghoshal, Sumantra, 55
GII, 18, 320
    defined, 7
    as innovation infrastructure, 8
Global holonomy, 325–27
Global Information Infrastructure.
    See GII
Global Knowledge Development
(GKD) project, 121, 122, 140, 263
Global Knowledge Innovation
    Infrastructure (GKII), 136–37,
    140
Global Knowledge Partnership
    (GKP), 262–65, 289–92
    action plan, 264
    consensus, 264
    defined, 262
    mission, 262–63
    organizations, 262
    story-telling method, 263
    vision, 262
    young people and, 289–90
    See also Innovation infrastructures
Global Valuation and Accounting
    Report, 56
Global Youth Action Network, 290

Goals to aspirations meta-view, 178–79
    comments, 179
    defined, 178
    questions, 179
    See also Meta-views
Gordon, Cindy, 238–39
    as author, 238–39
    background, 238
    with Xerox, 238
    See also Ken practitioners
Granell, Elana, 76

Health care, in WHKP vision, 16
Hochleitner, Albert, 173–74
Homeland security principles, 321–24
    battle is economic, 322
    best defense is offense, 322
    innovation is process by which
knowledge is created/harnessed, 323
    knowledge is engine of economic
        prosperity, 322–23
    national strategy must by
        international and collaborative,
        323
Human capital, 59
Human focus, 57

Implementation, 344
Information
    as basis in decision-making, 120
    begets information, 85
    contextual, 110
    as development factor, 64
    "pull" strategy, 120
    systematisation of, 104
    technology, 118
Information and communication
    networks (ICNs), 272
Information and communications
    technologies (ICTs), 123, 289,
    291
Inman, Admiral Bobby Ray, 239–40
    background, 239–40

Inman, Admiral Bobby Ray (continued)
Microelectronics and Computer
Technology Corporation
(MCC), 239–40
with start-up technology companies,
240
See also Ken practitioners
Innovation
atlas for, 37–40
case for, 302–3
as common language, 26
community, 146
as core value, 42
culture, 74
defined, 17, 335–37
enterprise vision, 312–14
five-stage analysis, 26–27, 28
as glue that bonds, 214
improvisational aspect, 101
as "knowledge in action," 30
language, 214, 308
learning nodes, 95–96
as learning process, 9–10
management, 309
as management problem, 32
mindset, 74
of others, embracing, 107
process, 98, 100, 103, 174
on the radar screen, 106–8
redefined, 29–32
sample definitions of, 335–37
source of, 101
technology, 124
twenty-first century, 301–15
as underlying theme, 9
value system, 100, 160
Innovation infrastructures, 261–78
CBIRD, 274–75
Development Gateway, 265–66
GKP, 262–65
KALiF, 266–67
Knowledge Wave, 267–69

NEPAD, 275–76
ShareNet, 271–74
Singapore, 270–71
summary, 277–78
United Nations, 276–77
Innovation strategy, 37–45
actualizing, 40–44
business strategy to, 186–87
calibrating, 338–40
case study, 192–99
collaborative process focus, 180–81
competitive intelligence focus,
186–87
computer/communications
technology focus, 191–92
dimensions, 40
distributed networks focus, 184–85
education/training focus, 183–84
knowledge economy enabled by, 76
leadership/leverage focus, 190–91
market/customer interaction focus,
189–90
migration to, 38
new products/services focus, 187–88
performance measures focus, 181–83
strategic alliances focus, 188–89
summary, 44–45, 199
ten dimensions of, 179–92
trends of, 173–99
*Innovation Strategy for the Knowledge
Economy,* 26, 40
Innovation superhighway
characteristics, 330–31
defined, 7
nine-box blueprint, 313
people-intensive, 22
proposal, 328–29
technical underpinning of, 29
toward, 330–31
Insight, 343
Intellectual Capital, 27–28
Intellectual capital (IC)

calculation/monitoring, 24
Denmark, 59
as driving force, 57
as financial concept, 49–50
harnessing, 21
index, 13
of Israel, 58
in knowledge value proposition, 23
measurement methods, 160
measurement steps, 57
reporting, 13
Intellectual property
honoring, 190
rights, in WHKP vision, 15
theft of, 151
International Institute for Sustainable
Development (IISD), 290
Internet
marketing, 117
viewed as promotion to viewed as
learning tool, 191
Intrapreneur, 86
Ishikawa, Akira, 115
Itami, Hiroyuki, 51

JADE network, 294–95
Jelcic, Karmen, 253–54
Jones, Keith, 241–42
with AVAC, 241, 242
background, 241
leadership, 242
See also Ken practitioners
Junior Alpbach, 294

Kaleidoscopic change, 20, 98
KALiF, 266–67
defined, 266
LTI and, 266–67
success, 267
See also Innovation infrastructures
Karl Wiig model, 102
"Keiretsu," 4
Ken, defined, 224

Ken practitioners, 223–60
Buma, Yvonne, 227–28
Carrillo, Dr. Javier, 228–30
Doering, Joachim, 230–31
Edvinsson, Leif, 232–33
Fernandez, Alejandro, 233–35
Formica, Dr. Piero, 235–36
Franco, Bob, 236–37
Gordon, Cindy, 238–39
Inman, Admiral Bobby Ray, 239–40
Jelcic, Karmen, 253–54
Jones, Keith, 241–42
Kozmetsky, Dr. George, 243–44
Lau, Chin Hoon, 244–46
Macnamara, Doug, 246–48
Malone, Dr. Tom, 248–49
Mercier-Laurent, Dr. Eunika,
250–51
overview, 224–25
Pasher, Dr. Edna, 251–53
Pulic, Dr. Ante, 253–54
Speh Birkenkrahe, Dr. Marcus,
225–26
Staeheli, Dr. Joerg, 255–56
Stanford, Xenia, 256–57
St. Onge, Hubert, 258–59
summary, 259
Know-How Company, 51
Knowing to imagining meta-view, 177
Knowledge
acquisition, 175
agenda, 9, 313
analysts, 87
brokers, 87
cells, 160
center, 109
commercialization, 29–30
conversion, 29–30
as decision-making basis, 120
as development factor, 64
distribution, 175
domains, mapping, 109

Knowledge (continued)
  ecology, 72
  editors, 87
  exchange, 27
  explicit, role of, 86
  five disciplines of, 89–90
  focus of, 149, 304
  high-leverage, 110
  how, 35–45
  identification, 175
  innovation analysis, 26–27, 28
  innovation systems, 27
  integration of, 39
  inventory, 109
  leadership, 203–20
  loss of, 101
  movement, 22–23, 85, 342
  navigators, 87
  as primary innovation driver, 39
  private, 286
  as production factor, 174
  programs, 211
  public, 286
  as source of economic wealth, 17
  tacit, role of, 86
  as underlying theme, 8–9
  valuing, 10–11
  visualization, 151
  See also Innovation
Knowledge assessment methodology
  (KAM), 63
Knowledge-based development strategy,
  121
"Knowledge Capital Scorecard," 52
"The Knowledge Capital of Nations," 56
Knowledge creation, 29–30
  conditions for, 75
  improving, 75
  role of, 71
Knowledge economies
  distinctive feature, 306–7

  enabled by innovation superhighway,
    76
  evolution of, 12
  interdependent, 99–100
  kaleidoscopic change, 98
  as matter of philosophy, 154
  policies, 13
  positioning, 36
  taglines in, 216
  visions of, 160–61
Knowledge for Development, 13
Knowledge for Development (K4D), 63
Knowledge-gathering tools, 114
Knowledge Innovation, 333–34
  defined, 334
  litmus test, 338
Knowledge Innovation Assessment, 218
Knowledge language, 214–15
  defined, 214
  defining, 214
Knowledge management (KM), 27
  benefits, 27, 105
  best practices, 118
  challenges, 21–22
  community, 146
  competency planning and, 88
  defined, 27
  driving force, 119
  momentum of, 341–46
  necessity, 345
  press, 320
  professionals, 91
  societies, 320
  success factors, 104–5
Knowledge-millennium generation,
  283–99
  arrogant certainty to humble doubt,
    285
  digital technology as knowledge
delivery mechanism to knowledge
    creation tool, 287–88

environmentally destructive
    knowledge to environmentally
    sustaining knowledge, 288
GKP, 289–92
individual points of view to group
    perspectives, 287
JADE network, 294–95
Junior Alpbach, 294
New Zealand, 296–98
organizations based on structures to
    based on cultures of
    relationships, 286–87
private knowledge to public
    knowledge, 286
progress to sustainability, 286
summary, 298–99
trends, 288–89
value based on money to based on
    wisdom, 285–86
vision of the future, 285
Young Entrepreneur Association
    World Congress, 292–94
See also OFW
Knowledge Networking, 101
Knowledge performance economics,
    49–66
action steps, 65
architectural considerations, 64
measurements, 66
national initiatives, 56–61
new foundations, 54–56
roots, 51–54
societal level, 62–64
summary, 65–66
Knowledge processes, 97–111, 318
action steps, 109–10
architectural considerations, 109
cross-organizational, 102–3, 105
dynamic, 203
emerging practices, 104–5
guidelines, 109
operationalizing strategies, 105–6

periodic review, 109
roots, 98–102
summary, 110–11
systematisation of, 104
underlying themes, 101–2
understanding, at multiple levels,
    104–5
Knowledge-processing technology,
    113–25, 318
action steps, 124–25
architectural considerations, 123–24
collaborative, 116
e-business implications, 116–18
emerging practices, 118–20
gateway, 120–23
roots, 114–16
summary, 125
Knowledge profession
classification schema, 91–92
knowledge academicians, theorists,
    visionaries, 92
knowledge and competitive
    intelligence professionals, 92
knowledge and expert system
    professionals, 92
knowledge and innovation
    professionals, 91
knowledge and strategic integration
    professionals, 92
knowledge catalogers, researchers,
    media specialists, 92
knowledge facilitators, trainers,
    corporate educators, 92
knowledge management
    professionals, 91
shaping of, 91–94
societies, 92–93
Knowledge-related advertising, 216
Knowledge sharing
benefits, 273
conditions for encouraging, 212
culture development, 80

Knowledge sharing (continued)
  vignette, 138–39
  See also ShareNet
Knowledge societies
  management, 320
  potential, 11–14
  professional, 92–93
Knowledge strategy, 105–6
  document, 106
  global momentum of, 149–71
  global response, 154–55
Knowledge structures, 69–81
  action steps, 80
  architectural considerations, 79–80
  culture and, 74–76
  platform for collaborative advantage, 77–79
  productivity paradox and, 72–74
  roots, 70–72
  summary, 80–81
Knowledge value proposition, 19–34
  behavior, 24
  creating, 22–25
  illustrated, 23
  knowledge movement subthemes and, 24
  performance economics, 23
  summary, 34
  technology, 24
Knowledge Wave, 267–69
  conference, 267–68
  conference attendees, 296–98
  defined, 267
  "Innovate" initiative, 269
  "Innovation Wave" project, 269
  recommendations, 268
  Trust, 267
  See also Innovation infrastructures
Knowledge workers, 50, 83–96
  action steps, 94–95
  analysts, 87
  architectural considerations, 94

  backgrounds, 155
  brokers, 87
  coaching/mentoring, 95
  editors, 87
  emerging practices, 87–91
  label, 83, 84
  motivation of, 94
  navigators, 87
  as new majority, 85
  profession, shaping, 91–94
  responsibilities, 155
  roots, 84–87
  self-managing, 206
  summary, 95–96
Kozmetsky, Dr. George, 243–44
  as author, 244
  background, 243
  research, 244
  with the University of Texas, 243
  See also Ken practitioners

Laggards, 348–49
Language, 174
Lau, Chin Hoon, 244–46
  background, 244–45
  as certified Internet Business Strategist, 246
  as Internet Biologists founder, 245
  See also Ken practitioners
Leaders
  inspirational, 207, 219
  knowledge, 219
  qualities of, 219–20
  as statesmen, 205
  ten characteristics of, 347–48
  vision and, 207
  See also Ken practitioners
Leadership, 143, 203–20
  in CAM-I case study, 197
  change and, 204
  competency map, 208
  focus, 190–91
  as function of listening, 217

as function of vision, 206
global knowledge map, 152
as innovation strategy dimension,
    190–91
in knowledge economy, 205
learning, 209–10
litmus test, 218
as matter of coaching, 217–18
as matter of communications, 215–17
as matter of communities, 212–14
as matter of competence, 207–10
as matter of context, 206–7
as matter of conversations and
    common language, 214–15
as matter of culture, 210–12
nature of, 191
obstacles, 211–12
required, 155
return-on (ROL), 204
starting with you, 218–20
strategy, 43
strategy as art of, 205
styles, 107
summary, 220
top-down, 343
training, 210
Learning
    contract, 209
    education to, 184
    e-learning, 108, 125
    focus, 88, 101
    global, 29
    Internet as tool, 191
    networks, 79
    nodes, 95–96
    on-the-job, 218
    organizations, 88
    process steps, 209–10
    real-time, 205
    role of, 71
    as rubric for change, 184
    strategy, 95

team, 90
time for, 95
Learning and training in industry
    (LTI), 266
*The Learning Organization: Managing
    Knowledge for Business Success,*
    307
Leonard-Barton, Dorothy, 55
Lev, Baruch, 52–53
Liaison relationships, 79
Limited to unlimited meta-view, 278
litmus test, 41
    leadership, 218
    questions, 338
*A Look to the Future: The Hidden Values of
    the Desert,* 58

Macnamara, Doug, 246–48
    background, 246–47
    as community participant, 247–48
    in executive capacity, 247
    as speaker, 247
    See also Ken practitioners
Macroeconomic (transnational) level,
    311–12
Malone, Dr. Tom, 14–15, 133
    background, 248–49
    as ken practitioner, 248–49
    positions served, 249
    publications, 249
    See also Ken practitioners
Management
    agenda, redefining, 206
    architectures, 344
    concept evolution, 203
    emerging sixth wave of, 303
    finance and, 50
    innovation, 309
    responsibilities, 315
    styles contrast, 33
    system attributes, 88
    See also Knowledge management
        (KM)

Managing Culture for Success, 76
Managing the Knowledge Assets of the 21ˢᵗ Century, 11
Market
  capital, 58
  customer interaction, 189–90
  focus, 57
  image campaign, 197
  perception, 189
Marketing
  Internet, 117
  proactive, 189
Mayo, Andrew, 93
Measurement, 342
  IC, 57, 160
  of impact, 210
  knowledge performance economics, 66
Media/advertising strategy, 43
Mental models, 89
Mercier-Laurent, Dr. Eunika, 250–51
  as author, 251
  background, 250
  founding EML Conseil, 251
  with Groupe Bull, 250–51
  See also Ken practitioners
Mesoeconomic (inter-organizational) level, 310–11
Meta-views, 175–79
  control to humility, 176–77
  defined, 175
  economy to holonomy, 176
  goals to aspirations, 178–79
  knowing to imagining, 177
  limited to unlimited, 278
  See also ENTOVATION 100
Metrics
  performance, 114
  reviewing, 43
  universal research, 64
Microeconomic (intra-organizational) level, 310

Microelectronics Computer and Technology Corporation (MCC), 4
  Austin roots, 4–5
  facility plans, 5
"The Momentum of Knowledge Management," 150

National Cooperative Research Act, 25
National income accounts, in WHKP vision, 15
National Information Infrastructure. *See* NII
National innovation systems (NIS), 63
NEPAD, 275–76
  defined, 175
  initiatives, 276
  See also Innovation infrastructures
Netherlands
  Benchmarking the Netherlands 2000: On the Threshold of the new Millennium, 60
  "innovation policy," 59
  KPMG, 60
Networks
  collaborative knowledge, 78, 320–21
  distributed, 184–85
  learning, 79
  management tools, 124
  nesting of, 318
  role of, 71–72
New Partnership for Africa's Development. *See* NEPAD
New products/services, 187–88
New Zealand, 296–98
NII, 320
  defined, 7
  perspective, 6
Not-invented here (NIH) syndrome, 151

OFW
  defined, 283

papers, 284
  speaker themes, 284
Organization network analysis (ONA), 256
Organization of Economic Co-operation and Development (OECD), 13, 304
  cross-divisional activity, 305
  economies, 63
  Observer, 62, 304
  reports, 62, 304
Organizations
  based on cultures of relationships, 286–87
  based on structures, 286–87
  connections, creating, 331
  innovation strategy perspective, 98–99
  knowledge-based, 87, 88, 119
  learning, 88
  networked, 98
  structure evolution of, 70
  trends, 288

Paradigm shift, 345
Paradox
  resolution, 20–22
  technology, 20, 34, 72–74
Participation, 143
Partnering role, 86–87
Pasher, Dr. Edna, 58, 251–53
  background, 252
  as NIMCube partner, 252
  as speaker, 252
  Status founder, 253
  See also Ken practitioners
Performance economics, 23
Performance measures, 181–83
  in CAM-I case study, 194–95
  guidelines, 181
  single to multiple, 182
Personal mastery, 89

Planning
  business, 37, 39
  competency, 88
  downside, 36–37
  innovation strategy and, 37
  re-entry, 210
Polanyi, Michael, 50
Por, George, 72
Porter, Michael, 98
Process capital, 58
Process focus, 57
Productivity paradox, 34, 72–74
  defined, 20
  resolving, 20–22
Products
  in CAM-I case study, 196–97
  intelligent, 188
  life cycles, 115
  from materials/technology, 188
  new, focus, 187–88
Prospectus, 327–31
  concept, 329–30
  defined, 327
  problem and opportunity, 330
  proposal, 328–29
  toward the innovation superhighway, 330–31
Pulic, Dr. Ante, 52
  as Austrian IC-Research Center co-founder, 254
  background, 253–54
  in Croatia, 254
  as ken practitioner, 253–54
  See also Ken practitioners

Quinn, James Brian, 30

Re-entry planning, 210
Renewal and development
  capital, 59
  focus, 57
Research-Technology Management, 26, 302

Return-on-leadership (ROL), 204
The Rise and Fall of Strategic Planning,
    36
The Rise of the Knowledge Worker, 85
Roles
    communities, 72
    competence, 86
    ecology, 72
    entrepreneurialism, 85–86
    knowledge creation, 71
    learning, 71
    networks, 71–72
    new, emergence of, 94, 95
    partnering, 86–87
    responsibilities, 94
    tacit and explicit knowledge, 86

Saint-Onge, Hubert, 105–6
    background, 258
    business philosophy, 258
    as ken practitioner, 258–59
    as LIIC recipient, 259
    presentations, 258–59
Senge, Peter, 88
Shared purpose, 309
Shared vision, 89
ShareNet, 271–74
    advantages, 273–74
    defined, 272
    focus, 272–73
    goal, 272
    urgent requests (URs), 273
    See also Innovation infrastructures
Singapore
    Asian Productivity Organization
        (APO), 270
    innovation culture cultivation, 16–17
    innovation infrastructure, 270–71
    Innovative Society, 271
Skyrme, Dr. David, 53–54, 101, 117
Sloan Management Review, 55
Social capital assessment tool (SCAT),
    144

Softbank, 320
Speh Birkenkrahe, Dr. Marcus, 225–26
    as author, 225–26
    background, 225
    as speaker, 226
    See also Ken practitioners
Staeheli, Dr. Joerg, 255–56
    background, 255
    organization network analysis
        (ONA), 256
    presentations, 256
    See also Ken practitioners
Stanford, Xenia, 142, 143
    background, 256–57
    education, 257
    as ken practitioner, 256–57
    research, 257
    See also Ken practitioners
Stata, Ray, 215
Stewart, Tom, 51
Storytelling, 101, 160
    as documentation/deployment
mechanism, 183
    GKP, 263
Strategic alliances, 43
    in CAM-I case study, 197
    focus on, 188–89
    as innovation strategy dimension,
        188–89
    internal knowledge to external
        knowledge, 189
    self-interest to group interest, 188–89
Strategic awareness, 104
*Strategic Learning and the Knowledge
    Economy*, 101
Strategy document, 106
Sustainability, 18, 143
    as interdependent variable, 18
    from progress to, 286
    WHKP outline, 15
Sustainable Development Networking
    Programme (SDNP), 140

Sveiby, Karl-Erik, 51, 55
Sweden, "Year of Innovation," 56
System thinking, 89

Taglines, 216
Team learning, 90
Technical infrastructure, 43–44
Technology
    computer/communications, 191–92
    as creation tool, 287–88
    exchange, 27
    exploiting, 120
    in functioning of knowledge
        enterprise, 344–45
    information, 118
    information and communications
        (ICT), 123
    infrastructures, 118, 119
    innovations, 124
    in knowledge value proposition, 24
    paradox, 20, 34
    solutions, 119
    transfer, 25, 26, 334
"Technopolis," 110
Thought, evolution of, 10
Time, 174
Transformation matrix, 314

United Nations, 276–77, 319

Value chain thinking, 99
Value Creation Efficiency Analysis
    (VAIC), 52
Value propositions, 19–34
    creating, 22–25

knowledge, 19–34
    traditional, 20
Value systems
    based on collaborative work, 160
    innovation, 100, 160
Vision
    enterprise innovation, 312–14
    Global Knowledge Partnership
        (GKP), 262
    knowledge economy, 160–61
    lack of, 212
    leadership and, 206, 207
    in progress, 319–21
    WHKP, 15–16
Voice of the Entovation 100, 179

Welfare and Security, 56–57
Wenger, Etienne, 213
Western hemisphere knowledge
    partnership (WHKP), 13–14,
    15
    sustainability outline, 15
    vision, 15–16
Wheatley, Margaret J., 205
Wisdom, 285–86
World Bank, 305, 319
World Economic Survey, 62

Young Entrepreneur Association World
    Congress, 292–94
    areas and themes, 293
    defined, 292
Youth Building Knowledge Societies
    (YBKS), 290